ORGANIZATION AND CHANGE IN HEALTH CARE QUALITY ASSURANCE

CONTRIBUTORS

R. Wayne Boss, D.P.A.
Verla Collins, R.N., Ph.D.
Joyce Crane, R.N., M.S.
William Feigin, M.B.A.
William R. Fifer, M.D.
Ann Barry Flood, Ph.D.
Phyllis B.J. Giovannetti, R.N., Sc.D.
Robert W. Hetherington, Ph.D.
JoAnne Horsley, R.N., Ph.D.
Arnold D. Kaluzny, Ph.D.
Rachelle Kaye, Ph.D.
James P. LoGerfo, M.D., M.P.H.

Catherine E. Loveridge, R.N., Ph.D.
Marie Michnich, R.N., M.P.H.
Sharon J. Reeder, R.N., Ph.D.
Sang-O Rhee, Ph.D.
William Richardson, Ph.D.
Harry Rosen, Ph.D.
W. Richard Scott, Ph.D.
Maryanne Shanahan, R.N., B.S.N.
Steven Shortell, Ph.D.
Sharon Stevens
Jean Watson, R.N., Ph.D.

T & A

ORGANIZATION AND CHANGE IN HEALTH CARE QUALITY ASSURANCE

Edited by

Roice D. Luke, Ph.D.
Department of Health Administration
Medical College of Virginia

Janelle C. Krueger, R.N., Ph.D.
Health Sciences Center
University of Colorado

Robert E. Modrow, Ph.D.
University of British Columbia
Graduate Program in Planning
and Administration

AN ASPEN PUBLICATION®
Aspen Systems Corporation
Rockville, Maryland
London
1983

Library of Congress Cataloging in Publication Data
Main entry under title:

Organization and change in health care quality assurance.

Bibliographies
Includes index.
1. Medical care—Quality control. 2. Quality
assurance. I. Luke, Roice D. II. Krueger, Janelle C.
III. Modrow, Robert E.
[DNLM: 1. Quality assurance, Health care—Trends.
W 84.1 068]
RA399.A1O73   1983   362.1   82-22825
ISBN: 0-89443-930-8

Publisher: John Marozsan
Editorial Director: Darlene Como
Managing Editor: Margot Raphael
Editorial Services: Dorothy Okoroji
Printing and Manufacturing: Debbie Collins

Library of Congress Catalog Card Number: 82-22825
ISBN: 0-89443-930-8

Printed in the United States of America

1 2 3 4 5

Table of Contents

Foreword

In January 1980, a national conference was held in Denver on quality assurance: The Administrative and Organizational Issues. It was sponsored by the University of Colorado School of Nursing and Division of Health Administration, the school of medicine, in conjunction with the Western Network for Education in Health Administration, the Association of Western Hospitals, and the Western Council on Higher Education in Nursing. The purpose of the conference was to examine the nurse administrator's role in the management of quality assurance. In November of the same year, a national invitational conference on Research in Quality Assurance was also held in Denver. It was sponsored by the University of Colorado Division of Health Administration, in conjunction with the Joint Commission on Accreditation of Hospitals (JCAH) and the Association of University Programs in Health Administration (AUPHA). Its purpose was to examine the state of the art in research on organizational and professional issues in quality assurance.

Many of the readings presented in this book are commissioned papers that were initially presented at these national conferences. These topics are particularly relevant because of the announcement in April 1979 by the JCAH regarding revised standards for hospital quality assurance. The intent of the new standards, in the Commission's words, "is to assist hospitals in implementing an overall quality assurance program designed to assure the delivery of optimal patient care." New quality assurance standards are a reflection of the Commission's concern that previous JCAH guidelines, rules, and regulations, which were developed to assure quality patient care, were not as successful as anticipated. Neither patient care nor clinical performance had been appreciably improved. Also, the focus in previous guidelines was on utilization review and medical audit. The new standards recommend a coordinated effort in assessment activities involving other health professions, as well as physicians. This provision presents a unique opportunity for hospital and nursing service administrators to play a more influential role in improving the quality of patient care. Along with this opportunity, a definite challenge has been placed before the health administration and nursing professions—that of sharing in the overall responsibility for high standards of patient care. To accept and meet the challenge requires no less than a total commitment from highly informed, well-prepared health administrators and directors of nursing services who will actively participate in implementing the revised JCAH standards.

Barbara J. Lee,
Program Director, ASC
The W.K. Kellogg Foundation
March 1982

Preface

Quality assurance has received increasing public attention since the Joint Commission on Accreditation of Hospitals (JCAH) was founded in the early 1950s. The roots of quality assurance, of course, predate this development, but it was not until the 1950s that extensive scientific experimentation with measurement and assessment strategies was begun. The 1960s and 1970s mark the entry of the federal government into the arena of quality assurance, notably with the funding of the Professional Standard Review Organizations (PSROs) in the early 1970s.

Ironically, it was during the late 1970s that quality assurance activities not only may have reached their greatest levels of maturation but also may have entered into what could be an extensive period of inattention. The PSROs came under increasing criticism because of their apparent ineffectiveness in controlling either the cost or the quality of care. This produced a continuing reappraisal of the role of the PSRO, as well as a high degree of uncertainty about continued federal funding. In April 1979, the JCAH also went through a reversal of direction by backing away from its prior emphasis on medical audits and approving its new standard on quality assurance. The new standard gave explicit emphasis to the programmatic rather than methodological aspects of quality assurance.

Such developments are symptomatic of the need for a redirection in quality assurance activities in this country. It is clear that quality assurance has until now been both expensive and, in general, marginally effective. We suggest that this is primarily attributable to a misplaced emphasis on assessment and measurement technique and to a failure to give sufficient attention to the problem of bringing about needed organizational and behavioral change.

As teachers of both health and nursing administration students, we became critically aware of the dearth of literature on the behavioral and organizational aspects of quality assurance. We found a considerable literature on measurement techniques, on the conceptualization of quality, and on the variety of assessment techniques, but little on the relationship between cost and quality, on the problems of structuring quality control at the institutional level, and on the application of change theory to quality assurance.

With this book we hope to begin the development of a literature on the organization/behavior side of the quality assurance problem. We have selected for inclusion readings drawn from both the published literature and several conferences on quality assurance. Other criteria used in the selection of readings were that they provide a clinical perspective to the organization/behavior problem, a research orientation, and an overview or summary content.

Particular attention was also given to the future role nursing might play in the development of quality assurance programs. We believe that nurses will be pivotal in the design and operation of such programs. The rationale for this is that nurses represent the largest group of care providers, are full-time employees of the institutions where they work, are present in those institutions on a continuous basis, and are becoming increasingly involved in managerial activities within health care institutions. Traditionally, nurses have also tended to view patients as both groups and individuals, and thus they are oriented toward a more organizational approach to patient care. We suggest, therefore, that nursing may have the greatest potential for creating stable structures for and assuring a leadership role in integrated quality assurance programs.

The papers included as readings in this book are organized into four parts. In the first part, a conceptual orientation to the book is provided by contrasting a traditional professional model of control to another model, called the Performance Accountability Model, which may need to be followed if institutional quality assurance programs are to be effective. In effect, it is suggested that if professional expectations for autonomy are to be reconciled with evolving institutional accountabilities, there must be an expansion of the domain of professional accountability to include a concern for both cost and quality and the development of explicit mechanisms of control both within and external to health care institutions. The latter suggestion is developed in greater detail by the readings included in the remainder of the book.

The second part focuses on what may be the two most important and challenging issues in quality control: (1) the problem of structuring control mechanisms in an environment dominated by professionals and (2) the problem of bringing about human and organizational change. These are the issues that must be addressed if quality assurance is to shift from a mere system of measurement and assessment to an effective mechanism for assuring that a high quality of care is provided to patients.

In the third part, data and measurement concerns that may need to be considered if quality assurance is to assume a more programmatic form are addressed. In addition, several of the authors conceptualize the quality assurance function from the perspectives of program evaluation and multi-institutional systems.

The last part of the book includes a brief capsulization of key educational, research, and policy recommendations identified by the contributors.

Organization and Change in Health Care Quality Assurance combines research and its applications to the design and analysis of quality assurance programs. It also uniquely locates quality assurance as an organization/behavior problem. This book should therefore be suitable for use both by students of health and nursing administration and by administrators who have responsibility for organizing quality assurance programs, as well as by their quality assurance staffs. In view of the considerable emphasis given by many of the authors to the research and conceptual sides of quality assurance, the material presented here should be of value to both clinical and social science researchers concerned with quality assurance. Finally, individuals in policy positions may also find this book to be of interest because of its emphasis on the necessity for charting new directions in quality assurance.

Acknowledgments

Appreciation is expressed to the organizations that provided support for the various conferences from which many of the readings included in this book were drawn: the W.K. Kellogg Foundation, the Joint Commission on Accreditation of Hospitals (JCAH), the Western Network for Education in Health Administration, the Nursing Council of the Western Interstate Commission for Higher Education (WCHEN), and the University of Colorado Schools of Nursing and Medicine. We thank Professor Eunice Blair for her thoughtful encouragement as this book was being developed as well as for her perceptive emphasis on the necessity for interdisciplinary collaboration in the area of quality assurance. To Tica McCollom we are indebted for her steady and valued assistance in editing, typing, and attention to the many administrative details involved in the preparation of this book.

Part I

Performance Accountability and Quality Assurance

1. Professionalism, Accountability, and Peer Review

ROICE D. LUKE and ROBERT E. MODROW

If there is a single feature distinguishing quality assurance activities in health care from those in other industries it is the exercise of autonomy embodied in the concept of peer review. The technical aspects of quality assurance per se, i.e., defining and measuring quality and designing assessment systems, do not set the health care system apart [1]. The problem of determining whether one good or service is qualitatively different from another is just as challenging for banking and the automotive industries as it is for the health care field. But each industry's mechanisms for implementing change, once qualitative differences are identified, differ significantly. In health care, these have evolved from a profession structured to insulate providers from the scrutiny and intervention of the institutions within which they work [2, 3]. Thus buffered from organizational interference, the health professional's work is difficult to evaluate and difficult to control. Therefore, professional autonomy may represent one of the most important impediments to health institutions becoming more fully accountable for the care they provide.

It is primarily this problem that led the Joint Commission on Accreditation of Hospitals (JCAH) to approve a new Standard on Quality Assurance in April of 1979 [4]. The new standard reflects the observation that considerable progress has been achieved in monitoring patient care activities, though little measurable change in overall institutional performance has resulted from quality assurance activities [5, 6, 7]. The standard focuses on the structure of professional/organizational relationships in an attempt to reconcile the emerging accountability requirements of health institutions with the traditional professional autonomy requirements of clinical decision making. It thus shifts the locus of concern for quality to

This paper was originally presented at the Invitational Conference on Research in Quality Assurance sponsored jointly by the University of Colorado Health Sciences Center, the Association of University Programs in Health Administration, and the Joint Commission on Accreditation of Hospitals, November 7, 1980 in Denver, Colorado.

the institutional level where issues of resource allocation, organization structure, and provider behavior are addressed within a common framework. The purpose of this reading is to present a general orientation within which a reconciliation of organizational and professional concerns for quality might be accomplished.

AUTONOMY

The autonomy accorded health professionals, in particular members of the medical profession, represents a general societal recognition that to be carried out effectively, the work of health professionals must be conducted in an environment of patient-provider confidentiality and mutual trust. The autonomy of health professionals is not something won through the industriousness and determination of individual professional groups. Rather, it represents the willingness of society to grant that autonomy, if assured that its interests will be protected by self-regulatory or peer review monitoring of the profession's members. In other words, the expectation is that health professionals will ultimately be accountable for their own actions.

It is important to note, of course, that changing societal expectations can lead either to strengthening or levying restrictions on that autonomy. Clearly, over the last 15 to 20 years we have been willing to restrict the autonomy of both professionals and institutions, when in doing so the public interest was better served. This is starkly reflected in the increasing structure of regulation in the areas of cost and quality control, the growing reliance on legal remedies to resolve a vast array of health care conflicts, the continuing experimentation and tinkering with the organization of the health care system (ranging from increased use of new practitioners to stimulation of competition), and the increasing readiness of industry, unions, third party payers and other nongovernmental interest groups to assume an active role in health care affairs.

The effect of these developments has been to formalize the accountability obligations of health institutions, particularly hospitals, thus increasing the potential for conflict between institutional goals of self-regulation and the autonomy requirements of health professionals. The potential for such conflict is perhaps the greatest when designing the institutional mechanisms for quality assurance since these, by definition, reach to the very core of professional work.

Strategies for Assuring Quality

From the perspective of developing public policy, it would appear that there are at least three major strategies for assuring the quality of care: regulation, competition and voluntary self-regulation [8, 9, 10, 11, 12]. Regardless of which of these approaches to control is emphasized in public policy, we suggest that none of them directly addresses the essentially organizational problem of integrating the emerging accountability obligations of institutions with the traditional autonomy requirements of professionals. Of the three, *regulation* offers the most formalized and potentially coercive approach to quality control. If it is effective, it is very likely to threaten the autonomy necessary for professional work. In actual practice, its effectiveness, especially in the area of quality assurance, is greatly limited because of the ability (and often, need) of professionals (or institutions, for that matter) to moderate or escape the demands of regulation through claims of "patient uniqueness" or "medical emergency" [2].

Competition is less likely to threaten professional autonomy since it focuses less on individual patient-provider relationships and more on institutional performance. Competitive pressures should stimulate health institutions to assure that the care offered is perceived as high in quality. On the other hand, competition shifts the burden of assessment to the consumer, a strategy with a long tradition in the economies of western societies, but obviously limited when applied to the health care field [13].

Volunteerism is the approach that has long been the hallmark of the health care field. Interest in it has recently renewed [10]. When applied at the institutional level, it becomes the very embodiment of the professional concept of autonomy. If volunteerism were implemented at the institutional level merely as an approach to "self-protectionism," it would assure the autonomy of professional work, yet be unlikely to serve the public interest any more than traditional approaches to professional self-regulation. On the other hand, if volunteerism leads to the design of formal mechanisms of control that, though implemented and directed by health professionals, were continuously subjected to public review, theoretically it could serve the public interest while protecting the autonomy requirements of health professionals [14]. Operationalized in this manner it might produce less rhetoric for self-protection and more self-directed efforts toward public accountability at both the institutional and patient-provider levels.

To a degree, voluntary self-regulation is reflected in such well-established mechanisms as professional certification boards, the JCAH, foundations for medical care, and the quasi-public PSROs and licensure boards. While all of these serve important functions, with few exceptions they do not monitor patient care delivery on a continuous basis or implement change as problems are identified and analyzed. The PSROs and the JCAH are set up, in part, to assure that this is done; but they represent external enforcers and not on-line implementers of needed change.

We suggest that solutions to the problem of self-regulation are not likely to emerge from developing public policy, but instead from the development of organizational structures and managerial techniques that directly address conflicting accountability and autonomy requirements. The challenge is to identify the characteristics of quality assurance mechanisms most likely to contribute to the reconciliation of such conflicts.

ACCOUNTABILITY

Accountability is a general concept referring in this case to the obligations of health professionals and institutions to assure responsible performance in the conduct of professional duties [14, 15, 16, 17]. How such obligations are specified and what forms the mechanisms of control take vary across individuals and organizations. Differences in content and structure are likely to differentiate successful from unsuccessful quality assurance programs. To capture such differences we introduce two important dimensions of accountability:

1. *domain* of accountability—the content or constituent elements of accountability which include *quality,* i.e., technical performance, accessibility, continuity/wholism, humanism, etc., and *cost;* and
2. *structure* of accountability—the configuration of professional and bureaucratic mechanisms for assuring responsible performance.

Traditionally, health professionals and institutions have tended to restrict their perceived domain of accountability to the assurance of *quality* [18, 19]. Concerns for the cost of care or even its accessibility have generally not been considered within their scope of accountability, but treated primarily as matters of public concern. Physicians, for example, have been expected to provide the best care available, regardless of cost; when such care was not accessible, government funds provided the additional financing.

It has also been traditional for the structures of accountability to take an implicit form, typified by loosely organized, often informal mechanisms of control. The structure of such mechanisms is illustrated in Figure 1-1.

Until the late 60s and early 70s the control of health institutions was left primarily to the JCAH and institutional licensure. While these have, perhaps, upgraded the "environment" of delivery they have not created a capability to monitor and control the everyday provision of health services. The same is also true for the health professions. The medical profession has relied primarily upon implicit mechanisms of accountability, turning to explicit forms of control only at well defined points in the educational process and in practice. The monitoring of performance, for example, has been conducted primarily during the initial training period and at the point of entry into the profession. The sanctioning of deviant performance has been a rare event, due largely to the lack of effective ongoing monitoring and an unwillingness to interfere in the work of "colleagues" [20, 21].

In general, the medical profession's expression of accountability has been direct to the public, through the doctor-patient relationship at the individual level, and licensure and certification at the societal level. Such direct links to the public enabled the profession, at least until the mid-60s, to minimize its accountability to health care institutions. They also offered the profession the leverage to resist

Figure 1-1 Traditional Accountability Model

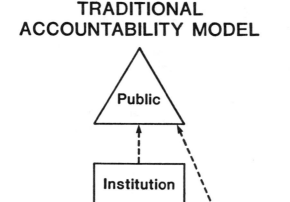

TRADITIONAL
ACCOUNTABILITY MODEL

⟶ **Explicit accountability**
---➤ **Implicit accountability**

efforts to expand its domain of accountability beyond a primary concern for the quality of care.

By contrast, the nursing profession has traditionally been directly and explicitly accountable to institutions for the cost of care, and to physicians for the quality of care. In part, the lack of functional autonomy for nurses may be attributable to an absence of explicit accountability to the public. While nursing has evolved a licensure relationship with the public, the ongoing control of both the cost and quality of care has been handled primarily through administrative and clinical channels. In effect, nursing licensure laws have served to control entrance into the profession, but have not provided the leverage to offset the control which administration and medicine have had over nursing.

Over the past 10 to 15 years the model illustrated in Figure 1-1 has come under increasing public criticism. The reason for this has been the public's concern over the rising costs of care, though the quality of care has continued to be a matter of public interest. As government contributions to the financing of health services increase, and as the economy continues to experience an inflationary spiral, concern over the motives underlying professional and institutional decision making is likely to intensify. The effect of this is already rather visible in the variety of specific legal and regulatory mechanisms focused on institutional performance.

As health institutions become increasingly accountable for both the cost and quality of care, the autonomy of health professionals who work within them will be threatened. The public is no longer likely to accept, at face value, mere reassurances that the autonomy it guarantees serves the public interest. Requirements that reassurances (implicit accountability) be validated through measures of demonstrated performance and the use of formal mechanisms of control (explicit accountability) will likely constitute the emerging form of professional and institutional accountability. It follows that if health professionals are to retain control over their work, they must evolve new approaches to self-regulation. Specifically, it is suggested, they must 1) expand their domain of accountability to include both cost and quality and 2) develop more explicit structures of accountability for both internal and public purposes.

The challenge facing the health professions is, perhaps, best illustrated by again comparing nursing and medicine. Because of its limited power base both within and outside of health institutions, nursing is less able to resist public pressures to account for the services the profession provides. Rather than resist such pressures, a more viable strategy for increasing autonomy would be to embrace, as a profession, the obligation of assuring the cost-effectiveness of nursing care. While this departs from the traditional approach to professionalism, it serves to reconcile public demands with the profession's striving for increased functional independence.

As public pressures on health institutions increase, the structure of nursing accountability may also need to be transformed. Should nursing fail to respond to changing public expectations, it is reasonable to expect that one of the following two scenarios might emerge. First, given the increasing obligations for health institutions to assure the cost-effectiveness of care, lay administrators can be expected to fill the vacuum for control on the cost side, thus solidifying their dominance over budgetary matters affecting nursing. A probable outgrowth of this could be increased reliance on negotiated solutions to the inevitable cost/quality trade-offs. It is not unreasonable to expect that this would move nursing further away from the professional model toward one involving collective bargaining.

Should nursing defer to administration the implementation of accountability structures, a second scenario could be one in which administration replaces medicine as the agency to which nursing is explicitly and directly accountable. This could be accomplished in many ways, but is likely to involve a cooptation strategy of including administratively trained nurses as members of the administrative team, with responsibility for the cost effectiveness of nursing services. In other words, hospital nurses may have control structures imposed on them, especially if they choose not to assume the responsibility for structuring the control of both the costs and quality of care.

Given these scenarios, it seems incumbent upon nursing, medicine and other health professional groups to reevaluate their approach to accountability. The structure of this approach we label the *Performance Accountability Model,* and illustrate in Figure 1-2.

As indicated, if nursing and medicine are to counter the increased accountability obligations of health institutions, and respond to equivalent obligations imposed on their respective professions, combinations of direct and indirect (the latter through health institutions) accountability to the public may need to be structured. These should be explicit (not based on reassurances and trust) and should address, at least, the domain areas of *cost* and *quality*. With these in place, health institutions could satisfy public expectations by holding physicians and nurses explicitly accountable for their work. In turn, the professional groups could structure explicit and direct accountability mechanisms (e.g., PSROs for nursing

---

Figure 1-2 Performance Accountability Model

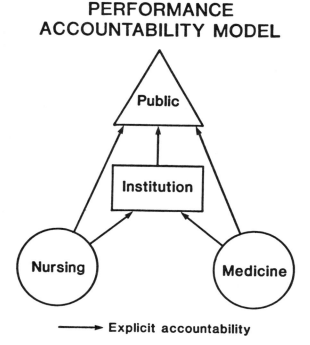

PERFORMANCE ACCOUNTABILITY MODEL

⟶ **Explicit accountability**

and medicine, especially if they are directed more toward the respective professions and less toward the work settings—a direction that runs counter to current trends for existing PSROs [22]), thus providing balance for the growing power of health institutions.

CONCLUSION

This paper has attempted to call attention to the interdependence of changing institutional accountability expectations and professional autonomy requirements. It is suggested that as health institutions experience increasing public scrutiny and control, the health professions must expand their accepted domain of accountability to include control over costs as well as quality, and create more explicitly structured mechanisms of control. Such mechanisms must link the professions directly to the public through externally based control structures generated by the professions, and indirectly through the use of formal structures established within health institutions. By evolving both direct and indirect mechanisms of control, the professions will balance the rising power of health institutions with countervailing structures of explicit self-regulation.

Quality assurance may be the vehicle through which professional mechanisms of control might best be introduced, particularly since it focuses on the primary obligation of the health professions to assure proper performance. By expanding quality assurance to include the cost of professional work, the health professions respond directly to changing societal expectations, while assuring the privilege of professional self-regulation.

Specifics about necessary structural features, methods for accomplishing behavioral change and interrelating cost and quality, however, remain to be developed. These essentially organizational and economic aspects of quality assurance have received little analytic and research attention. We thus have in quality assurance a classic example of the "horse and cart" reversal in priorities. Since the 50s, the literature has focused almost exclusively on the technical aspects of definition, measurement and information systems. Clearly, such is premature if we do not yet know how the mechanisms of control should be operationalized. Data do not bring about change, they merely facilitate the change process [23]. The challenge, then, is to design mechanisms of control that are sensitive to the unique characteristics of health professionals and institutions.

REFERENCES

1. Juran, J.M., F.M. Gryna, Jr., and R.S. Bingham, Jr. (eds.). *Quality Control Handbook*. New York: McGraw-Hill Book Co., 1974.
2. Freidson, E. *Profession of Medicine: A Study of the Sociology of Applied Knowledge*. New York: Dodd, Mead & Co., 1973.

3. Scott, R. Managing professional work: three models of control for health organizations. *Health Services Research* 17(3), Fall 1982 (forthcoming).

4. New Quality Assurance Standard Approved. *Perspectives on Accreditation* (3):1, May/June 1979.

5. Health Services Administration, Office of Planning, Evaluation, and Legislation (OPEL). *PSRO: An Initial Evaluation of the Professional Standards Review Organization.* Vol. 1, February 1978.

6. Ginsburg, P.B. and D.M. Karetz. *The Effects of PSROs on Health Care Costs: Current Findings and Future Evaluations.* The Congress of the United States, Congressional Budget Office, June 1979.

7. Anderson, O.W. and M. Shields. Quality measurement and control in physician decision making: state of the art. *Health Services Research* 17(2):125, Summer 1982.

8. Ellwood, P.M. Models for organizing health services and implications of legislative proposals. *Milbank Memorial Fund Quarterly* 52:67, 1974.

9. Enthoven, A.C. *Health Plan: The Only Practical Solution to the Soaring Cost of Medical Care.* Reading, MA: Addison-Wesley, 1980.

10. McNerney, W.J. Control of health care costs in the 1980's. *The New England Journal of Medicine* 303:1088, November 6, 1980.

11. Altman, S.H. and S.L. Weiner. Regulation as second best. In W. Greenberg (ed.). *Competition in the Health Care Sector: Past, Present, and Future.* Germantown, MD: Aspen Systems Corp., 1978.

12. Schultz, C.L. *The Public Use of Private Interest.* Washington, DC: The Brookings Institution, 1977.

13. Pauley, M.V. Is medical care different? In W. Greenberg (ed.). *Competition in the Health Care Sector: Past, Present, and Future.* Germantown, MD: Aspen Systems Corp., 1978.

14. Matek, S.J. Accountability: Its Meaning and Its Relevance to the Health Care Field. USDHEW, PHS, HRA, Pub. No. (NRA) 77-72, September 1977.

15. Etzioni, A. Alternative conceptualizations of accountability: the example of health administration. *Public Administration Review* 35:279, May/June 1975.

16. Greenfield, H.I. *Accountability in Health Facilities.* New York: Frederick A. Praeger Publishers, 1975.

17. Luke, R. and R. Modrow. An accountability framework for the measurement of quality. In E.J. Hinman (ed.). *Advanced Medical Systems: Health Decisions Systems.* Chicago: Year Book Medical Publishers, Inc., 1980.

18. Havighurst, C.C. and J.F. Blumstein. Coping with quality/cost trade-offs in medical care: the role of PSROs. *Northwestern University Law Review* 70:6, March/April 1975.

19. Donabedian, A. *The Definition of Quality and Approaches to its Assessment.* Ann Arbor, MI: Health Administration Press, 1980.

20. Bosk, C. *Forgive and Remember, Managing Medical Failure.* Chicago: University of Chicago Press, 1979.

21. Freidson, E. *Doctoring Together: A Study of Professional Social Control.* New York: Elsevier, 1975.

22. Goran, M.J. The evaluation of the PSRO hospital review system. (Supplement to) *Medical Care* 17:1, May 1979.

23. Luke, R.D. and R.W. Boss. Barriers limiting the implementation of quality assurance programs. *Health Services Research* 16(3):305, Fall, 1981.

2. Delivery and Assurance of Quality Health Care: A Rights-Based Foundation

JEAN WATSON

Quality assurance is a troubling area to consider because of the conceptual and operational problems it creates for health care providers and institutions. While quality of care has for a long time been a direct concern of providers, the management of the phenomenon has only recently been addressed. The assurance of quality of care has now become a task for providers, as well as for systems engineers, behavioral scientists, management administrators, economists, and others.

Perhaps the most dramatic concerns, however, involve the related ethical duties, responsibilities, and obligations imposed on providers and institutions, and perhaps on society at large. Such concerns are reinforced by the prevailing consumer rights and entitlements to quality care that health care providers and institutions must consider in the conduct of their duties.

The ethical aspects of quality assurance, however, tend to be lost in the maze of conceptual and operational problems that so often dominate quality assurance activities. It is the purpose of this reading, therefore, to draw attention to some of these ethical considerations. It is suggested that as health care professionals and institutions experiment with quality assurance mechanisms, they should be aware of the ethical implications of the measurement and assessment strategies they evolve.

BIOETHICS AS AN AREA OF INFLUENCE

Before examining some ethical positions that may help to clarify some of the ethical claims in the area of quality assurance, we will examine briefly what is meant by health ethics or bioethics. Bioethics is a concern that spans professional groups and disciplines and attempts to nourish science, medicine, and health care with human values. According to LeRoy Walters of the Kennedy Institute in

Bioethics, it involves systematic study; an attempt to relate and apply ethical and moral traditions to new developments in science and technology (for example, quality assurance); and an attempt to institutionalize bioethical concerns and to bring institutions under study, examination, and change in regard to human values.[1] Bioethics raises questions about what is *right* or *ought* to be done in a health science situation. In effect, it calls for decisions to be examined in moral or value terms, rather than merely as professional or technical considerations.[2(p4)]

In a broad sense, one begins to see that an ethical dilemma can emerge because of different moral claims on what is right, good, or ought to be done in a given situation. For example, it is often the case that cost, quality, or access cannot be optimized at one time. Thus, different moral or ethical claims on the ensuing trade-offs can emerge because of the differing ethical perspectives of institutions, professionals, consumers, and society. An ethical dilemma has been defined as a difficult problem seemingly incapable of a satisfying solution or a choice or a situation involving a choice between equally unsatisfactory alternatives.[2(p6)] For example, quality care may be considered "right" in an individual institution but not considered "good" if it conflicts with institutional cost-effectiveness objectives. Thus it is possible to have a "health practice success" but an "ethical failure."

Professional codes of ethics govern the usual and ordinary encounters between practitioners and clients. However, when those codes are applied to the social system or to the common good, a breakdown occurs, and the "archaic state" of codes of ethics becomes evident when applied to the larger social institution of health care delivery systems. This breakdown is often evidenced by the consumer's lack of trust of practitioners and by the conflicts that emerge between professionals and the institutions within which they work.

The ethical dilemmas inherent in quality assurance can be examined from the perspectives of three major theoretical positions: (1) teleology, (2) deontology, and (3) an alternative rights-based position.

Utilitarian Teleological Ethical Position

The teleological position is a consequential theory of ethics that looks at purposes, ends, and aims. This leads to a utilitarian view of quality assurance based on early positions of Jeremy Bentham (1748–1832) and John Stuart Mill (1806–1873). An action is considered right if it produces good consequences. The criteria used to examine consequences, however, may be subject to change, depending on the framework or the objectives. Is the desired consequence quality assurance or some spinoff criterion such as patient satisfaction or cost containment? Regardless of the criteria chosen, a utilitarian-based ethical decision would be based on outcomes or on the consequences produced, rather than on the process itself.

Nonutilitarian Deontological Position

A second major ethical framework may be labeled deontology. This view is considered a nonconsequential or nonutilitarian position or a theory of duty. One's duty is to act rightly, the assessment of which is not determined by the consequences of one's acts. For example, in the quality assurance area, one's professional duty may be perceived as providing quality health care regardless of the ability to ensure, measure, or control the outcome. An action would be considered right and good if it recognized the rights of individuals. According to this ethical position, humans are treated as ends in and of themselves and not as means to an end. This is based on Immanuel Kant's (1724–1804) view of duty; for example, Kant said, "One has a duty not to lie even if the world would perish."[3] Translated to quality care, one might say that health care providers have a duty to provide quality health care, even if the hospital would go bankrupt.

Means/End and Individual Versus Collective Good Problems

Underlying both of these ethical frameworks is the means/end problem. If quality assurance is a means to an end, how is the human client to be viewed: as a means to a system end, or as an end in and of himself or herself?

When associating quality assurance with what is best for an individual, a different set of values and norms operates than when it is associated with what is best for the common good. Values and goals associated with *excellence* and values and goals tied to *accountability* behavior may be very different. An inherent conflict may exist between professional values of excellence of care and behaviors of measurement, monitoring, and evaluation for which they are accountable. A still larger ethical dilemma occurs if one asks, not only for what is one accountable, but to whom? Society? Institution? Administrator? Profession? Client?

Is the locus of concern on the "individual good" or on the "common good"? The value differences between the two are not easily reconciled. The individual good emphasizes individual quality and excellence; the common good must emphasize control of quality for the whole and its impact on the professions, the institutions, and society. It is at this point that the difficult trade-offs between cost and quality, between individuals and groups, and between different groups become matters of ethical concern to those involved in quality assurance activities. We can see that both utilitarian and nonutilitarian ethical positions operate simultaneously in all of us, even though we may use one or the other to justify our positions, depending on our unique setting, circumstances, and involvements.

An Alternative Rights-Based Position

A third and last ethical framework has been proposed that may provide a structure for guiding one's commitment to quality assurance in health care.

According to Miller,[4] Rawls,[5] and others, an alternative ethical theory must deal with three things: (1) duties (as with a deontological position), (2) goals-consequences (as with a teleological position), and (3) *rights*. (Human rights is added as an important consideration for an alternative position.) An effective ethical framework would need to show a relationship between the three, because each affects the other and they often are not mutually exclusive. An alternative ethical framework may help establish some conceptual clarity for justifying an ethical position regarding quality assurance.

The alternative rights-based framework indicates that one can view either goals or rights as the fundamental issue. If one adheres to a rights- or goals-based theory, then the rights or goals are primary and duties would be derived accordingly. However, in examining quality assurance from a strict goals-based position, the operational outcome variables (goals) would direct quality assurance decisions. Individual rights and professional institutional duties would be determined by the designated goal. If the goal were *assurance* of quality, assurance would be an end in and of itself, not a means to an end (to provide quality). A goals-based assurance position could provide a professional-institutional success but could result in an ethical failure for individual clients. If, on the other hand, the agreed-upon goal were quality, then the rights and duties of the professions and institutions would flow from the pursuit of providing quality health care. The consequences or assurance outcomes would become secondary to the primary goal of quality outcomes. Either way the goal in quality assurance is defined there is a potential ethical dilemma, because with quality assurance both areas are necessary and any choice between the goals results in equally unsatisfactory alternatives. If, however, a rights-based ethical framework is selected under the alternatives proposed, primary attention is directed toward individual rights.

Historically, policy makers and institutions have tended to avoid or eliminate rights, rather than to allow them, thus providing "grounds" for the emergence of the document, "A Patient's Bill of Rights."[6,7] The document merely restores rights that people had in the first place but were denied in favor of the institutional-professional goals that were considered first. Thus, one can see how a goals-based theory led the health care system "astray," because the goals were system, not client, related. The very foundation of quality assurance programs cautions that the same mistake not be repeated.

ADVANCEMENT OF LEGAL RIGHTS

If one considers a rights-based ethical position for quality assurance, then one selects the most fundamental perspective to guide ethical decisions. A rights-based position is a Kantian, deontologically based view, mentioned earlier. In this ethical view, people are ends in and of themselves. The presupposition of a rights-based theory is inherent in Western philosophy; it is seemingly demanded by consumers and now is required by legislation. P.L. 92-603, the law establishing the PSRO program, simply allows citizens to establish a claim to their fundamental right to quality health care and the right to its assurance. A rights-based theory is hard to overlook in considering ethical issues in quality assurance programs. If quality health care is viewed as a fundamental right, then the primary duty would be to provide quality care and the goal of assurance would fall to a lower level of priority.

The irony of a rights-based position today is that the establishment of Professional Standards Review Organizations in effect moved the right to quality health care from a negative right status for an individual to a positive right status. For example, prior to the enactment of P.L. 92-603, quality health care was considered a right of all people—but a negative right; that is, everyone and anyone was free to pursue it, but there was no absolute mandate that society, institutions, or providers actually guarantee that the right be provided. In a positive right context, a "right to assurance of quality health care" is more than just a belief or interest an individual may have about receiving quality health care. The positive right resulting from legislation invokes entitlements. Entitlements "mean not those things which it would be nice for people to have, or which they would prefer to have, but which they must have and which if they do not have they may demand, whether we like it or not."[8] Now quality of health care appears to have moved beyond something that is preferred, to something to which everyone is entitled. This means that the institution and the provider have a duty not only to provide quality health care but also to take measures to ensure that it is provided.[9,10]

ADVANCEMENT OF CONSUMER RIGHTS

The consumerism movement is an important incident that should be considered when addressing some of the ethical concerns inherent in the assurance of quality health care. Society, health care institutions, and professionals have done such a good job of convincing everyone that they have extensive rights as consumers of health care that they now seek it, demand it, and are outraged if they are denied access, inconvenienced, or injured in the process. In a very real sense, consumers have begun to lay claim to their entitlements to quality health care irrespective of the legal requirement to provide the right.

On the one hand, consumers are demanding a right they believe they have, and which our Western philosophy supports; on the other hand, P.L. 92-603 and our legal system regulates and ensures that right. In a basic ethical sense the right to quality health care already exists and has existed; however, now citizens are claiming it and the law is demanding it.

Compounding these events is the fact that consumers of health care seem to have changed their expectations regarding quality health care more rapidly than have health institutions and providers. The social concerns of the 1970s led to a conviction by citizens that they must participate in decisions affecting their lives. Since this perspective has been slow in coming in the traditional health care delivery system, various alternative health care systems are emerging that are largely independent of professional-institutional bureaucracies. These systems, which are primarily sponsored by consumer groups, have attracted up to 20 million people in some 500,000 self-help—mutual aid groups that in the past would have been handled by natural support systems or health care professionals.[11]

Today, consumers are trying to renegotiate their relationship with health care providers and the system. They show interest in personalized, decentralized delivery of service, and they request a wider range of choices and more participation and control over decisions.[12-15]

The consumer movements have responded more quickly and more effectively than the established groups; consequently, the prevailing attitudes and assumptions of institutions and providers are seriously out of phase with the social, legal, and consumer demands. The current concerns for change in the health care delivery systems are even now largely due to the legal and consumer demands and not to any ethical conviction or awareness that prevailing attitudes and assumptions may be stale or that quality health care is a fundamental right to begin with.

CONCLUSION

It could be argued that structural defects in the system must be repaired if the system is to deal with present and coming problems associated with assuring the quality of health care.[16] We suggest, however, that the structural defects are not incompetence or lack of knowledge, technology, or even lack of commitment to change, but rather a crisis in the underlying values, assumptions, and functions of our health care delivery system.[17,18] Assurance of quality health care will not be forthcoming until individual consumer rights as well as provider rights are acknowledged.

If health care programs are to demonstrate true concern for the quality of health care, institutions and providers must acknowledge the basic human right to quality health care, repair the medical model system of delivery, promote the advancement of *health* professional groups, and restore to patients the right to humanistic care.

It is hoped that in the 1980s a new awareness of the fundamental defects of our health care delivery system will evolve. As this nation moves into its role as a mature postindustrial society, a reexamination of its rights-based foundation must be directed toward its health care quality assurance programs; only by doing so can provider and institutional duties be ethically determined for both the individual and the common good.

REFERENCES

1. Walters L: Seminar Notes: Intensive Session in Bioethics. Washington, DC, Kennedy Institute in Bioethics, Georgetown University, July 1978.
2. Davis A, Aroskar MA: *Ethical Dilemma and Nursing Practice.* New York, Appleton-Century-Crofts, 1978, pp 4 and 6.
3. Kant I: *Foundations on the Metaphysics of Morals: Text and Critical Essays,* Wolff RP (ed). New York, Bobbs-Merrill Co Inc, 1969.
4. Miller B: Course Presentation—Hasting Conference on Ethics in Public Policy. Boulder, University of Colorado, July 1979.
5. Rawls J: *A Theory of Justice.* Cambridge, Mass, Belknap Press, 1971.
6. Gaylin W: The patient's bill of rights, editorial. *Saturday Rev Sci,* March 1973, p 22.
7. Schwartz DH: The patient's bill of rights and the hospital administrator, in Bandman EL, Bandman B (eds): *Bioethics and Human Rights.* Boston, Little Brown & Co, 1978, pp 277-280.
8. Fried C: Equality and rights in medical care. *Hastings Center Rep* 1976; 6(February):29-34.
9. Fried C: Equality and rights in medical care, in Beauchamp T, Walters L (eds): *Contemporary Issues in Bioethics.* Belmont, Calif, Dickenson Publishing Co, 1978; pp 364-370.
10. Fried C: Rights and health care: Beyond equity and efficiency. *N Engl J Med* 1975; 293:241-245.
11. Bandman B: The human rights of patients, nurses, and other health professionals. *Am J Nursing* 1978; 78:84.
12. Sidel V: The right to health care: An international perspective, in Bandman EL, Bandman B (eds): *Bioethics and Human Rights.* Boston, Little Brown & Co, 1978, pp 341-350.
13. Braden W: Changes on the way: Rose colored crystal ball offers hope for 1980s. *Denver Post–Chicago Sun Times,* January 1, 1980, p 11.
14. Illich I: *Medical Nemesis: The Expropriation of Health.* New York, Pantheon Books, 1976.
15. Kass LR: The pursuit of health and the right to health, in Beauchamp T, Walters L (eds): *Contemporary Issues in Bioethics.* Belmont, Calif, Dickenson Publishing Co, 1978, pp 352-363.
16. Outka G: Social justice and equal access to health care, in Beauchamp T, Walters L (eds): *Contemporary Issues in Bioethics.* Belmont, Calif, Dickenson Publishing Co, 1978.
17. Pelletier KR: *Mind As Healer, Mind As Slayer.* New York, Delta Books, 1977.
18. Reston J: Where are we going. *New York Times,* December 23, 1979, p 13.

3. The Quality Assurance Standard of the JCAH: A Rational Approach to Patient Care Evaluation

MARYANNE SHANAHAN

Anyone who is aware of the evolution of quality assurance efforts and evaluation requirements realizes that the new quality assurance standard of the Joint Commission on Accreditation of Hospitals (JCAH) was prompted and supported by health care professionals and that the standard attempts to reflect the state of the art in quality assurance. In developing the standard, the JCAH responded to the need for a comprehensive and practical approach to quality assurance. The quality assurance standard is the current phase of an evolutionary process that began in 1917 when the American College of Surgeons published the Minimum Standard for hospitals. The initiation of voluntary accreditation, the establishment of the JCAH, and the development of the quality assurance standard are all part of this process. The evolution of quality assurance in this century, the intent of the quality assurance standard, and the features of the standard that make it a useful management tool will be discussed in this reading.

EVOLUTION OF QUALITY ASSURANCE

The idea underlying what eventually became the JCAH received its first official expression in a resolution made on November 15, 1912, at the Third Clinical Congress of Surgeons of North America. The resolution stated, in part, that

> some system of standardization of hospital equipment and hospital work should be developed, to the end that those [sic] institutions having the highest ideals may have proper recognition before the profession, and that those of inferior equipment and standards should be stimulated to raise the quality of their work. In this way patients will receive the best type of treatment, and the public will have some means of recognizing those institutions devoted to the highest ideals of medicine.[1]

This resolution was made to correct unacceptable conditions in many hospitals in the United States and to improve the quality of patient care being delivered. In many cases, professional services in hospitals were not properly supervised; medical staffs were not organized; hospitals lacked clinical laboratory, radiology, and other necessary services for conducting proper preoperative and postoperative studies of surgical patients; and medical records were unsatisfactory. The American College of Surgeons (ACS) became aware of the need to establish standards for hospitals during the first three years of its existence. During these years, the College rejected over 60 percent of otherwise qualified candidates for fellowship because their medical records were insufficient to form a basis for determining their surgical and technical ability. To correct this and other deficiencies in hospitals, the ACS published the Minimum Standard in 1917 (Figure 3-1), and, in 1918, the ACS inaugurated a voluntary accreditation program called the Hospital Standardization Program.

The Minimum Standard contained the first formal requirements for the review and evaluation of the quality of patient care. The standard required the medical staff to review and analyze at various intervals its experience in clinical departments and to base its review and analysis on the clinical records of patients (see standard 3b, Figure 3-1). The Minimum Standard also addressed the quality of the medical record, the quality of clinical performance, and the requirements for medical staff membership.

The quality of care in hospitals that participated in the Hospital Standardization Program improved noticeably, and the medical records of physicians in approved hospitals became more acceptable. Over the years more and more hospitals sought the benefit of the voluntary survey process. The number of approved hospitals rose from 89 during the program's first year of operation to more than 3,000 in 1951.

By 1950, the Hospital Standardization Program had grown to the extent that the cost of operation was prohibitive. To succeed, voluntary accreditation had to be vested in an independent organization that could devote all of its efforts to improving and promoting voluntary accreditation, and it needed the support and cooperation of the entire medical and hospital field.

The ACS enlisted the support of other national organizations and, in 1951, the JCAH was established by the American College of Surgeons, the American College of Physicians, the American Hospital Association, the American Medical Association, and the Canadian Medical Association. (The Canadian Medical Association withdrew in 1959 to participate in its own national accreditation program.) In 1979, the Board of Commissioners of the JCAH accepted the American Dental Association as its fifth corporate member.

Under the direction of the Board of Commissioners, the JCAH continued to expand and improve the Hospital Standardization Program. In 1953, it published the *Standards for Hospital Accreditation,* an updated and expanded version of the Minimum Standard. This edition included brief standards on governing body,

Figure 3-1 The Minimum Standard of the American College of
Surgeons' Hospital Standardization Program

The Minimum Standard

1. That physicians and surgeons privileged to practice in the hospital be organized as a definite group or staff. Such organization has nothing to do with the question as to whether the hospital is "open" or "closed," nor need it affect the various existing types of staff organization. The word STAFF is here defined as the group of doctors who practice in the hospital inclusive of all groups such as the "regular staff," "the visiting staff," and the "associate staff."

2. That membership upon the staff be restricted to physicians and surgeons who are (a) full graduates of medicine in good standing and legally licensed to practice in their respective states or provinces, (b) competent in their respective fields, and (c) worthy in character and in matters of professional ethics; that in this latter connection the practice of the division of fees, under any guise whatever, be prohibited.

3. That the staff initiate and, with the approval of the governing board of the hospital, adopt rules, regulations, and policies governing the professional work of the hospital; that these rules, regulations, and policies specifically provide:

   (a) That staff meetings be held at least once each month. (In large hospitals the departments may choose to meet separately.)

   (b) That the staff review and analyze at regular intervals their clinical experience in the various departments of the hospital, such as medicine, surgery, obstetrics, and the other specialties; the clinical records of patients, free and pay, to be the basis for such review and analyses.

4. That accurate and complete records be written for all patients and filed in an accessible manner in the hospital—a complete case record being one which includes identification data; complaint; personal and family history; history of present illness; physical examination; special examinations, such as consultations, clinical laboratory, X-ray and other examinations; provisional or working diagnosis; medical or surgical treatment; gross and microscopical pathological findings; progress notes; final diagnosis; condition on discharge; follow-up and, in case of death, autopsy findings.

5. That diagnostic and therapeutic facilities under competent supervision be available for the study, diagnosis, and treatment of patients, these to include, at least (a) a clinical laboratory providing chemical, bacteriological, serological, and pathological services; (b) an X-ray department providing radiographic and fluoroscopic services.

bylaws, buildings, food preparation, dietary services, drug control, and nursing services.

Although this edition did not have a standard that specifically related to requirements for quality review, the quality of patient care was addressed in requirements for tissue review, medical record review, review of medical staff credentials, and coordination by the executive committee of all activities and general policies of the various clinical departments. The medical staff executive committee was also required to receive and act on reports of all hospital and medical staff committees. It is interesting to note that there were no specific quality review requirements for the nursing department at that time.

The 1953 edition of the standards underwent constant revision, and by 1966 more specific standards had been developed for the review of care. For the medical staff, the JCAH required the "review and clinical evaluation of the quality of medical care provided to all categories of patients on the basis of documented evidence" (typically, functions of the medical record, tissue, and medical audit committees).[2] These and other functions, such as surveillance of pharmacy and therapeutics, policies and practices, hospital admissions (utilization review), and hospital infections were to be conducted frequently enough to "assure that their objectives were being achieved."[2] Written reports were to be submitted for follow up and disposition by the executive committee of the medical staff.

For the nursing department, "constant review and evaluation of the nursing care provided patients" was to be conducted. According to the standards, this review and evaluation necessitated "written nursing care procedures and written nursing care plans for patients, either on an individual or nursing unit basis."[2]

In 1966 the Board of Commissioners voted to rewrite the standards to raise them from minimal essential to optimal achievable standards. These optimal achievable standards were published in the 1970 *Accreditation Manual for Hospitals (AMH)* and represented a landmark achievement for the JCAH. Review and evaluation requirements in the 1970 *AMH* reflected the new optimal achievable philosophy of the JCAH. The new standards included an interpretation and explanation of medical care evaluation and directed the medical staff to take all reasonable steps to ensure clinical practice of the highest quality.

For the medical staff to carry out this responsibility properly, each staff member had to "assist in promoting and maintaining high quality care, through the analysis, review, and evaluation of clinical practice that exists within the hospital."[3] Medical care evaluation was described as a fact-finding and educational function, an analysis of medical practice based on criteria established by the medical staff. The JCAH did not suggest any methodology by which care should be evaluated; in fact, the standard stated that "the formal means established to accomplish medical care evaluation is dependent upon, and varies with, the size and organizational structure of the hospital."[3] Whatever the organizational structure, however, the medical staff was to conduct evaluations of the medical, surgical, and obstetrical functions (including tissue review and analysis of necropsy reports) at least monthly. In addition, medical care evaluation was to include periodic review of utilization of the facility's beds.

Although the standards for nursing services had been expanded to include five standards that focused on nursing direction and staffing, organization and administration, policies and procedures, the nursing care plan, and educational programs, there was still no specific requirement for formal evaluation of patient care and nursing practice. Written nursing procedures and written nursing care plans were compulsory, however, and nursing procedures were required to be consistent with professionally recognized standards of practice and in accordance with the nurse practice act of each state.

By 1975, the *AMH* had been updated three times and a supplement was published in March of that year. This supplement included the new Quality of Professional Services (QPS) standard that had been approved by the Board of Commissioners in April 1974. The QPS standard required hospitals to "demonstrate that the quality of patient care was consistently optimal by continually evaluating care through reliable and valid measures."[4] The interpretation of the QPS standard required the medical and other professional staffs to evaluate the quality of patient care and to establish or adapt explicit, measurable criteria by which to evaluate that care—including expected patient outcomes. Numerical requirements for audit were established, and methodologies for retrospective outcome-oriented audit swept the land. In the next few years, the QPS standard was expanded and modified and the JCAH developed and conducted workshops throughout the country to teach physicians, nurses, and medical record personnel a method of outcome-oriented audit that would assist them to evaluate systematically the outcomes of patient care.

The next major development occurred in April 1979, when the Board of Commissioners approved the quality assurance standard for hospitals. At the same time, the Board eliminated the QPS section of the *AMH* and the numerical requirements for audit. The quality assurance standard represented a completely new orientation to the evaluation of patient care. The new standard for hospitals, which became effective for accreditation decision purposes on January 1, 1981,

- emphasized the value of a coordinated, hospital-wide quality assurance program
- allowed greater flexibility in approaches to problem identification, assessment, and resolution
- emphasized the importance of focusing quality assurance activity on problems whose resolution will have a significant impact on patient care outcomes
- emphasized the importance of focusing quality assurance activity on areas where demonstrable problem resolution is possible

- encouraged the use of multiple data sources
- discouraged the use of quality assurance studies only for the purpose of documenting high quality care.[5]

THE EVOLUTION—WHY CHANGE?

Each time the JCAH revised, updated, deleted, or expanded its standards, it was responding to evolutionary forces and to movements for change within the health care community. Such responsiveness is essential in an organization that is at the forefront of the voluntary accreditation movement and that intends to remain the leading voice for quality in health care.

The Minimum Standard was right for its time. It reflected the state of the art of health care delivery in 1917 when medical technology was limited, when medical staffs were small, and when other professional disciplines other than nursing were nonexistent. By 1953, the state of the art of health care delivery had advanced dramatically and the *Standards for Hospital Accreditation* reflected that advancement. By the time the *AMH* was published in 1970, the health care industry was a highly sophisticated, complex field. New health care professions had emerged, and the focus of medical care delivery had changed with the proliferation of medical specialties. The 1970 edition of the *AMH* was again right for its time, since it included standards that reflected the proliferation of health care professions and specialties, for example, standards for anesthesia, radiology, respiratory therapy, and social services). Because the medical profession was responsible for the overall quality of patient care, specific requirements for patient care evaluation were directed toward the medical staff, although responsibility for quality patient care was implicit in the standards for all disciplines.

In 1972, when the JCAH developed its audit methodology, specified the number of medical audits required, and stressed the importance of criteria-based medical care evaluation, it was responding to the need to quantify, in some tangible manner, the outcome of patient care and medical performance. In the ensuing years, health care professionals came to know audit intimately, modified methodologies to meet their needs, and both loved and hated the JCAH for promulgating a more specific approach to patient care evaluation. Many of the disciplines that were not required to conduct audits embraced the practice of retrospective outcome-oriented audit and became more involved in the activity than the physicians to whom the requirement had been directed. During this time, new ideas proliferated, new approaches emerged, new constraints arose, and health care professionals and the JCAH began anew to question the manner in which patient care was and should be evaluated.

Both the JCAH staff and health care professionals who were evaluating care began to realize that medical audit requirements were self-limiting. Strict adherence to numerical requirements limited the amount and scope of care evaluated. In addition, emphasis on the broad diagnosis-based review specified by the JCAH methodology encouraged hospitals to focus only on diagnostic topics rather than on identified or potential problems in patient care or clinical performance. Other quality assessment and quality-related activities that had been long required by the standards (for example, tissue, antibiotic, and blood utilization review; review of nursing care and support services; delineation of clinical privileges; and monitoring of clinical practice) were not coordinated with audit activities or recognized as part of an overall quality assurance effort.

Researchers and evaluators also began to realize that evaluation was more quantitative than qualitative; that evaluation efforts were fragmented and duplicated throughout the hospital; that greater authority was needed to implement corrective actions; that adherence to a strict retrospective approach limited the use of a variety of important data sources; and that problem resolution was not monitored. Further, evaluations of patient care were not representative of all types of practice and their effect on improving patient care and clinical performance was difficult to determine. Some hospitals did demonstrate impressive results in the evaluation and improvement of care. In other hospitals, however, changes in patient care were not in proportion to the amount of time and work invested and the costs associated with audit activity. Many individuals perceived that it was time to give evaluation activities a wider perspective, one which encompassed all hospital quality assurance activities.

The quality assurance standard for hospitals (see Appendix A) is the result of that evolutionary process. The standard is necessary and appropriate for the times. In an age of increased sophistication and specialization of health care technology, inflationary costs, escalating utilization of services, and greater consumer awareness and expectations from the health care field, hospitals need a mechanism that will enable them to administer and manage quality assessment activities effectively and efficiently. Hospitals must streamline functions, eliminate duplication, contain costs, and, above all, ensure that problems in care are identified and corrected. The quality assurance standard provides a mechanism whereby hospitals can bring together, in one comprehensive program, all quality-related activities. The focal point of all other standards, the quality assurance standard illustrates once again how the JCAH responds to forces for change that necessitate a reexamination of requirements.

INTENT OF THE STANDARD

The clamor over the new standard reflects a normal response to change. A large portion of health care professionals had only recently become accustomed to previous requirements. Many felt that the new requirements were applied without consideration for the capacity of hospitals to assume more responsibility. Still others assumed that additional staff time and resources would be required. It should be noted, however, that many applauded the JCAH's decision and understood and supported the philosophy and concept of the standard. These people had long recognized the need for change; in fact, some had already pioneered similar changes in their facilities. These practitioners understood the intent of the standard.

The intent of the standard is to

- allow greater flexibility in quality assurance activities
- encourage innovation and creativity in the evaluation process
- encourage the elimination of duplicative committees, activities, and functions
- encourage the coordination of fragmented activities throughout the hospital
- promote systematic and effective evaluation of overall patient care
- encourage communication about the results of evaluation so that improvement in patient care and clinical performance can be assured.

The standard is not intended to create a greater burden on hospital staffs; rather, it was designed to relieve the burden of ineffectual evaluation activities and provide management with an incentive to administer all related assessment activities in a systematic, effective manner.

The quality assurance standard requires hospitals to integrate or coordinate all quality assurance activities in a comprehensive program that focuses on problems in care, and this is designed to improve patient care and clinical performance. To provide evidence that such a program has been instituted, the hospital is asked to develop a written plan. This plan is important! It provides structure and guidelines for communication, authority, accountability, and administration of the program. It also provides a mechanism for reporting results of quality assurance activities and for feedback. However, the development of a plan is not the primary requirement of the standard and should not be the primary concern of a hospital.

The requirement for a plan, and the requirements for integration, comprehensiveness, and annual reassessment of the quality assurance programs, should be viewed as the system through which problems are identified, assessed, resolved, and monitored. At the heart of the new quality assurance standard is the improvement of patient care through the identification and resolution of problems. The quality assurance program, and the plan that defines that program, should be developed in terms of problem resolution and identification—how, what, when, where, why, by whom, and with what communication, feedback, and authority.

The innovation and flexibility encouraged by the standard promotes an organizational philosophy that allows hospitals to shape and mold quality assurance programs to their unique needs. The standard encourages careful analysis of current quality assurance activities to determine how these activities can be integrated or coordinated to meet the intent of the standard. It also encourages careful planning to ensure that changes in current activities are implemented systematically and effectively, with the complete support of appropriate hospital authorities and staff.

ANALYZING CURRENT QUALITY ASSURANCE ACTIVITIES

One of the first steps toward developing a comprehensive quality assurance program is the analysis of current quality assurance activities. This analysis is conducted

> to identify the scope, purpose, and effectiveness of current activities; to ascertain whether such activities meet all JCAH requirements for review and evaluation; to identify strengths and weaknesses in the overall QA program; to determine whether duplication in activities, overlap in authority and responsibility, or unnecessary expenditures in staff time and resources exist; and to determine whether expansion, reorganization, or streamlining of the current program is necessary and appropriate.[5]

Besides assessing activities that are routinely considered quality assurance activities (for example, medical care evaluation; tissue, antibiotic, and blood utilization review; and support services review), hospitals should analyze medical staff functions, such as departmental meetings, continuing education activities, and credentialing and hospital-wide activities such as risk control, safety programs, and infection control. By looking at these activities separately and in the aggregate, quality assurance planners can identify appropriate components of a comprehensive quality assurance program and initiate efforts to integrate systematically quality assurance activities and functions.

The extent of analysis will vary in each facility because of size, number of quality-related committees and functions, extent of fragmentation and duplication, and current delineation of authority and responsibility for quality assurance activities. Several organizations have developed mechanisms for analyzing quality assurance activities,[5,6] and hospital personnel can adapt these mechanisms to meet their own needs or can develop their own assessment tools. These tools are also useful for ongoing assessment and annual evaluation of established quality assurance programs.

Once the organization of all quality assurance activities is analyzed, relationships among committees are defined, lines of authority and responsibility are designated, and sources of information on patient care are defined, the problem-solving mechanism—that is, the quality assurance program—becomes the hub of the wheel around which all quality-related activities revolve and from which techniques for evaluating and improving care evolve.

THE RATIONALE FOR PROBLEM SOLVING

Quality assessment and assurance activities exist for the same reasons hospitals exist—to care for patients and to assure that health care professionals fulfill their responsibility to maintain and, when possible, improve the quality of that care. In the best of worlds, such an ideal could be attained without hospital-wide mechanisms for ongoing identification and correction of problems in care. The best of worlds does not exist in most hospitals, however. Like all other organizations, hospitals are places in which the hazards of human error, equipment failure, and environmental imperfections precipitate problems that affect patient care. Consequently, the essential requirement of the standard is that hospitals identify, assess, and resolve problems in care that exist throughout the hospital.

The requirement that quality assurance activities be problem focused is not negative, nor does it presume that hospitals are necessarily replete with severe problems. It does presume that quality control is a necessary feature of any industry and that problems affecting the product of that industry must be recognized and eliminated. In the health care industry, whose product is people, problem solving is a critical aspect of the overall quality of patient care.

Numerous internal and external sources of information on problems and potential problems exist. (Examples of these sources are listed in lines 21 to 34 of the 1981 standard.) In a well-organized quality assurance program, information channeled from all units and departments of the hospital becomes the basis for identifying problems and patterns of problems, for determining the cause and scope of such problems, and for correcting them as quickly and efficiently as possible.

THE QUALITY ASSURANCE STANDARD AND SUPPORT SERVICE REVIEW

If one accepts the premises that the quality assurance standard is the focal point from which all standards emanate and that it serves as the mechanism whereby hospitals bring together, in one comprehensive management system, all quality-related activities, one can accept the reasonableness of the requirements for support service review.

After the QA standard was established and numerical requirements for audit were eliminated, hospital personnel throughout the country looked to the JCAH in disbelief: Requirements for support service review and evaluation stipulated time frames, use of the medical record, and preestablished criteria. To many, this signified audit and numerical requirements. From a management perspective, however, these requirements do not stipulate the need for formal, structured studies, nor do they require a discrete number of studies. Rather, like the quality assurance standard itself, these requirements provide a framework and guidelines for evaluating the overall management of individual support services. The standard in each of the support services section that requires review and evaluation of the service can be seen as the focal point from which all other standards in the section emanate—each support services section is a microcosm of the entire *AMH*. The nursing services standards are good examples of this concept (see Figure 3-2 for an illustration of the relationships among the seven standards in the nursing services section of the *AMH*). Nursing care should be delivered in a department that is organized to ensure delivery of high quality care and fulfillment of nursing functions delineated in the first six standards. This care, and the management functions that support its delivery, must be assessed on an ongoing basis to determine whether goals and objectives of the department are being met.

The nursing service standards can be translated into procedures for care or objectives for the department, and they could easily serve as criteria to apply against and fulfill the review and evaluation requirements of standard VII. The request that this management oversight function be conducted quarterly does not indicate a need to perform formal, structured studies based on a specific topic. It does indicate the need to look at the overall management of the department and at the attainment of objectives for the department at least quarterly in a formal manner (for example, documented through reports of department heads or minutes of department meetings). In the course of this management review and in the course of other quality-related activities, problems will be identified and should be solved in the manner recommended by the quality assurance standard. The data generated by the nursing department and the findings of quality assurance activities conducted by the nursing department are channeled to the overall quality assurance program. This communication of information is essential to the effective operation of a comprehensive quality assurance program. In other words, the nursing department is one of the important spokes of the wheel of which the quality assurance program is the hub: When the nursing department, other support services, and other medical and hospital departments fulfill their management responsibilities and quality assurance activities, the wheel turns smoothly and efficiently, and the total quality assurance management system operates successfully.

Figure 3-2 The Relationship That Exists Between the Nursing Standard
That Requires Review and Evaluation of Nursing Care
(Standard VII) and the Other Six Nursing Standards.

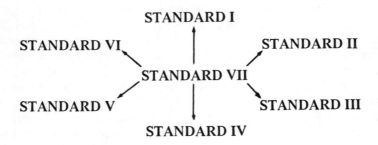

I. The nursing department/service shall be directed by a qualified nurse administrator and shall be appropriately integrated with the medical staff and with other hospital staffs that provide and contribute to patient care.

II. The nursing department/service shall be organized to meet the nursing care needs of patients and to maintain established standards of nursing practice.

III. Nursing department/service assignments in the provision of nursing care shall be commensurate with the qualifications of nursing personnel and shall be designed to meet the nursing care needs of patients.

IV. Individualized, goal-directed nursing care shall be provided to patients through the use of the nursing process.

V. Nursing department/service personnel shall be prepared through appropriate education and training programs for their responsibilities in the provision of nursing care.

VI. Written policies and procedures that reflect optimal standards of nursing practice shall guide the provision of nursing care.

VII. The nursing department/service shall provide mechanisms for the regular review and evaluation of the quality and appropriateness of nursing department/service practice and functions. Such mechanisms shall be designed to attain optimal achievable standards of nursing care.

REFERENCES

1. Davis L : *Fellowship of Surgeons: A History of the American College of Surgeons.* Chicago, Charles C Thomas, Publisher, 1960, p 476.
2. *Standards for Hospital Accreditation.* Chicago, Joint Commission on Accreditation of Hospitals, 1965.
3. *Accreditation Manual for Hospitals,* 1970 edition. Chicago, Joint Commission on Accreditation of Hospitals, 1970, p 43.
4. *Supplement to the Accreditation Manual for Hospitals.* Chicago, Joint Commission on Accreditation of Hospitals, March 6, 1975.
5. Kaplan KO, Hopkins JML: *The QA Guide: A Resource for Hospital Quality Assurance.* Chicago, Joint Commission on Accreditation of Hospitals, 1980.
6. Stearns G, Imbiorski W, Fox LA: *Solutions.* Chicago, Care Communications Inc, 1979.

Appendix

Quality Assurance

PRINCIPLE

The hospital shall demonstrate a consistent endeavor to deliver patient care that is optimal within available resources and consistent with achievable goals. A major component in the application of this principle is the operation of a quality assurance program.

STANDARD

There shall be evidence of a well-defined, organized program designed to enhance patient care through the ongoing objective assessment of important aspects of patient care and the correction of identified problems.

INTERPRETATION

It is the governing body's responsibility to establish, maintain, and support, through the hospital's administration and medical staff, an ongoing quality assurance program that includes effective mechanisms for reviewing and evaluating patient care, as well as an appropriate response to findings. The plan for assuring the comprehensiveness and integration of the overall quality assurance program and for delegating responsibility for the various activities that contribute to quality assurance must be defined in writing. The mechanisms for assuring the accountability of the medical and other professional staffs for the care they provide should be described in the plan. The quality assurance program should be comprehensive, and it should be flexible enough to permit innovation and variation in assessment approaches. This does not imply that a totally new system should replace existing committees or functions concerned with quality assurance. To obtain maximal benefit, any approach to quality assurance must focus on the resolution of known or suspected problems (that impact directly or indirectly on patients) or, when indicated, on areas with potential for substantial improvements in patient care. It is incumbent on a hospital to document evidence of an effective quality assurance program.

The essential components of a sound quality assurance program-in-the-aggregate shall include:

- Identification of important or potential problems, or related concerns, in the care of patients.
- Objective assessment of the cause and scope of problems or concerns, including the determination of priorities for both investigating and resolving problems. Ordinarily, priorities shall be related to the degree of impact on patient care that can be expected if the problem remains unresolved.
- Implementation, by appropriate individuals or through designated mechanisms, of decisions or actions that are designed to eliminate, insofar as possible, identified problems.
- Monitoring activities designed to assure that the desired result has been achieved and sustained.
- Documentation that reasonably substantiates the effectiveness of the overall program to enhance patient care and to assure sound clinical performance.

The mechanisms for assuring that the components of the quality assurance program are used *as indicated* in specific studies or other quality assessment activities should be described in the plan.

The medical record remains an important data source in the identification of problems. However, other potentially useful sources include morbidity/mortality review; monitoring activities of the medical and other professional staffs; findings of hospital committee activities (for example, safety, infection control); review of prescriptions; profile analysis, including PSRO and other regional data; specific process-oriented/outcome-oriented studies; incident reports relating to both individual safety and clinical care; review of laboratory, radiologic, and other diagnostic clinical reports of services rendered; financial data (for example, hospital charge data on services rendered, liability claims resolutions); utilization review findings; data obtained from staff interviews and observation of hospital activities; patient surveys or comments; and data originating from third party payers/fiscal intermediaries.

Once an actual or potential problem is identified, it may be assessed prospectively, concurrently, or retrospectively. Whatever time frames for review and whatever quality assessment activities are used, representative care (that is, adequate sampling) provided by all clinical departments/disciplines and individual practitioners must be evaluated. While the evaluation of physician-directed care must be performed by physician members of the medical staff, nonphysician health care professionals should assess those aspects of care that they provide. However, the participation of both physicians and other health care professionals in the same quality assessment activities, when appropriate, is strongly encouraged.

Written criteria that relate to essential or critical aspects of patient care and that are generally acceptable to the clinical staffs shall be used to assess problems and measure compliance with achievable goals. These criteria should be clinically valid in that, when applied to actual practice, they can be expected to result in improved patient care/clinical performance. Structure, process, or outcome criteria; standards of practice of professional organizations; or criteria developed within the hospital or in cooperation with local hospitals may be utilized as appropriate. Although the use of criteria is required, there is no requirement to employ any specific method in the review or evaluation of patient care, nor is it implied that a specific number of criteria shall be employed.

Appropriate action must be implemented to eliminate or reduce the identified problem. Such action may include, but is not limited to, educational/training programs, new or revised policies or procedures, staffing changes, equipment or facility change, or adjustments in clinical privileges. Periodic monitoring of the results of the corrective action taken must be conducted to assure that the identified problem has been eliminated or satisfactorily reduced.

Pertinent findings of quality assurance activities throughout the hospital shall be reported to one, two, or all of the following, as appropriate, through their designated mechanisms: the medical staff, the chief executive officer, and the governing body. Findings related to the quality of care provided by a clinical unit that is not represented in a specific assessment activity shall be made available to the director of the unit.

Although each clinical discipline is responsible for identifying and resolving problems related to patient care, administering or coordinating the overall quality assurance program may be performed through a committee, group, or individual. The role of the patient care monitoring activities of the medical and other professional staffs that are already in effect, for example, the medical staff and clinical department rules and regulations relating to patient care requirements, must be identified within the quality assurance program.

Quality assurance activities proven to be effective should be integrated coordinated to the degree possible. To the extent that such integration coordination preserves any productive interrelationships, minimizes duplication, and assimilates information gathered, communication should be greatly enhanced and, in addition, there may be a potential for cost savings. Although some overlap between two or more activities is frequently desirable, any unnecessary or nonproductive duplication should be avoided. In the interest of consistency, terminology used to describe studies performed or methods employed in quality assessment activities should be defined.

As appropriate, the administration and medical staff shall determine the extent, if any, to which outside aid (consultants, voluntary or mandatory review bodies, and so forth) is used in the performance of quality assessment activities to identify and assess problems. However, attaining a suitable solution to problems is a function and responsibility, as appropriate, of the governing body, medical staff, or hospital administration.

In the coordination/integration of a hospital's quality assessment and control activities, related requirements specified in the following sections of this *Manual* should be considered: Anesthesia Services, Dietetic Services, Emergency Services, Functional Safety and Sanitation, Governing Body, Home Care Services, Hospital-Sponsored Ambulatory Care Services, Infection Control, Medical Record Services, Medical Staff, Nuclear Medicine Services, Nursing Services, Pathology and Medical Laboratory Services, Pharmaceutical Services, Radiology Services, Rehabilitation Programs/Services, Respiratory Care Services, Social Work Services, Special Care Units, and Utilization Review.

The quality assurance program shall be reappraised through a designated mechanism at least annually. The reappraisal should identify components of the quality assurance program that need to be instituted, altered, or deleted. Resultant recommendations, when instituted, should assure that the program is ongoing, comprehensive, effective in improving patient care/clinical performance, and conducted with cost-efficiency.

The effectiveness of a hospital's quality assurance program shall be emphasized in determining a hospital's accreditation status.

Part II

Issues in Quality Control

4. Managing Professional Work: Three Models of Control for Health Organizations

W. RICHARD SCOTT

Reprinted with permission from *Health Services Research* 17(3). Copyright © 1982, 213-240.

From a sociological point of view, there are three primary arrangements for structuring the work of professional participants within organizations. I will discuss each of these structural types as a vehicle for describing and assessing the relation between physicians and administrators, and to a lesser extent, trustees in U.S. hospitals. I will attempt to avoid caricature and overstatement but must note at the outset that the great variety of hospital forms and practices militates against detail and precision in any brief, general treatment such as this.

The three structural models to be described are the *autonomous,* the *heteronomous,* and the *conjoint* professional organization. By a professional organization, I mean simply an organization in which the primary or core tasks are performed by professional participants. For each of the three models of professional organizations, I will describe the rationale, the support structures that have fostered its development, the organizational features, the advantages—and for whom they are such—and the problems or issues associated with its operation. More so than most such treatments, I will underscore the extent to which each of these structural arrangements is driven by forces external to the organizations which manifest them.

AUTONOMOUS PROFESSIONAL ORGANIZATIONS

By definition, an autonomous professional organization exists to the extent that "organizational officials delegate to the group of professional [participants] responsibility for defining and implementing the goals, for setting performance

This paper was originally presented at the Invitational Conference on Research in Quality Assurance sponsored jointly by the University of Colorado Health Services Center, the Association of University Programs in Health Administration, and the Joint Commission on Accreditation of Hospitals, November 7, 1980 in Denver, Colorado.

standards, and for seeing to it that standards are maintained'' [1, p.66]. Examples of types of professional organizations that are likely to conform to the autonomous pattern include general hospitals, therapeutic psychiatric hospitals, medical clinics, elite colleges and universities, law firms, and scientific institutes oriented to basic research [2, 3, 4, 5, 6].

Rationale

The most widely accepted explanation for the distinctive structures supporting professional work is that they constitute a response to the special characteristics of the work performed: work regarded as unusually complex, uncertain, and of great social importance. To insure the best possible outcomes under these difficult circumstances, the strategy pursued is to couple capability with discretion in one responsible actor and place him or her as close as possible to the problem situation. Individual professionals are subjected to a prolonged period of socialization and training in which they are expected to internalize standards, acquire a repertoire of skills, and master a general set of theoretical principles that will enable them to make decisions and act autonomously in a responsible and expert fashion. These internalized controls are supported and reinforced by collegial associations. Colleagues are viewed as (a) capable of exercising control since they have acquired similar skills and standards, and (b) motivated to exercise control since they have a personal stake in maintaining the reputation of their profession. It is asserted that clients or other recipients of services benefit by these arrangements; unable to evaluate directly the quality of the services they receive, they rely on the assistance of a set of highly qualified individuals who are collectively committed to protecting their interests [7, 8].

The professional association not only serves as an instrument of internal control but as a political body seeking to advance the interests of its members. These associations, when successful, obtain state backing to defend their monopoly position with respect to the provision of specified services. Thus, physicians are licensed to practice medicine, and all unlicensed persons are specifically prohibited from performing this work. The power of the profession to determine working arrangements for their members extends beyond private practice into organized settings. As Freidson [9, p.24] notes:

> The effectively organized professional occupation controls even the determination and demarcation of tasks embodied in jobs supported by employers. . . . Through their influence on regulatory agencies, the organized professions (and the crafts) are often responsible for writing the job descriptions for their members and determining the employer's training and educational requirements as well as the kind of special skill imputed to the qualified worker.

An alternate explanation for the special arrangements enjoyed by professional workers focuses on their power as an occupational group. Analysts such as Friedman [10, p.137-160] and Freidson [11] point out the substantial economic and social advantages stemming from such a monopoly position and suggest the possibility of a reverse causal process: rather than power resulting from the special nature of the work performed, occupational groups enjoying power may define their work as having special characteristics. As is often the case in such lively controversies, the truth may lie somewhere between the two extreme positions. In any event, in the case of powerful professional groups like physicians, such claims have been successfully made.

Support Structures

As suggested, primary support for autonomous structures for professionals within organizations stems from the power of the organized occupational groups to define the nature and conditions of their work. Beginning early in this century, professional groups of physicians such as the American College of Surgeons and the Council on Medical Education and Hospitals of the American Medical Association began to promulgate procedures and standards defining the terms under which physicians should practice in hospitals [12, pp.102-107; 13, pp.33-39].

In addition to such direct efforts to define work arrangements, a fully developed profession is capable of mobilizing support for its cause from many sources: political—as it helps to shape relevant legislative, licensure, and regulatory activities [14, 15, 16, 17]; economic—as it exercises the power stemming from its monopoly status [18, 19]; and legal—as its dominance over an area of activity is protected by statute [20].

The extraordinary power of this constellation of forces is captured in Alford's description of a *dominant structural interest*. As Alford [21, p.14] points out, there are many interest groups in a complex social system but they are not all of equal power. The *dominant* groups are those whose interests are "served by the structure of social, economic, and political institutions as they exist at any given time." Their position is sufficiently entrenched and their legitimation so secure that they "do not continually have to organize and act to defend their interests; other institutions do that for them." Physicians are viewed by Alford as a classic case of a "professional monopoly" that has gained the position of a dominant structural interest in our society.

Organizational Features

Two features distinguish the structure of autonomous professional organizations. The first is a sharp demarcation between professional and administrative zones of control; and the second is the organization of the professional staff.

Administrative-Professional Sectors

In organizations of this type, legitimate control over the nature and quality of professional practice is vested in the professional staff, not in the administration. Although the situation is changing, as will be described in connection with the heteronomous and conjoint models, hospitals still conform substantially to this pattern.

Legal responsibility for the care of patients is lodged in the governing board of hospitals; nevertheless, most readily delegate responsibility for the setting and enforcing of professional standards of patient care to the medical staff [12, 13]. Rules forbidding the "corporate practice of medicine"—the doctrine that only an individual, not an organization, can be legally licensed to practice medicine—reinforce the authority of the individual physician and the collegial body of which he or she is a member. Lay control over professional discretion—whether client or administrative—is viewed as inappropriate.

The separation of professional and administrative jurisdictions is more clearly exemplified by U.S. hospitals than any other type of organization. Physicians have insisted on their prerogative to assume control over output (patient care) goals; and administrators have tended to accept the definition of their own domain as limited to organizational support or maintenance objectives. Physicians perform the key patient care tasks within hospitals which administrators maintain. Both groups generally endorse the validity and the propriety of the distinction in spite of the obvious overlap in the actual functions of physicians and administrators and the impact of administrators and those serving under their direction on the provision of patient care.

Organization of the Professional Staff

The second hallmark of the autonomous professional organization is that the dominant professional group organizes itself as a professional staff to support and police the performance of its members. In this discussion, we shall concentrate attention on the organization of physicians in hospitals; but it is instructive to note that the nursing staff in a few hospitals have taken steps to organize themselves as an autonomous professional staff, paralleling the structure adopted by the physicians [22, 23].

The primary tasks carried on within hospitals are diagnostic and therapeutic activities for specific patients. For the most part, individual professional practitioners, the most important of whom are physicians, conduct or direct these activities. Physicians organize themselves as overseers of these activities to ensure patient/client needs are met and to protect individual practitioners from inappropriate control attempts by nonpractitioners.

This key system of professional control has only gradually evolved in hospitals. As physicians began to conduct an increasing proportion of their practice in hospitals after the turn of the century, the predominant mode of professional care—independent, entrepreneurial, fee-for-service practice—was simply extended into the hospital. Wilson [24, p.178] comments on this arrangement:

> When the independent practitioner came to the hospital, he essentially wished to preserve this doctor-patient relationship undisturbed. If he could keep the relationship free from unsought incursions by the organization, while at the same time taking advantage of what the hospital could offer in the way of technical facilities and therapeutic environment, the physician would clearly enjoy the best of both worlds. To a fairly considerable extent, of course, this is precisely what occurred.

With the stimulation and encouragement of such professional associations as the American College of Surgeons, an increasing number of hospitals met the Minimum Standard for Hospitals requiring physicians to organize a "definite medical staff" to determine the physicians to be admitted to staff and the level of their privileges [13, p.36]. Such developments have continued so that, according to Somers [12, p.22], the medical staff which once was

> a collection of unrelated individuals who brought their private patients into the hospital for nursing care . . . has become a highly organized unit that is increasingly held collectively responsible for the total quantity and quality of care rendered in the hospital, and hence for its reputation and financial status. The medical staff is, in truth, the *sine qua non* of any hospital. It determines the institution's image of itself, its basic philosophy, and its effectiveness.

Somers correctly describes the *direction* of change—from aggregation of individual physicians to organized medical staff—but overstates the *amount* of change. At this point, there still remains great variation in the extent to which the medical staff in hospitals functions as "a highly organized unit" [13, 25].

Several layers of control may be identified in connection with the professional staff system [26, pp.47-51]. We describe four.

Peer Group Control. As already noted, part of the rationale underlying the structure of professionals is the expectation of direct collegial controls—one practitioner observing, correcting, and, if necessary, sanctioning another. However, the few studies we have of these processes question whether physicians (a) have sufficient opportunity to observe the work of their colleagues; (b) possess the particular competence—medicine is so highly specialized—to evaluate the work observed; and (c) have a sufficiently varied arsenal of effective sanctions at their disposal to back up their evaluations [27, 9]. Although questions arise concerning the efficacy of peer group control among professionals, these processes are certainly more likely to operate in collective settings (like hospitals) where practitioners work in close proximity, than in situations characterized by independent, decentralized practice—situations which are still the modal settings for the delivery of medical services in this country.

Differential Peer Group Controls. In virtually all occupations, the seniority principle operates as an important basis of control; professional occupations are no exception. In this connection, Etzioni [28, pp.256-259] points to three major rankings of professionals: professionals in training, pre-tenure professionals, and professionals with tenure. For professionals who are in training, e.g., interns and residents in hospitals, "it is obvious that their income, promotion, prestige, privileges, and facilities are controlled to a considerable degree by higher ranking professionals." Tyro-professionals provide care under the direct supervision of other professionals and are explicitly evaluated for the quality of the services they deliver.

Tenured professionals exert important controls over non-tenured staff members. Every hospital staff is required by the Minimum Standard for Hospitals (1919) and by the Joint Commission on the Accreditation of Hospitals (JCAH, 1952) to develop criteria for selecting medical staff members and, in particular, for awarding them privileges in the hospital [29; 13, pp.36-43; 30]. Moreover, probationary periods are imposed during which more active controls and surveillance are practiced. In these and other ways, differential peer control is exercised in hospitals, providing a modified system of echelon authority. Again, however, the actual amount of control exercised in this manner varies greatly from one hospital to another.

Formalized Peer Group Controls. Once the professional staff becomes formally structured within a specific organizational context—as compared with informal structure within a community setting [31]—a specialized set of control mechanisms becomes available [11, pp.185-201]. A number of formally defined positions are created whose responsibilities include the exercise of professional control.

Many of these positions are nominally administrative arising in connection with the creation of specialized units and departments, e.g., chief of staff, departmental chair, director of a clinic, and often entail a combination of administrative and professional duties. Most analysts, beginning with Parsons [32, pp.58-60] and Gouldner [33, pp.22-23] have emphasized the difference between administrative and professional control, even when combined in a single office. In this vein, Goss [34], in her description of control patterns among a group of hospital clinic physicians, reported that a physician acting as clinic director exercised "authority," i.e., issued directives to which compliance was expected, regarding administrative matters like the scheduling of patients, but only proffered "advice" to professional colleagues in the area of patient care. This distinction is both time-honored and useful for differentiating administrative from professional control; but it may cause us to overlook the equally important distinction between informal and formalized peer group control. From the latter standpoint, what is important to note in the situation described by Goss is the extent to which surveillance duties have been concentrated in a few positions rather than distributed evenly throughout the colleague group, so that physicians occupying these positions are granted the "right" (and accept the "obligation") to routinely review all case records and make suggestions to individual practitioners concerning patient care. Moreover, as Goss [34, p.44] admits: these rank-and-file physicians "considered it their duty to take supervisory suggestions about patient care into account, and in this sense they accepted supervision." These represent important modifications in the structure of peer group controls.

In addition to the "departmentalization" of the medical staff leading to the creation of these administrative/professional positions, other formalized positions are created in connection with the medical staff's committee system. Most of the business of the medical staff is conducted through an elaborate set of committees. Functions performed range from liaison with the hospital administration through the oversight of ancillary departments to the evaluation of physician performance in specific areas of patient care. The functioning of such committees is mandated by accreditation requirements so that virtually all hospitals exhibit a varied array of medical staff committees. Of particular importance for control purposes are the medical audit committees mandated in the 1950s by the JCAH and the utilization review committee requirements of Medicare.

The departmentalization of the medical staff combined with its elaborate committee structure clearly moves away from the model of a collegial structure toward that of a bureaucratic hierarchy. In appearance, however, these structures tend to be somewhat misleading.

Two important factors modulate their effects. First, the types of control exercised over individual practitioners are restricted primarily to: (a) selection, based on training, certification and other evidence of past performance; and (b) retrospective audits, based on a review of medical records or pathological evidence. That is, the controls exercised tend to occur before or after, not during the performance. This is consistent with professional norms mentioned earlier that grant a large measure of discretion to individual practitioners in the day-to-day management of patient care activities. Second, professional participants tend to circulate fairly rapidly through the formal positions, each occupying an office for a limited and specified period. Professionals do not generally perceive their career mobility as linked to advancement in administrative positions, and most are reluctant to take on such responsibilities and are more than willing to relinquish them at the end of their term of office. This continuous circulation of personnel both weakens the effectiveness of the formalized control system—in that participants are forever learning the job or preparing to leave it—and regularly infuses professional values into the system. Without question, it enhances the acceptability of the control apparatus to those practitioners subject to it.

Externally Authorized, Formalized Peer Group Controls. With the advent of the Professional Standard Review Organizations (PSRO) system, came the creation of a new layer of professional controls [35]. In principle, this system is designed to organize physicians on an area-wide basis in order to monitor the costs (appropriateness of hospitalization and length of stay) and quality of care provided by the institutions within that area. This system is described as externally authorized because its legitimacy stems from federal statute, not primarily from endorsement by those whose behaviors are to be controlled [36, pp.37-64]. At the same time, the principle of peer group controls is reaffirmed. By insisting that specified crucial roles (e.g., medical director, physician advisor) in the local PSROs be filled by physicians, the hope is that physicians' collegial norms will be harnessed, augmenting the legitimacy of the control system [37].

A variety of sanctions are available to PSROs to enforce their evaluations. Primary among these is decertification of care delivered for reimbursement from federal sources. Although they are rarely employed, more extreme financial sanctions are also available, e.g., suspension or revocation of a physician's right to be reimbursed for care delivered under the Medicare/Medicaid Act.

Individual PSROs do not operate in isolation but as part of a nationwide system: in all, some 200 local PSRO organizations have been developed and are organized into 10 regional areas, each of which is overseen by a regional office. A National Professional Standards Review Council of 12 physicians develops and distributes information to individual PSROs and reviews regional norms of care. Thus, the PSRO system is designed to coordinate and standardize controls within health care institutions on an area-wide basis and to link this review process into a national system. The hierarchy within the PSRO is designed to improve the technical capability of local PSROs to monitor and regulate the cost and quality of health care and, at least in the long run, influence the standards used by these agencies in carrying out their functions [38].

Advantages and Problems

A major strength of the autonomous professional control system is that it places primary responsibility on the person to whom is granted greatest discretion. This arrangement is compatible with the physician's training and self-image, so that he or she does not attempt to resist or subvert it. Though control processes are supposed to operate somewhat automatically as part of the interactions associated with everyday work routines, the few studies we have suggest that a major weakness of the autonomous system is that informal peer controls are relatively ineffective. Among physicians, the efficacy of collegial control appears to be undermined by the "ethics" of professional courtesy [6, 39].

The effects of more formally structured control arrangements are well summarized by Palmer and Reilly [40].

> There is a strong body of opinion and a little evidence that a highly structured medical staff organization is associated with a high level of care and that a loosely structured medical staff organization is associated with a lower level of care.

Empirical evidence supporting this proposition is reported by Morehead [41], Roemer and Friedman [13], and Flood and Scott [25]. Much more research is needed, however, before the opinion can be regarded as justified.

Another advantage of the autonomous professional system is the high priority which it places on the needs of individual clients. Physicians are under a number of pressures—economic, interpersonal, normative—to service the needs and, to some extent, the wishes of their individual patients. This strength is balanced by an associated cost: a focus on the needs of an individual client may benefit one patient at the expense of others. This is a manifestation in the health care arena of the micro-macro dilemma [42]. Since this is a distinction to be used throughout our analysis, it is important to define it clearly.

Micro care is focused on the needs and interests of individual patients; it is governed by a principle that assesses the needs of an individual as a basis for determining appropriate action and desired outcomes. The clinical orientation of physicians is one that places great emphasis on individual patient needs, their assessment and satisfaction [11]. By contrast, *macro* care focuses on the characteristics of populations of patients and is governed by principles applicable to that aggregate, e.g., the overall shape of the distribution of desired outcomes or the specification of minimum or modal levels of services [42, 43, 44]. It is important to stress that micro and macro principles may conflict: the latter is not simply an aggregated version of the former but represents a new and different basis for determining the distribution of services. For example, a macro-level rule specifying that a given proportion of hospital beds be set aside for Medicare patients may conflict with admission criteria focusing on the needs of individual patients.

Closely related to the micro-macro distinction is the cost-quality trade-off. If resources are unlimited, then micro concerns about individual patient care are less likely to impinge on macro issues relating to the distribution of care (e.g., issues of access and equity). However, as health care administrators are expected to give greater attention to cost containment, constraints are tightened on care decisions at the individual level. Put another way, restrictions on costs cause micro-level care choices to be increasingly interdependent with macro-level care issues.

The PSRO system is a recent development, and it is much too early to draw any firm conclusions. However, the apparent advantages of this new program include the promise of an arrangement for gathering comparable information on aggregate performance characteristics of hospital systems. This promise is supported by the development of more uniform patient abstracts, the availability of technical assistance and computer services for managing data, and the organization of performance characteristics on an area-wide basis, i.e., external to any specific hospital. The prospects are dimmed by such considerations as the lack of clear or widely accepted standards of care [45, p.246], the disinterest and, in some instances, active resistance of physicians, the absence of any specific role or voice for hospital interests [46], and most significantly, the changed political climate in Washington.

Additional comments on PSROs are made in the following section. While some aspects of the PSRO program are consistent with the autonomous model, others reflect the heteronomous model of professional organizations.

HETERONOMOUS PROFESSIONAL ORGANIZATIONS

In the heteronomous professional organization, by definition, "professional participants are clearly subordinated to an administrative framework," and the amount of autonomy granted them is somewhat circumscribed [1, p.67]. Participants in these settings are more constrained by administrative controls than their counterparts in autonomous structures: they are subject to routine supervision. This type of organizational form is exemplified by many public agencies—libraries, secondary schools, social welfare agencies—and by private organizations like small colleges, engineering firms, applied research organizations, and accounting firms. In acute care hospitals, it also characterizes the situation of nursing personnel, physical therapists and similar types of professionals [47].

Rationale

Although historically the heteronomous form has been associated with weaker or less fully developed professional groups like nurses, engineers and social workers [48], patterns of patient care in hospitals have been moving in directions which make the heteronomous alternative more applicable to the work of physicians. Among the most important of these changes are:

- the increasing specialization of care among physicians (in response to the growing scientific and technical sophistication of medical practice) that replaces the medical generalist responsible for the "whole patient" with a collection of highly refined and restricted specialists

- the increasing dependence of physicians on hospitals as reflected in both the proportion of medical practice taking place within the confines of this institution and in the growth of salaried or contract physicians
- the increasing use of paraprofessional and technical personnel as vital and indispensable contributors to the delivery of medical care
- the expanding conception of the meaning of health, e.g., "the medicalization of social problems," [49] and of the legitimate arena of health services, which extends to include more types of conditions, e.g., alcoholism, sexual adjustment, shyness and obesity, and more modes of practice, e.g., education, acupuncture, nutrition and biofeedback
- the rapidly increasing costs of hospital care, sufficient to evoke the label "crisis," resulting in greater external pressures for cost containment and improved efficiency in the operation of hospitals.

All of these and related developments over the past three decades have led to the growth of power of hospital administrators and medical managers within hospitals [50]. They are increasingly expected to adjudicate differences among conflicting physician groups, coordinate the work flow among interdependent professional specialists and technical personnel, and pursue cost-containment strategies. They are also encouraged and required to assume greater responsibility for the quality of the health care delivered by the institution.

Courts of law both acknowledge and legitimate the increasing responsibility of medical institutions for the quality and appropriateness of the medical care delivered. The Darling case, "widely recognized by legal, professional, and public opinion as a landmark in the evolution of hospital corporate responsibility" [12, p.32], is but one of several specific rulings that recognizes the transition from independent professional to institutional accountability [12, 51, 52].

Many observers of the medical care scene have concluded that the physician's independence needs to be subordinated to organizational controls in the interests of improved quality and efficiency of medical care. Whether these controls are to be lodged in the hands of "lay" administrators or of medical professionals is less important than the growing consensus that such controls are required. As Somers and Somers [53] point out:

> The controversy over full-time medical directors and chiefs of service suggests that the basic issue is not so much physician versus lay management as between those in both groups who believe that the doctor's individual entrepreneurial role has to be considerably modified in favor of strong responsible management and institutionalized teamwork and those who do not believe this.

Those advocating the extension of heteronomous professional controls to all participants in hospitals, in particular to physicians, clearly subscribe to this former view.

Support Structures

Support for this view of the changing nature of medical care and the role of hospitals may be found primarily among administrators, medical and administrative educators, and governmental health authorities. All of these actors share a common interest in what Alford [21] terms an ideology of "corporate rationalization." That is, emphasis shifts from a reliance on professional autonomy and individual discretion to organizational arrangements supporting a well-defined division of labor together with structural devices to insure coordination and control of the individual contributions. Greater efforts are expended to codify, standardize and quantify procedures to insure improvements in the modal level of practice and greater consistency among practitioners.

There is considerable evidence to suggest that this coalition of structural interests is gaining ground in its efforts to challenge and curb the power of the professional monopolists. We have already noted the increasing professionalization of the hospital administrators, reflecting an effort to develop a base of expertise and legitimacy for managers of health care institutions independent of the medical community. The growing power of the American Hospital Association (AHA) is indicated by such events as the creation of the JCAH in 1952 which provided an organizational framework for recognizing the legitimate role of administrators, along with physicians, in assuring the quality of care in hospitals. These organizations have become increasingly active in their efforts as indicated by the Quality Assurance Program, TAP Institutes, and continued upgrading of accreditation requirements for the standards of quality for professional services.

It is also important to recognize that no profession is a monolithic group; all represent collections of varying subgroups characterized by differences in their relation to clients, other practitioners, and supporting institutions [54]. Academic physicians, full-time physicians who are salaried or under contract to hospitals, and physicians engaged in medical and health care research are among the types of physicians who may be expected to promote the rationalization of health care. Given the widely shared belief that physicians should be controlled only by other physicians, the existence of physician groups who share the ideology of rationalization is a supporting resource of critical importance.

As is well known, government officials have also become increasingly interested and active in health care matters. Early interests in equity of access have blossomed into a growing concern for the efficiency and quality of health care services that are increasingly purchased with federal dollars. The creation of

PSROs to monitor the appropriateness of hospital care is the most recent but should not be regarded as the final effort by the government to regulate the cost and quality of health services. The fact that the form of the mechanism employed takes into account the interests and claims of the dominant professional monopolists—physicians—should not obscure recognition of the larger truth that federal officials are now involved in systems designed to oversee the quantity and quality of health services in hospitals.

PSROs represent a compromise between the dominant structural interests of the professional monopolists and the challenging structural interests of the corporate rationalizers. The ideology underlying the program is one of rationalization: codification and standardization of quality of control procedures; however, the mechanism—local physicians' organizations—acknowledges the power of the professional monopolists by granting them the central roles in the operation of the system. As already noted, the compromise is possible because the medical profession is comprised of many factions, some of which share the goal of rationalization [55].

Finally, it is instructive to note that efforts to rationalize the delivery of social services are now very widespread in our society: the movement in health services is part of a much broader pattern [56]. Rationalizers in the health arena gain ideas and support from their counterparts working in other areas.

Organizational Features

Heteronomous professional organizations lack the two features that distinguish autonomous forms: the professional staff is not allowed to organize as a distinct corporate body, and sharp distinctions are not made between professional and administrative spheres of action. While U.S. hospitals tend to reflect the autonomous model, in most European hospitals, the medical staff is not organized separately from the administrative structure of the hospital [57, 58]. In many of the more recently evolved hospital forms with full-time medical staff, as well as in academic medical centers and the VA setting, we tend to see a blurring of the professional/administrative distinction. Though, at this point, few U.S. hospitals are actually heteronomous forms, we believe the direction of change is toward the heteronomous structure. Its major features are described below.

Conventional Hierarchical Form

Outwardly, heteronomous professional organizations appear to be conventional bureaucratic structures with horizontal division of labor—usually along functional lines—and vertical hierarchies to direct and coordinate the flow of work. However, there are also important differences between bureaucratic and heteronomous forms.

Delegation to Performers

Much more so than in the conventional bureaucratic organizations, decision-making autonomy is granted to individual, professionalized participants. Although they work within a general framework of institutional rules and hierarchical structures, individual performers are granted considerable discretion over task decisions, in particular, decisions concerning means or techniques.

Augmentation of Hierarchy

Conventional wisdom might lead us to expect that, given increased delegation of decision making to individual performers, the hierarchical arrangements can be "lean," with few supervisors and broad spans of control. On the contrary, numerous studies have shown that heteronomous organizations exhibit a relatively high proportion of administrators and supervisors [59, pp.222-224]. In general, the more complex the nature of the work and the higher the qualifications of workers, the larger and more elaborate the hierarchy [60, 61]. Augmenting the hierarchy is simple: increase the number of managers and reduce their spans of control. However, the terms "manager" and "span of control" are somewhat misleading since in almost all cases, the managers are themselves professionals and the proportional increase in their numbers signifies not increased closeness of supervision but an attempt to improve the transmission of information and the decision-making capacity of the organization. Galbraith [62] has pointed out that the more complex, uncertain and interdependent the work carried on within organizations, the greater the information that must be transmitted during the course of the task performance. Augmentation of the hierarchy is an important device for increasing both the communication and decision-making capacity of the system.

An oversized administrative component also assists in handling the problems of coordination. In comparison with autonomous professional organizations, coordination requirements are substantially increased in heteronomous organizations. This occurs because in the latter form, physicians are no longer viewed as *the* provider of medical services, only as *a* provider. The organizational implications of this change are enormous. Generalist professionals are expected to perform a variety of services and to coordinate those that are provided—both their own and those of ancillary personnel [63]. Specialist professionals, in contrast, perform only a subset of the required tasks so that they contribute to the problem of coordination rather than toward its solution. Others, i.e., managers, administrators, directors, clerks, must orchestrate and integrate their specialized contributions.

Teams

A structural form found more and more often in these settings is the team or project group. A variety of types of teams are found in medical care settings, ranging from the semi-permanent groups that regularly perform specific functions, such as heart transplants, to the highly transitory systems developed to minister to the particular needs of a single patient. Teams are usually composed of persons from varying occupations; ideally, team composition and leadership, as well as duration, vary depending on the requirements of the tasks performed [64].

There is little doubt that the use of teams builds more flexibility into the system, permitting relatively rapid changes in the deployment of personnel. Nevertheless, the use of teams remains consistent with the hierarchical principle: the team leader is held responsible for the work performed by the team. (The fact that the identity of the leader may change from time-to-time or by situation does not alter that conclusion, but underlines the extent to which leadership has become formalized; i.e., separated from persons and associated with positions.) The continuity between team-based and more traditional hierarchical forms becomes more apparent when we recognize that the shift from conventional to team arrangements is basically equivalent to a shift from a functional to a product mode of organization.

Advantages and Problems

A number of important issues arise when the heteronomous form is applied to the organization of professional work. In medical care organizations, most of these become issues of "the bureaucratization of medicine." As analysts and critics have noted, the use of large-scale organizations for health care delivery introduces a new element, i.e., the organization or institution itself, that may intrude into the practitioner-patient relationship. Mechanic has studied this problem and assessed its consequences for care. His conclusions, based on a review of others' as well as his own research, are as follows:

> Increasingly, the physician and other health workers are employees of a bureaucratic organization, resulting in a shift in their loyalties from the individual patient providing the fee to the organization, the profession, or the physicians' sponsors. Although the character of such shifts needs more careful study, indications are that the technical quality of care is enhanced, but that patients are dealt with more impersonally. Patients are more likely to feel that physicians are inflexible, less interested in them, and less willing to take time to listen to them. There is a tendency in such organizations to give relatively less attention to the patients' concerns and relatively more attention to the problems of organization and work demands [65, p.15].

A closely related issue pertains to the locus of decision making and responsibility for patient care. Again, Mechanic [65, pp.54-55] calls attention to dangers inherent in the heteronomous system:

The bureaucratization of medicine also has the effect of diluting the personal responsibility of the provider, making it more likely that interests other than those of the patient will prevail. By segmenting responsibility for patient care, the medical bureaucracy relieves the physician of direct continuing responsibility. . . . It is far easier for patients to locate and deal with individual failures where responsibility is clear, than to confront a diffuse organizational structure where responsibility is often hazy and the buck is easily passed.

We have here the obverse side of the micro-macro dilemma noted earlier. If the autonomous structure gives priority to micro concerns of quality service to individual clients to the neglect of macro concerns of equity and distributional aspects of care, the heteronomous structure reverses the priorities, favoring macro over micro criteria of care.

More generally, designing control systems is always problematic. Heteronomous structures, like all hierarchical systems, presume that those designing the control system know better than the performers what types of decisions and behaviors are necessary or preferred. All performers resist this assumption to some degree; and it is always a risky assumption to some extent. There will always be some types of information available locally that are not available to those who design and maintain the control system. In the case of professional performers, external control systems are likely to be seen as inadequate, misguided, and illegitimate. Professionals see themselves as moral, autonomous actors, responsible and accountable for their own decisions, hence, needing to resist all efforts to regulate their actions. They emphasize the critical importance of decision making on a case-by-case basis and resist the notion that there are abstract or all-purpose formulas adequate to regulate their work. Thus, they are likely to resist external control arrangements on principle, believing that even if a particular rule may not be objectionable, the idea of administrative rules and the precedent for them must be resisted.

In addition to resistance to hierarchy, rules, and supervision in heteronomous systems, we would expect to observe difficulties in the use of teams, especially in medical care systems. Smoothness of team functioning presumes relative equality in the skills and power of participants, but this feature is lacking in most medical teams. Pellegrino [66, pp.310-311] upholds the value of flexibility in team leadership, noting:

The captain of the team should be determined by the dominant features essential in the management of the patient. The captain should be the person who possesses the skill and knowledge most consonant with the dominant features of the clinical condition exhibited by the patient.

but then goes on to acknowledge:

> Most physicians do not as yet accept the idea of a shifting captaincy or of truly shared responsibility and decision-making authority.

Though one of the chief advantages of the team arrangement is supposed to be the flexibility it permits in the use of personnel of varying skills and levels of training, the promise of flexibility is seriously curtailed because of the rigidities introduced by the licensing of almost all occupational categories. Neither tasks nor personnel can be redeployed to enhance the effectiveness and efficiency of care delivery without posing some conflict with licensure restrictions [12, 67]. The continuing importance of occupational licensure as the exoskeleton of health care delivery is a sure manifestation of the enduring power of the occupations and professions (as opposed to the administrators and managers) in determining the arrangements under which health care is dispensed.

CONJOINT PROFESSIONAL ORGANIZATIONS

More so than the other two models, the conjoint model describes a possible rather than an existing model of professional organization. Although some health care organizations appear to be moving in this direction, it is not easy to point to specific forms which conform to this model. For this reason, it is more difficult to provide concrete descriptions of the structural features, advantages and problems, etc., associated with this model. And, more seriously, our treatment of it may tend to be somewhat utopian, emphasizing its strengths and ignoring its deficiencies. In spite of these problems, I believe that the conjoint model is a potential model for structuring professional work.

The conjoint professional organization is one in which, by definition, professional participants and administrators are roughly equal in the power that they command and in the importance of their functions. Instead of one or the other group dominating, they coexist in a state of interdependence and mutual influence. (The conjoint model can accommodate more than two centers of power. Some may desire to see power shared with patients or their representatives. Such arrangements are possible, but more complex. I will not attempt to describe them within this reading.)

Tannenbaum [68] has pointed out that organizations vary not only in the relative amount of power or control exercised by one set of participants over another but also in the total amount of control exercised by participants. Thus, the conjoint model is characterized by more equal distribution of power and more total power exercised by each group. Professionals have greater influence on administrators, and vice versa, i.e., the professional/administrative functions are more highly interdependent than is the case in the autonomous or the heteronomous forms.

Rationale

As in the autonomous and the heteronomous forms, there is considerable differentiation in the functions of professional practitioners and administrators, with each enjoying primacy in certain arenas. The basic distinction, however, is no longer one of support (i.e., maintenance goals) attended to by administrators, and patient care (i.e., output goals) presided over by the medical staff. Instead, physicians and other health care practitioners specialize in the delivery of micro patient care, and administrators and medical managers attend to the delivery of macro care.

Because micro and macro principles governing care may conflict, those representing these principles must also expect to experience and wrestle with conflict, i.e., genuine differences in choice criteria, not simply misunderstandings or failures of communication. The recognition of the presence and the legitimacy of conflict is one of the features that sets off the conjoint from the previous models of professional organization. Rather than being suppressed in the dominant professional or dominant administrator form, the built-in conflict is expressed in the structural characteristics of the conjoint organization.

Support Structures

Support for the emergence of conjoint structures comes partially from the working out of processes previously described. As noted, professional participants, especially physicians, are increasingly involved in administrative and management responsibilities within medical care organizations, and the nature of these positions is such that macro issues dominate the agenda. Similarly, administrative officials are increasingly drawn into medical care delivery problems because of the specialization and complexity of coordination requirements.

However, the major impetus for increasing collaboration of professional and administrative factions within health care organizations is action taken by the federal government. (One might almost refer to the conjoint structure as the result of a shotgun marriage with the weapon held by Uncle Sam!) Much recent legislation requires better cooperation between administrators and physicians in curbing costs and assuring quality. The implicit threat is one of increasing governmental intervention and controls. Increasing pressures for external accountability have been a powerful force encouraging a more "cooperative" attitude on the part of physicians [46, p.106]. It also seems apparent that the new JCAH standards for quality assurance—standards that stress the combined responsibilities of trustees, administrators, and physicians—represent an "industry" response to the threat of increased federal controls.

Yet another source of external pressure for increased collaboration on quality control is the increasing number of court decisions which hold the hospital, not just the physician, liable for the quality of care dispensed. Kinzer [46, pp.125, 126] comments on these developments and their implication for internal collaboration between administrators and physicians:

> Court precedents, from Darling vs. Charleston Community Hospital up to Gonzales vs. Nork and Mercy General Hospital, seem to firmly establish hospital responsibility and accountability for the performance of members of its medical staff.
>
> One of the constructive outgrowths of the Darling-Nork trend in court decisions has been the persistent effort to meld the hospital into one legally accountable entity, instead of what has often been described as "a three-legged monster without a head." The hard part of this has been to get members of the medical staff to believe that they function as an integral (and accountable) part of the hospital organization, and not as a separate power block functioning within the hospital walls. Progress in this area has been slow but steady.

Organizational Features

Our discussion of the structural features associated with conjoint professional organizations is necessarily vague and somewhat general since relatively few organizations of this type presently exist. If our analysis is correct, more are currently in the process of "becoming."

A Pluralist Structure

Conjoint professional organizations are expected to exhibit a pluralist form. Kornhauser [69, p.197] has portrayed this type of structure in his description of the structural features of scientific research organizations:

> Where participation is mediated by partly autonomous relations and where at the same time there is access to the organization, the system tends to acquire a *pluralist* character. This means that there are multiple centers of power. The organization does not wholly absorb professionals, nor do professionals wholly absorb the organization. To the extent that a system of relations is pluralist, it tends toward a balance of freedom and power or, in functional terms, between the conditions conducive to creativity and those conducive to control.

Ideally, we would expect to see some relatively independent and autonomous structures embodying the diverse and sometimes conflicting interests of administrators and practitioners, and we would also expect to see some relatively interdependent structures created to allow the conflicting parties to come together to express and deal with their differences. In particular, quality assurance programs that often consist of a set of diverse and uncoordinated medical staff committees and PSRO-mandated units, need to be gathered into broader and more articulated frameworks supporting the involvement of medical and hospital administrators together with practitioners in a standard setting, data gathering and interpretation, and appraisal and feedback activities. These are the settings and these are the types of issues around which macro and micro care interests and concerns should come together in health care organizations. For the conduct of such programs, the skills of integration, negotiation, bargaining and conflict resolution will be in great demand.

On the other hand, one of the hallmarks of the pluralist structure is that all activities and units need not be tightly linked and coordinated. The presence of highly professionalized participants who have their own norms of practice and modes of control means that many units and subdivisions may be allowed to function relatively autonomously. Most treatment and care units are parallel rather than interdependent units, organized to meet the needs of patients within their own boundaries. Only the more complex cases require the joint collaboration of two or more specialty groups. Thus, pluralist structures are in many respects and for many types of activities, "loosely coupled" systems [70] comprised of relatively independent and autonomous units and programs that do not require tight controls or high levels of coordination. Since many arenas of autonomous functioning remain, we need to supplement the integrating skills listed above with a set of buffering, differentiating, insulation and segregation skills and tactics.

Matrix Structures

For those issues and areas of maximum interdependence across specialty groups and levels that require extensive coordination efforts, matrix structures may be the most suitable form [71, 72]. The matrix structure is appropriate when most or all of the organization's or unit's work is carried on within a shifting set of project teams. The hallmark of the matrix is the simultaneous use of two competing bases of authority, typically a project or product base and a functional or disciplinary base. Thus, a physician will be responsible to both the project leader of his team (e.g., the chief surgeon on the operative team) and the department head (e.g., chief of surgery). The project interests are more likely to encompass micro patient care goals; the departmental interests, macro concerns. By requiring participants to take both into account simultaneously, matrix structures elevate these conflicts into a structural principle. While institutionalizing conflict in this manner does not resolve it, it does insure that both project (micro) interests, and departmental (macro) interests receive attention. Matrix forms eschew the unity of command principle in order to stress that under some conditions, decisions and actions must serve multiple, sometimes conflicting, objectives.

Concentric Spheres

The autonomous and heteronomous models presume a hierarchical arrangement within which either the professionals or the administrators are dominant. The conjoint model has sometimes been conceptualized as a side-by-side system offering differentiation and parity to each sector. But this image is misleading. It is more useful to visualize the conjoint professional organization as composed of a series of concentric circles [73]. The innermost circle represents the technical core of the organization. In hospitals it includes the settings in which care is actually dispensed: examination rooms, operating theaters, patient care wards. It is within this zone that the autonomous professional interests and values may be expected to dominate. However, they do so within constraints set by the outer circles. The second circle is comprised of the medical managers and support systems providing backup to the patient care workers. Managers not only coordinate and control the interdependent units providing direct services to patients but also administer more remote but essential support programs: personnel, admitting, accounting. The third and outer circle includes general administrators, both hospital and medical, and administrative units that relate to the hospital environment, e.g., third party payers, regulatory groups, and finally, the hospital board. All of these officials and groups relate primarily to the hospital environment and mediate its impact on the hospital's structure and services. In many ways, the outer circle orients out toward the environment as much or more than it faces in toward the hospital's technical work. The primary task of managers in this sphere is to build bridges between their organizations and relevant environmental units, while seeing to it that processes within the technical core are buffered or insulated from these perturbations and uncertainties [74, 75, 59].

As we move from the core to the peripheral structures, we would expect to see the changing mix of administrative and professional values noted by Kornhauser [69, p.201 (The term "medical" has been substituted for Kornhauser's "scientist" administrator)].

> The role of [medical] administrator has been discussed thus far as if it were a single position. But there is actually a hierarchy of positions of [medical] administration. The adaptation of the [medical] administrator tends to vary according to his rank: the higher the position, the more controlling are the norms of management and the organization; the lower the position, the more responsive is the [medical] administrator to professional norms and demands.

Kornhauser emphasizes the changing mix of values. This is valuable, but so also is the more general point that all positions contain some measure of both values. In a professional organization, no administrator should be completely governed by administrative (macro) values; and no practitioner should subscribe exclusively to professional (micro) values. In a healthy professional organization, intra-role conflicts will be as numerous as, if not outnumber, inter-role conflicts.

A Strengthened Board

In our discussion of support systems for the emerging conjoint structure, we emphasized the importance of the threat posed by an increasingly active federal bureaucracy. Physicians have been "encouraged" to collaborate with administrators in the development of more effective and efficient health care delivery systems. These alliances are at least partially defensive ones. A second tactic in a local hospital's defensive strategy is to strengthen its board of trustees.

Although, in the beginning, the boards of general hospitals were the centers of power [76], they have until recently been relatively weak. They are now growing in strength for at least three reasons—the first, general to many organizations, the others, specific to hospitals.

Initially, they can serve as important resource-gathering and protective mechanisms for organizations [75]. In times of growing environmental turbulence, when more opportunities and dangers are found in systems and events external to the organization, boards serve in several ways. They become important sources for information, connecting links to critical environmental elements, and sources of legitimacy and good will. Studies by Pfeffer [77] support the thesis that hospitals use board appointments to establish a relationship with important segments of their environment, and specific appointments vary to reflect the particular needs of different types of hospitals.

The second factor encouraging the development of stronger boards is the recent stream of legal decisions placing responsibility for the quality of care delivered in hospitals on the trustees. There is nothing quite like holding a group responsible for a set of behaviors, to motivate it to increase its control over those behaviors.

Third, both hospital administrators and the medical staff look increasingly to the hospital board as a voice for community and localized interests and, in this sense, a bulwark against centralized, federal controls. As noted, the PSRO program may be viewed as moving the health care system toward a more centralized and uniform set of care standards and practices. Many local physicians and hospitals are resisting this pressure, and are doing so under the banner of preserving local community control. Strengthened boards increase the power and legitimacy of these efforts.

Advantages and Problems

The conjoint professional organization represents an approach that recognizes both the autonomy requirement of professionals and the increasing interdependence of the work they perform. It attempts to combine the administrative forms essential for coordinating and attaining macro-care goals with the spheres of autonomy essential for pursuing micro-care goals. It provides overlapping roles and structures that allow administrators to co-opt professionals in the decision bodies stressing macro-care goals, and professionals to co-opt administrators in decision areas stressing micro-care goals.

Micro- and macro-care concerns need to be kept in close proximity to one another. If they are separated, unrealistic and inappropriate "solutions" are likely to result. Those attempting to devise the constraints and incentives to shape the distribution of care at the macro level must take into account the manner in which their directives will be received and responded to by those delivering micro care. In their enthusiasm to rationalize and quantify, reformers may impose inappropriate requirements that can result in sterile and non-therapeutic standardization of care and impersonal inflexibility of services. Decisions made or rules promulgated far from delivery sites can engender a variety of problems when implemented. At this point, that conjunction of events does not appear to be too widespread. In part, this is due to the continuing power of professional practitioners. Few attempts at rationalization and reform have considered how practitioners may be expected to interpret and react to administrative goals or "the specific mechanisms by which policy goals are to be reached" [44, p.47]. In addition, administrative controls developed thus far—both incentives and sanctions—have not been powerful enough to cause major behavioral changes in practitioners who have their own ideologies and justifications for care decisions.

There may also be a defensive response to external regulatory attempts at the *organizational* level. Externally imposed requirements defined by organizational managers as inappropriate or misguided often receive a symbolic response—assurances of cooperation, gestures of support, reports of attempts to comply—accompanied by little change in the specific behaviors that were the target of the change attempt [78, 79]. Symbolic changes may even take the form of structural modifications in which new committees or offices are created signaling to the environment the organization's responsiveness, the signal being accepted at face value as an indicator of compliance in the absence of data regarding the efficacy of the new forms [80].

I do not wish to condone duplicity or to praise noncompliance with externally imposed regulations, but I cannot refrain from noting that all organizations devise tactics and structures to protect their core activities from undue influence from their environments. Professional organizations in particular may be expected to be highly creative and resourceful in buffering and sealing off their central work processes. That is why we would not expect change efforts to be effective unless they take into account the specific characteristics of these organizations with their unusual participants and distinctive structures.

NOTES

1. Scott, W.R. Reactions to supervision in a heteronomous professional organization. *Administrative Science Quarterly* 10:65, 1965.

2. Stanton, A.H. and M.S. Schwartz. *The Mental Hospital.* New York: Basic Books, 1954.

3. Clark, B.R. Faculty organization and authority. In T.F. Lunsford (ed.), *The Study of Academic Administration.* Boulder, CO: Western Interstate Commission for Higher Education, 1963.

4. Smigel, E.O. *The Wall Street Lawyer: Professional Organization Man?* New York: Free Press, 1964.

5. Georgopoulos, B.S. (ed.). *Organization Research on Health Institutions.* Ann Arbor, MI: Institute for Social Research, The University of Michigan, 1972.

6. Freidson, E. *Doctoring Together: A Study of Professional Social Control.* New York: Elsevier, 1975a.

7. Goode, W.J. Community within a community: the professions. *American Sociological Review* 22:194, 1957.

8. Vollmer, H.K. and D.L. Mills (eds.). *Professionalization.* Englewood Cliffs, NJ: Prentice-Hall, 1966.

9. Freidson, E. The Future of Professionalization. In M. Stacey et al. (eds.), *Health and the Division of Labor.* London: Croom Helm, 1977.

10. Freidman, M. *Capitalism and Freedom.* Chicago: University of Chicago Press, 1962.

11. Freidson, E. *Profession of Medicine.* New York: Dodd, Mead, 1970.

12. Somers, A.R. *Hospital Regulation: The Dilemma of Public Policy.* Princeton, NJ: Industrial Relations Section, Princeton University, 1969.

13. Roemer, M.I. and J.W. Friedman. *Doctors in Hospitals.* Baltimore, MD: The Johns Hopkins University Press, 1971.

14. Garceau, O. *The Political Life of the American Medical Association.* Cambridge, MA: Harvard University Press, 1971.

15. Hyde, D.R. (ed.). The American Medical Association: Power, purpose and politics in organized medicine. *The Yale Law Journal* 63:938, 1954.

16. Stevens, R. *American Medicine and the Public Interest.* New Haven, CT: Yale University Press, 1971.

17. Krause, E.A. *Power and Illness: The Political Sociology of Health and Medical Care.* New York: Elsevier, 1977.

18. Monsma, G.N., Jr. Marginal Revenue and the Demand for Physicians' Services. In H.E. Klarman (ed.), *Empirical Studies in Health Economics.* Baltimore, MD: The Johns Hopkins University Press, 1970.

19. Reinhardt, U.E. Alternative methods of reimbursing non-institutional providers of health services. In Institute of Medicine, *Controls on Health Care.* Washington, DC: National Academy of Sciences, 1975.

20. Dolen, A.K. Antitrust law and physician dominance of other health care practitioners. *Journal of Health Politics, Policy and Law* 4:675, 1980.

21. Alford, R.R. *Health Care Politics: Ideological and Interest Group Barriers to Reform.* Chicago: University of Chicago Press, 1975

22. Christman, L. The autonomous nursing staff in the hospital. *NAQ/Leadership in Nursing Administration* 1:37, 1977.

23. Sample, S.A. Development of organizational by-laws: an approach to accountability. *Nursing Clinics of North America* 13:91, 1978.

24. Wilson, R.N. The physician's changing hospital role. *Human Organization* 18:177, 1959-60.

25. Flood, A.B. and W.R. Scott. Professional power and professional effectiveness: The power of the surgical staff and the quality of surgical care in hospitals. *Journal of Health and Social Behavior* 19:240, 1978.

26. Scott, W.R. Some implications of organization theory for research on health services. *Milbank Memorial Fund Quarterly* 44, part 2:35, 1966.

27. Freidson, E. and B. Rhea. Processes of control in a company of equals. *Social Problems* 11:119, 1963.

28. Etzioni, A. *A Comprehensive Analysis of Complex Organizations.* New York: Free Press of Glencoe, 1961.

29. Eisele, C.W. *The Medical Staff in the Modern Hospital.* New York: McGraw-Hill, 1967.

30. Joint Commission on the Accreditation of Hospitals. *Accreditation Manual for Hospitals.* Chicago: Joint Commission on the Accreditation of Hospitals, 1971.

31. Hall, O. The informal organization of the medical profession. *Canadian Journal of Economics and Political Science* 12:30, 1946.

32. Parsons, T. Introduction to Max Weber. *The Theory of Social and Economic Organization.* Glencoe, IL: Free Press, 1947.

33. Gouldner, A.W. *Patterns of Industrial Bureaucracy.* Glencoe, IL: The Free Press, 1954.

34. Goss, M.E.W. Influence and authority among physicians in an out-patient clinic. *American Sociological Review* 26:39, 1961.

35. Goran, M.J., et al. The PSRO hospital review system. *Medical Care* (supplement) 13:1, 1975.

36. Dornbusch, S.M. and W.R. Scott. *Evaluation and the Exercise of Authority.* San Francisco: Jossey-Bass Publishers, 1975.

37. Freidson, E. Speculations on the social psychology of local PSRO operations. *Proceedings: Conference on Professional Self-Regulation.* Washington, DC: HEW Publ. No. 77-621, June 1975b.

38. Scott, W.R., R. Bies and M. LaPlante. Organizational Effectiveness: Models and Measures for Assessing PSRO Effectiveness. In Health Care Financing Administration, *Health Care Financing Research Report: Professional Standards Review Organization 1979 Program Evaluation.* Washington, DC: DHHS, HCFA Pub. No. 03041, 1980.

39. Millman, M. *The Unkindest Cut: Life in the Backrooms of Medicine.* New York: William Morrow, 1977.

40. Palmer, R.H. and M.C. Reilly. Individual and institutional variables which may serve as indicators of quality of medical care. *Medical Care* 17:693, 1979.

41. Morehead, M.A. *Quality of Medical Care Provided by Family Physicians as Related to Their Education, Training and Methods of Practice.* New York: Health Insurance Plan of New York, 1958.

42. Brickman, P., R. Folger, E. Goode and Y. Schul. Micro and Macro Justice. In M.J. Lerner (ed.), *The Justice Motive in Social Behavior.* New York: Plenum, 1980.

43. Havighurst, C.C. and J.F. Blumstein. Coping with quality/cost trade-offs in medical care: the role of PSROs. *Northwestern University Law Review* 70:20, 1975.

44. Taft, C. and S. Levine. Problems of Federal Policies and Strategies to Influence the Quality of Health Care. In R.H. Egdahl and P.M. Gertman (eds.), *Quality Assurance in Health Care.* Germantown, MD: Aspen Systems Corp., 1976.

45. Health Care Finance Administration. *Professional Standards Review Organizations: 1978 Program Evaluation*. Washington, DC: DHEW, HCFA Pub. No. 03000, January, 1979.

46. Kinzer, D.M. Inpatient Quality Assurance Activities: Coordination of Federal, State, and Private Roles—The Hospital's Views. In R.H. Edgahl and P.M. Gertman (eds.), *Quality Assurance in Health Care*. Germantown, MD: Aspen Systems Corp., 1976.

47. Mauksch, H. Organizational Context of Nursing Practice. In F. Davis (ed.), *The Nursing Profession*. New York: John Wiley, 1966.

48. Etzioni, A. (ed.). *The Semi-Professions and their Organization*. New York: The Free Press, 1969.

49. Fox, R.C. The Medicalization and Demedicalization of American Society. In J.H. Knowles (ed.), *Doing Better and Feeling Worse: Health in The United States*. New York: W.W. Norton, 1977.

50. Wilensky, H.L. Dynamics of professionalism: The case of hospital administration. *Hospital Administration* 7:6, 1962.

51. Greenfield, H.I. *Accountability in Health Facilities*. New York: Praeger, 1975.

52. Halbert, G. The Legal Aspects of Physician Credentialing. In R.H. Egdahl and P.M. Gertman (eds.), *Quality Assurance in Health Care*. Germantown, MD: Aspen Systems Corp., 1976.

53. Somers, H.M. and A.R. Somers. *Doctors, Patients and Health Insurance*. Garden City, NY: Doubleday (Anchor), 1961.

54. Bucher, R. and A. Strauss. Professions in process. *American Journal of Sociology* 66:325, 1961.

55. Stevens, B. Academic physicians versus community practitioners: PSROs and the regulation of the medical profession. Unpublished paper, Department of Sociology, Harvard University, January 15, 1980.

56. Scott, W.R. Reform Movements and Organizations: The Case of Aging. In R.W. Fogel, E. Hatfield, S.B. Kiesler, and E. Shanas (eds.), *Aging: Stability and Change in the Family*. New York: Academic Press, 1981a.

57. Glaser, W.A. American and Foreign Hospitals: Some Sociological Comparisons. In E. Freidson (ed.), *The Hospital in Modern Society*. New York: Free Press of Glencoe, 1963.

58. Glaser, W.A. *Social Settings and Medical Organization: A Cross-National Study of the Hospital*. New York: Atherton, 1970.

59. Scott, W.R. *Organizations: Rational, Natural and Open Systems*. Englewood Cliffs, NJ: Prentice-Hall, 1981b.

60. Bell, G.D. Determinants of span of control. *American Journal of Sociology* 73:100, 1967.

61. Blau, P.M., W.V. Heydebrand and R.E. Stauffer. The structure of small bureaucracies. *American Sociological Review* 31:179, 1966.

62. Galbraith, J. *Designing Complex Organizations*. Reading, MA: Addison-Wesley, 1973.

63. Heydebrand, W.V. Autonomy, Complexity, and Non-bureaucratic Coordination in Professional Organizations. In W.V. Heydebrand (ed.), *Comparative Organizations*. Englewood Cliffs, NJ: Prentice-Hall, 1973.

64. Nagi, S.Z. Teamwork in health care in the U.S.: A sociological perspective. *Milbank Memorial Fund Quarterly/Health and Society* 53:75, 1975.

65. Mechanic, D. *The Growth of Bureaucratic Medicine*. New York: John Wiley, 1976.

66. Pellegrino, E.D. The Changing Matrix of Clinical Decision Making in the Hospital. In B.S. Georgopoulos (ed.), *Organization Research on Health Instituions*. Ann Arbor, MI: Institute for Social Research, The University of Michigan, 1972.

67. Hershey, N. The inhibiting effect upon innovation of the prevailing licensure system. *Annals of the New York Academy of Science* 166:951, 1969.

68. Tannenbaum, A.S. *Control in Organizations*. New York: McGraw-Hill, 1968.

69. Kornhauser, W. *Scientists in Industry: Conflict and Accommodation*. Berkeley: University of California Press, 1962.

70. Weick, K.E. Educational organizations as loosely coupled systems. *Administrative Science Quarterly* 21:1, 1976.

71. Knight, K. Matrix organization: a review. *Journal of Management Studies* 13:111, 1976.

72. Neuhauser, D. The hospital as a matrix organization. *Hospital Administration* 17:8, 1972.

73. Parsons, T. *Structure and Process in Modern Societies*. Glencoe, IL: Free Press, 1960.

74. Thompson, J.D. *Organizations in Action*. New York: McGraw-Hill, 1967.

75. Pfeffer, J. and G.R. Salancik. *The External Control of Organizations*. New York: Harper and Row, 1978.

76. Perrow, C. The analysis of goals in complex organizations. *American Sociological Review* 26:854, 1961.

77. Pfeffer, J. Size, composition, and function of hospital boards of directors: A study of organization-environment linkage. *Administrative Science Quarterly* 18:349, 1973.

78. Edelman, M. *The Symbolic Uses of Politics*. Urbana, IL: University of Illinois Press, 1964.

79. Etzioni, A. Epilogue: Alternative Conceptions of Accountability. In H.I. Greenfield, *Accountability in Health Facilities*. New York: Praeger, 1975.

80. Meyer, M.W. Organizational structure as signaling. *Pacific Sociological Review* 22:481, 1979.

5. Quality Assurance and Organizational Effectiveness in Hospitals

ROBERT W. HETHERINGTON

Reprinted with permission from *Health Services Research* 17(2). Copyright © 1982, 185-201.

INTRODUCTION

Current emphasis on competition instead of regulation may result in the federal government's curtailing requirements for quality assurance programs in hospitals. Evidence is not overwhelming that these programs have been cost-effective, and without this evidence, they are difficult to defend in times of declining resources. However the failure of health services research to identify real benefits from quality assurance programs may be due as much to a scattered approach to the problem as to an absence of benefits. Whether or not external pressures continue for the regulatory programs, it is important to consider the range of possible benefits before concluding that the hospital industry would be better off with less regulation of quality of care. Also, the primary targets of regulation—physicians—may be shortchanging themselves by supporting retrenchment to an environment where less regulation prevails.

The "scattered" approach we have mentioned rises primarily from lack of agreement among researchers on how best to measure the impact of quality assurance programs. Different measures can demonstrate different results. It becomes necessary, then, to adopt a theoretical framework to guide assurance research and to direct attention to areas of performance requiring further study.

This paper describes one such theoretical framework. It is based on the problem-solving concept of organizations originated by Parsons for social systems [1], and later applied to organizations by Georgopoulos and Tannenbaum [2] and Georgopoulos [3, ch.2; 4]. In this framework, quality assurance programs introduce structural problems for the hospital; specifically, quality assurance research requires increased formalization of some procedures and the creation of new authority structures. It is evident the attendant changes in structure have other impacts, e.g., on costs, interpersonal relationships within the organization, and the hospital's public image. Responding to the problem of how best to organize a quality assurance program, management must consider the simultaneous impact of each of these factors. In general, research aimed at evaluating the impact of quality assurance on organizational performance fails to measure this range of outcomes, i.e., quality, organizational structure, interpersonal relationships, community relations.

Our emphasis on research using multiple performance measures is referred to in the general organizational literature as the "effectiveness" approach [5,6]. When this approach is combined with the problem-solving framework, an effective organization is defined as one which performs well across all problem areas simultaneously. In research, this proves to be a difficult concept to deal with. However, if the simultaneous presence of these problems represents the real world for organizations, health services research (and organizational research in general) should not, as some would suggest, abandon the concept because it is difficult to operationalize.

THEORETICAL MODEL

The theoretical framework identifies four types of problems encountered by all social systems. Problems are defined as either *internal* or *external* to the organization (external meaning the problem concerns exchanges between the organization and its relevant environment), and involving activities which are either *instrumental* or *affective* in nature. Instrumental activities are those valued primarily as means to organizational ends or goals. Affective activities may also contribute to achieving goals, but are primarily valued as ends in themselves. They embody the societal values and norms which govern human relationships.

The problems are defined by the intersection of these dimensions: the *internal-external* and the *affective-instrumental*. The *external-instrumental* problem is concerned with *adaptive* mechanisms the organization can employ to obtain needed resources from the environment (e.g., finances, labor, raw materials) and to market the products of the organization. The *internal-instrumental* problem involves defining *goal-attainment* structures in such a way that the connection between resources and product is most efficiently/effectively made (the arrangement of offices in hierarchical relationships and formal coordination of activities, for instance). The intersection of *internal* and *affective* dimensions defines the *integration* problem, wherein relationships among workers and subunits of the organization are dealt with and motivation is created to maintain productive effort within the organization. Finally, the *affective-external* dimensions pinpoint the problem of making the goals and values of the organization consistent with those of the larger society, i.e., *pattern maintenance.*[1]

Diagrammatically, the four system problems may be represented as follows:

LOCATION OF THE ACTIVITY/PROBLEM

		INTERNAL TO THE ORGANIZATION	EXTERNAL TO THE ORGANIZATION
NATURE OF THE ACTIVITY/PROBLEM	INSTRU-MENTAL	*Goal Attainment* (structuring resources to best achieve organizational goals)	*Adaptation* (procuring resources and disposing of products)
	AFFECTIVE	*Integration* (motivating personnel to work toward organizational goals)	*Pattern Maintenance* (attaining and assuring congruence between organizational values and those of the larger society)

An assumption implicit in the framework is that the four types of problems are interdependent. Change in any one area will create pressures for adjustments in the other three. If appropriate adjustments are not made, the change may lead the organization to crisis. For instance, if a decrease in employee morale occurs (*integration* problem), this may lead to lowered productivity (*adaptive* problem), a breakdown of the authority structure (*goal-attainment*), and an altered public perception of the organization (*pattern-maintenance*). Assessment of the effectiveness of the organizational solution to the morale problem must take into account its impact on the other three problems.[2]

QUALITY ASSURANCE

How can quality assurance programs be studied within the above framework? These programs call for modifications in the structure of the organization in order to achieve greater control over the activities of its members.[3] These modifications in structure are defined by the framework as *goal-attainment* problems. They are concerned with rules and regulations, hierarchical relationships, centralization-decentralization of power, and so on. They are *internal* to the organization, and *instrumental* in that the justification for the existence and persistence of any given structural arrangement is that it is seen as essential for efficiently achieving the goals of the organization.[4]

The ''modifications in structure'' brought about by quality assurance programs may be more precisely referred to as increases in the formalization of procedures, particularly with regard to activities of the medical staff. Formalization is defined as the extent to which rules exist in an organization, and the extent to which they are enforced [10]. Formalization is a key characteristic of the concept of "bureaucracy" so that an increase in formalization means the organization becomes more bureaucratic.

At the heart of the quality assurance program in a hospital are rules specifying procedures which operationalize the concept of quality of care. There are two aspects to this specification: the definition of criteria by which medical care may be judged adequate or not, and the establishment of standards of expected performance. This specification can deal with process or outcome, or both. Accompanying these are other new rules and regulations governing such diverse behaviors as medical records documentation, preparation of reports, recording minutes of committee meetings, and specifying the relationships among offices in the quality assurance program and those between the program and the existing structure of the hospital.

Besides the institution of new rules and regulations, quality assurance programs require alterations in the formal authority structures of the organization—namely, the creation of new roles and the fitting of these new roles into the existing power structure. Although it is possible that the way in which things actually get done as a result of quality review depends to a large extent on the existing power structure, certain new features become necessary [11, Ch.9]. For instance, referring to new roles, attention is drawn to the need for a quality coordinator whose job is to note discrepancies with established standards (for instance, length of stay exceeding authorized limits without justification), and the physician-advisor who provides the initial link between the assessment and the corrective action phase. New centers of power are created through the institution of the quality assurance committee.

Organizational change always creates certain strains and tensions, because the status quo is supported by those whose primary rewards depend on it [12, p.508; 13, p.179]. Change of the nature described above, however, engenders more than the usual amount of tension since it deals directly with a long-standing, unresolved issue in organizations: the conflict between the norms of professional freedom and the norms of bureaucratic structure [14, pp.60-74]. In the hospital setting, the increase in bureaucracy means quite simply that the technical experts (physicians) may lose some power and status [13, p.49] through the process of specification of procedures which is the integral part of the quality assurance program. Once procedures are specified and the visibility of performance vis-à-vis those specifications is raised, information regarding activities of the medical staff are "demystified" to a certain extent. Power then may slide towards those in charge of the bureaucratic power structure—the administration and the board of directors who formerly relied largely on the application of implicit standards by the medical staff itself to judge quality of care. The so-called "three-legged stool" of the hospital structure (board of directors, administration and medical staff) has traditionally suffered from a lack of integration due to this structural issue; quality assurance programs directly address the lack of integration of the three sources of power and decision making [15].

In terms of the framework, then, the crux of the matter is a *goal-attainment* problem—quite simply, what rules and regulations shall be adopted and how shall they be enforced in order to maximize the primary goal of the organization and the new program: high quality care. Due to the interdependence of problems, however, the solution to this problem involves not merely defining a well-articulated structure for attaining quality, but also attending to the other three system problems. For instance, most obviously, how is the good will of the medical staff to be retained in the face of these changes, and how can the physicians' commitment to making the new program work be obtained (*integration* problem)? Further, where does the organization find adequate resources for the program without threatening current levels of productivity, and how is the new "product" to be marketed and at what cost (*adaptation*)? Finally, how does the quality assurance program affect the reputation of the hospital among relevant constituents—physicians, consumers, insurance agencies, government and civic agencies (*pattern maintenance*)?

THE GOAL-ATTAINMENT PROBLEM: STREAMLINING THE BUREAUCRACY

If the conceptual essence of quality assurance programs is increased formalization of medical care activities, the essence of the research question within the *goal-attainment* problem area is: what is the relationship between increased formalization and quality of care? The answer to this question must consider the nature of payoffs to be expected from an organization in which the basic characteristics of bureaucracy are maximized (e.g., formalization), and the types of problems inherent in bureaucracy which must be overcome if the payoff is to be realized.

The concept of bureaucracy has been described in terms of six dimensions, based on Weber's [16] original work: hierarchy of authority, division of labor, presence of rules, procedural specifications, impersonality, and technical competence. Taken together, these dimensions suggest a system whose members, unlike members of a professional group, can be held accountable. Those in autonomous groups can in no real sense of the word be held accountable except to their colleagues, but those in bureaucracies can be held accountable to the extent that their actions are in all instances defined by a formal rational and legal structure. Failure of the individual in a bureaucratic structure is due to his noncompliance with rules and regulations defining his duties and obligations—for this, the individual is held responsible and may be disciplined or removed from the office. If the failure is in the rules themselves, these are subject to alteration to correct the problem situation.

The emphasis in an effective bureaucratic structure is on rationality; the payoff expected is that activities which are in conformance with rules, and therefore directly in support of *goal-attainment,* are rewarded; a further payoff is that activities are specified and programmed to the degree possible, leading to coordination of the total organizational effort.

Bureaucracy sounds ideal, but incorporates several unrealistic assumptions. One of these assumptions is that there is adequate socialization into compliance with bureaucratic rules. The person in a bureaucracy quickly learns that power resides in the domain of the bureaucrat who understands all rules pertaining to a given situation. He becomes the "expert." The more complex the situation, the greater his power. Many rules can be safely ignored provided that this does not result in visible adverse consequences, and he may allow rules to be ignored except in instances where he wishes to exert his power. Since the application of rules is a punishment in this sense, socialization which occurs is based on the lack of marginal return to those who attempt to follow rules closely. A second assumption is that it is possible to devise rules to deal with all circumstances. In complex situations, this becomes burdensome ("red tape") and in uncertain situations the best rule is simply unknown. Consequently, there may be instances where the rules do not apply or do not exist, but the person whose action is governed by the rules can be held formally accountable for actions which are specified. Finally, there is the assumption that relevant behaviors are visible or documented so that compliance can be determined. This places unreasonable demands on supervisors to observe, or on the workers to document activities which are not easily counted or evaluated. Under such circumstances, what is being reported may or may not represent actual behaviors.

The hypothesis emerging from this discussion, in response to the research question concerning the relationship between increased formalization and quality of care, is that quality of care will be favorably affected by increases in formalization to the extent that the above problems are minimized. Central to this argument is that the natural tendency of professionals to avoid bureaucratic constraints, coupled with the power of the medical profession to maximize its autonomy, can work towards this minimization. This is a significant departure from the original hypothesis suggested by Weber's theory, that colleague control (wherein peers review and advise, but do not command) reduces the effectiveness of organizations. It builds upon recent arguments regarding the accommodation of professional and bureaucratic norms [17-22].

The hypothesis is thus that increased formalization (i.e., quality assurance programs) will favorably affect quality of care to the degree that the organization is structured to foster professional autonomy through meaningful involvement of professionals in evolving regulations defining the innovative program, and meaningfully involved in their administration.[5] Members of the profession will naturally bend all efforts to avoid problems normally associated with unwieldy bureaucracies—red tape, passing of power to rules experts, emphasis on regulations and documentation—and not clearly relevant to the goal of high quality care. Those directly involved in the care of patients in a hospital are in the best position, by virtue of their expertise and their motivation to be free of meaningless rules, to define a most efficient structure—a lean and mean formal structure which specifies meaningful activities and provides significant rewards for behaviors which comply with those specifications.

For instance, the professional can help ensure that organizational goals are in conformity with the legitimate function of the organization in society, and further that an efficient relationship between goals and bureaucratic means is preserved. In the former, there is the danger, with the transfer of power from the profession to the bureaucracy, that organizational goals of providing high quality institutional care will be displaced by politically popular goals of cutting costs. The profession, being constrained to maintain and document its dedication to service by the very structure of the hospital organization within which it functions, must in turn challenge the hospital, in particular the board, where ultimate power resides (see for example *Darling vs. Charlestown Community Hospital* [26; 27, p. 112]), to justify its policy decisions in terms of legitimate objectives. In the latter, bureaucratic efficiency will be enhanced if professionals apply pressure toward the rational operationalizing of policies. This implies a constant questioning of the need for more rules and procedural specifications, and of the effectiveness of hierarchical authority structures in enforcing regulations which are necessary [28; 29, p.56].

It is emphasized that the hypothesis does not ignore the "unrealistic assumptions" associated with efficient bureaucratic operation discussed earlier. Rather, the argument is that the strain towards professional autonomy which has been traditionally regarded as problematic for bureaucracies [30] may be regarded as an effective means for minimizing the problems associated with those assumptions, and moving the organization toward realization of the promise inherent in the predominant values of bureaucratic structure. Conversely, if the "dead hand" of bureaucracy is lifted from professional activities, certain adverse consequences for professional initiative, incentive and innovation [31] may also be avoided.

THE INTEGRATION PROBLEM: MOTIVATING PROFESSIONALS

The integration problem area raises the issue of compliance with rules devised in the *goal-attainment* problem area. There are two types of determinants of compliance: motivations and constraints [32]. In order for the latter to work, the former must be present to some degree. What would motivate professionals to participate in programs of quality assurance? More specifically, what characteristics of professionalism, considered by members of the profession themselves to be vital, are likely to be enhanced through interaction with bureaucracy? Just as the quality of care outcome was the criterion for successful solution of the *goal-attainment* problem, so commitment of professionals to the quality assurance program is the criterion for successful resolution of the integration problem.

Professionalism has been described [33] in terms of two central features, that of prolonged training in a body of abstract knowledge (expertise), and service orientation. The first of these leads to the rational demand of the profession for autonomy from outside direction, since presumably nobody else knows enough about what its members do to exercise knowledgeable judgment; the second legitimizes the first, in that professional values direct the members to act in the best interests of the public they serve, so that their actions, which are otherwise poorly understood, are nevertheless assumed to be collectively-oriented rather than self-oriented. This definition of professionalism has developed largely from the example of the medical profession, and, for the most part, survived since the era of World War II and before. The key characteristic embedded in the definition concerns power derived from expert knowledge. At the level of the individual professional, this means he is free to practice his profession with final reliance on, and responsibility for, his own judgment, although he may seek and/or be proffered advice by colleagues; at the group level, this means the professional group is self-governing with regard to practices within the realm of its collective expertise.

Within bounds of the ideal type described above, one would not wish to interfere in any way with the operation of professional practice. However, as with the bureaucratic ideal, this ideal type incorporates several unrealistic assumptions as well. The first is that each individual professional internalizes to the fullest extent the service orientation. In terms of socialization theory, this implies that society will provide its highest rewards for those members of the profession who demonstrate this orientation, and has effective sanctions against those who do not [34, Ch.2]. To the extent that noncompliant professionals achieve success through, for instance, maximizing their wealth and social position without demonstrating a particular concern for the welfare of those in need of their services, deviance will be encouraged. That is, if a physician who undertakes the wrong procedures, or undertakes the correct procedures carelessly, achieves material rewards and social status equivalent to or exceeding that of the more knowledgeable or conscientious physician, the absence of marginal gain in these terms leads to a withering away of professional dedication. Another major assumption is that in instances where the results of professional misconduct are not obvious to everybody, the professional group will not misuse its power to protect the reputation of the group rather than the welfare of the society. Since, by definition, only colleagues have the competence to judge each other, there exists a tendency to explain away behaviors which do not have highly visible adverse consequences. To do otherwise could result in creation of many internal strains within the profession itself as well as promotion of the view of the profession as either lacking the expert knowledge its professional status assumes, or lacking the dedication to apply that knowledge, or both. In any case, this is not a good position for the profession to get into, and may be avoided in the short run simply by appearing to police the conduct of individual professionals and finding for the most part that all is well.

Public, legal and governmental demands for increased regulation and accountability within the health care delivery system [35] rise to the degree that professional behavior becomes disassociated in the public eye with the service value, and to the degree that the profession is seen to protect its own interests versus those of society when they are in conflict. Professional resistance to providing evidence that the two assumptions are, if not totally accurate, at least reasonably approximate, results in the long run in increased public discomfort with professional autonomy. Using this line of reasoning, there may be increasing awareness among members of the medical profession that meaningful involvement and cooperation in quality assurance programs, rather than resistance, will eventuate in maximizing professional freedom.

The key to raising such awareness is the recognized strength of bureaucracies: the rational relationship between means and ends. By virtue of this structure, bureaucracy demands of professionals a set of explicit criteria by which their work may be judged and, to the extent that these criteria are related to the ultimate goals of the institution, can implement reward systems which are in direct support of behaviors which conform to those criteria. In this way, the bureaucracy can be used as an effective substitute for weak societal controls, to reward and facilitate behaviors that conform to professional service values [36, p.88]. In addition, since bureaucracies tend to keep rather detailed records, explicit evidence can be marshaled on performance, then used to great advantage by the profession to demonstrate to its own members and to the public that effective surveillance is in place.

The research question raised earlier concerns the impact of quality assurance programs on professional commitment to making those programs work. It is hypothesized here that professional commitment will vary directly with the professionals' perception that the assumptions underlying autonomy are not being met, and that the hospital quality assurance program effectively shores up those assumptions. Thus research directed at this problem cannot simply deal with the issue of professional satisfaction with the quality assurance program, but must develop measures of professional perception of the state of the profession in society relative to the characteristics of the quality assurance program under study. The underlying hypothesis of interest is that professional autonomy will be greater within bureaucracies where professionals themselves have taken a responsible role in developing and administering the regulations, than in bureaucracies where the professionals have attempted to remain outside this process.

THE ADAPTATION PROBLEM: QUALITY AT WHAT COST?

The central question raised in this problem area is: do quality assurance programs reduce the cost of hospital care? Some regard the development of new regulatory mechanisms as ultimately contributing to cost increases rather than decreases. This is of vital concern in assessing the contribution of quality assurance programs to organizational effectiveness. There can be little doubt that, no matter how streamlined the program or how well it fits with the existing hospital structure, quality assurance requires additional resources in terms of finances, personnel and organizational expertise and may incur certain types of indirect costs as well [37]. In an era of cost consciousness, these additional costs to the organization must be justified either by the savings which they introduce (e.g., shorter hospital stays, more appropriate use of facilities and treatments, fewer inappropriate admissions) or by the improved outcomes of those who are treated. Recent analysis of benefits from the PSRO program indicate a 1:1 ratio between costs and savings, and there is some indication of improvement in quality [38].

Theory [39] and research in industrial settings leads us to believe formalization is positively related to efficiency (defined as costs per unit of production). In the health care setting, while some of the same reasons for expecting this relationship are applicable (e.g., the clear definition of roles and responsibilities in an organization leads to efficiency through coordination), problems may arise with specifying expected behaviors of organizational members when the complexity and uncertainty of procedures rises. Under these circumstances, there is a tendency to collect more information than can be effectively used in decision making. To be effective, the new information generated by quality assurance programs must be kept to a minimum and accurately reflect significant activities.

The death knell for quality assurance programs frequently will be sounded by the "thud" of the latest report generated by that program. Without due caution and learned judgment, it will contain too much information, the majority of which will address tangential or trivial issues in quality of care. But the costs of that information are not trivial, considering that extremely expensive resources are expended in collecting, transmitting, and analyzing it. The efficiency loss in organizations due to information overload can be profound [40, Lect.III]. The "bounded rationality" of both individuals and organizations is quickly exceeded [41, p.xxiv].

Research in the *adaptation* problem area can be fruitfully directed towards efficiency as the dependent variable, and formalization of the quality assurance program as the independent variable. But characteristics of information must be considered as an important contingency. Thus, the hypothesis that formalization is positively related to efficiency will depend on several characteristics of information and communication, *viz:* overload, accuracy, significance of activities reflected in the data, mode of transmission (for instance, use of computerized information systems), and use in decision making [24; 42, p.66].

While the costs of patient care are directly affected by the characteristics of quality assurance information produced, organizational adaptation to the external environment is to a large extent mandated by requirements of external agencies for certain types of information (e.g., insurance companies, federal and state governments, law firms). If hospitals and their physicians have any particular fight on their hands with regard to these informational requirements, it is to convince the external agencies that a certain minimum of highly relevant information is sufficient. As experts in the practice of medicine, it is the physicians who must argue for a realistic, but effective, collection of data which will accurately reflect the nature of the care provided; as experts in the administration of hospitals, the executive officer and his board must argue similarly and supportively from the perspective of effective decision making and legal accountability. If the current political atmosphere prevails, the environment may be ripe for application of such efficiency principles. Failing this, administration and medical staff must bear the burden of the data-collection required by external agencies (since this will frequently be a condition for acquisition of resources), but can design data-handling mechanisms whereby the information which the institution itself regards as expendable for the purposes of quality control can be routed directly to those external agencies without occupying the time of those in higher decision-making roles in the quality assurance programs. *Adaptation* is precisely this: the adoption of flexible rules of procedure within the organization relative to the requirements of the environment.

To the degree that both administration and medical staff are committed to the *goal-attainment* structure devised for quality assurance, the battle against collection and processing of meaningless information can be won. Health services researchers can offer an important assist, since research in the *adaptation* problem area will relate directly to decisions regarding the utility of data collected. Research evidence is required to demonstrate the costliness of collecting information, and the relationship between information which is collected and improvements in quality of patient care (or, more proximally, improvements in decision making directly related to improvements in quality of care).

Beyond the economic consideration of fiscal exchange between the organization and its environment, assessment of the effects of adaptive adjustments arising from quality assurance programs must include the ability of the organization to attract professionals and foster their professional growth. Quality assurance programs which become known to professionals as unnecessarily burdensome and not promotive of professional behavior will decrease the attractiveness of the institution for the best physicians as well as increase the costs of the program to the institution. Physicians are not the only professionals affected; other providers of care and technical staff are involved in quality programs, along with people in the hospital who are responsible for administering the assurance program itself.

THE PATTERN MAINTENANCE PROBLEM: STUDYING LONG-TERM EFFECTS

Will quality assurance programs contribute to the maintenance of societal values normally associated with the hospital? Two such values have been discussed in this paper: professional freedom of physicians, and accountability of bureaucratic institutions.

Regarding professional freedom or autonomy, it has been argued here that professional freedom is conducive to efficient functioning of professional organizations. This is somewhat counter to the argument presented by Roemer and Friedman [43], whose data suggest that organizational functioning (in terms of quality of care) is enhanced through greater controls over the professional staff. This has not been supported by recent research [44], however, and one suspects from the perspective of the argument developed in this paper, that an organizational orientation which is generated by greater dependence on the bureaucracy does not support a professional orientation which is requisite to challenging inappropriate bureaucratic procedures. The "tie that binds" the professional to the organization is the legal responsibility of the hospital for his or her activities carried on within the institution; this key aspect of recent developments in the hospital's relevant environment provides the basis for the bureaucracy's power which is necessary to avoid domination by the profession. For both professionals and bureaucracy to realize their mutual benefits, their power basis must be kept at a countervailing level. They are thus effective foils.

Regarding *pattern maintenance*, then, the introduction of quality assurance programs, if appropriately handled in the *goal-attainment* problem area, can result in preserving important societal values with regard to professional activities and bureaucratic accountability. Changes in these values present the greatest challenge for assessment, since they must be looked at over time, and are difficult to measure. It is even more difficult to assess the determinacy of any given independent variable. In the long run, however, this is possibly the most important assessment, since it deals with the wider problem of the association between the survival of professional freedom and the machinations of an increasingly bureaucratic society.

SUMMARY

A general theoretical framework has been discussed for health services research on the impact of quality assurance programs on the effectiveness of hospitals. The problem-solving model identifies four types of problems to be considered in the assessment: *goal-attainment, integration, adaptation,* and *pattern maintenance.* These are interrelated problem areas, such that an organization must devise simultaneous solutions for all of them in order to achieve long-run effectiveness.

Quality assurance programs are conceptualized as increases in the bureaucratization of hospitals through effects on the hierarchy of authority, rules and regulations, and specification of procedures. The conflict of this increased bureaucratization and professional freedom suggests that the natural aversion of professionals for control can be exploited to maximize the efficiency of the bureaucracy, and conversely the rational means-ends structure of the bureaucracy can be exploited by professionals to promote and demonstrate compliance with professional values and hence minimize the demand for external controls.

In these terms, it is at least theoretically feasible for quality assurance programs to promote organizational effectiveness through increased bureaucratic responsibility (*goal-attainment*), increased physician motivation (*integration*), containment of costs and attraction of valued resources (*adaptation*), and preservation of values (*pattern maintenance*).

NOTES

1. The reader will note that this framework, while derived from the work of Parsons and Georgopoulos, involves interpretations and definitions of concepts which are somewhat different from those in the earlier works.

2. Several reviewers of this paper have pointed out the difficulties of the effectiveness approach in comparative studies of organizations [7]. Space does not permit detailed consideration of the issues; an important one, however, is the difficulty of empirically deciding whether organization A, which measures (1, 2, 3, 4) on the four areas by some metric is better off or worse off than organization B, which measures (4, 3, 2, 1) on the same metric. Presumably, both are required as a condition of survival to score better than (0, 0, 0, 0), but beyond this, what can be said beyond a normative judgment? One approach to the problem is to assume the industry represented by a sample of organizations is viable, and to allow respondents from these organizations to rate indicators from the four areas in terms of how they judge the success of their own organizations. Comparative studies of effectiveness then involve determining the distribution of studied organization vis-à-vis the mean ratings from the total sample.

3. Scott has advised that one should never underestimate the "power of social structures to create reality," and that modifications in structure of an organization can alter behaviors of organizational members [3, p.388]. His work on the Institutional Differences Study [8, 9] has implicated several structural characteristics of hospitals in accounting for differences in surgical outcomes which remain after careful controls are introduced for patient casemix.

4. Due to the separation of the *instrumental* and *affective* dimensions in this framework, it is stressed that assessment of one structural arrangement over another is based on value-free criteria; the only consideration is the logic of means-ends linkages. In reality, the structure adopted must take into account the *affective* dimension as well, but the degree to which logical means-ends linkages are modified by consideration of values will vary considerably, depending upon the perceived risk of ignoring those values versus the perceived payoff from instituting them.

5. Some research has been done on the impact of formalization on quality of care. Neuhauser [23] found a negative impact of increased specification of procedures, Shortell et al. [24] suggested that specification may be beneficial for less complex procedures, and Georgopoulos and Mann [25, p.497] concluded that formalization must be accompanied by effective communication systems in order to have a positive impact on quality via better coordination. Our own work in progress has found that extent of specification is positively related to quality, regardless of task and technological complexity. Analysis of the other half of the hypothesis—the impact of extent of enforcement coupled with participation in decision making—is underway.

REFERENCES

1. Parsons, T. (in collaboration with R.F. Bales and E.A. Shils). *Working Papers in the Theory of Action.* Re-issued in 1967, Glencoe, IL: The Free Press, 1953.

2. Georgopoulos, B.S. and A.S. Tannenbaum. The study of organizational effectiveness. *American Sociological Review* 22:534, 1957.

3. Georgopoulos, B.S. (ed.) *Organization Research on Health Institutions.* Ann Arbor, MI: The University of Michigan, Institute for Social Research. Chap. 2, 1972.

4. Georgopoulos, B.S. *Hospital Organization Research: Review and Sourcebook.* Philadelphia: W.B. Saunders Company, 1975.

5. Steers, R.M. *Organizational Effectiveness: A Behavioral View.* Santa Monica, CA: Goodyear Publishing Company, 1977.

6. Goodman, P.S. and J.M. Pennings and Associates. *New Perspectives on Organizational Effectiveness.* San Francisco: Jossey-Bass Publishers, 1979.

7. Hannan, M.T. and J. Freeman. Obstacles to comparative studies. In P.S. Goodman, J.M. Pennings and Associates (eds.), *New Perspectives on Organizational Effectiveness.* San Francisco: Jossey-Bass Publishers, 1979.

8. Forrest, W.H. Jr., W.R. Scott, and B.W. Brown, Jr. *Study of Institutional Differences in Postoperative Mortality.* Stanford, CA: Stanford University, Center for Health Care Research, 1974.

9. Scott, W.R., W.H. Forrest, Jr., and B.W. Brown, Jr. Hospital structure and postoperative mortality and morbidity. In *Organization Research in Hospitals (Inquiry* monograph). Chicago: Blue Cross Association, 1976.

10. Aiken, M. and J. Hage. Organization alienation: A comparative analysis. *American Sociological Review* 31:497, 1966.

11. Winsten, J.A. The Utah professional review organization as a prototype. In R. Greene (ed.), *Assuring Quality in Medical Care.* Cambridge, MA: Ballinger Publishing Co., 1976.

12. Parsons, T. *The Social System.* Glencoe, IL: The Free Press, 1951.

13. Pfeffer, J. *Organizational Design.* Arlington Heights, IL: AHM Publishing Corp., 1978.

14. Blau, P.M. and W.R. Scott. *Formal Organizations: A Comparative Approach.* San Francisco: Chandler Publishing Co., 1962.

15. Kinzer, D.M. Inpatient quality assurance activities: Coordination of federal, state and private roles—the hospital's view. In R.H. Egdahl and P.M. Gertman (eds.), *Quality Assurance in Health Care*. Germantown, MD: Aspen Systems Corp., 1976.

16. Weber, M. (translated by A.M. Henderson and T. Parsons). *The Theory of Social and Economic Organization*. New York: Oxford University Press, 1947.

17. Blau, P.M., W.V. Heydebrand and R.E. Stauffer. The structure of small bureaucracies. *American Sociological Review* 31:179, 1966.

18. Engel, G.V. The effect of bureaucracy on the professional autonomy of the physician. *Journal of Health Social Behavior* 10:30, 1969.

19. Hall, R.H. Professionalization and bureaucratization. *American Sociological Review* 33:92, 1968.

20. Goss, M.E.W. Patterns of bureaucracy among hospital staff physicians. In E. Freidson (ed.), *The Hospital in Modern Society*. New York: Free Press of Glencoe, 1963.

21. Scott, W.R. Reactions to supervision in a heteronomous professional organization. *Administrative Science Quarterly* 10:65, 1965.

22. Etzioni, A. *A Comparative Analysis of Complex Organizations*. New York: The Free Press, 1961.

23. Neuhauser, D. The Relationship Between Administrative Activities and Hospital Performance. Research Series 28. Chicago: University of Chicago Center for Health Administration Studies, 1971.

24. Shortell, S.M., S. Becker, and D. Neuhauser. The effects of management practices on hospital efficiency and quality of care. In *Organization Research in Hospitals (Inquiry* monograph). Chicago: Blue Cross Association, 1976.

25. Georgopoulos, B.S. and F.C. Mann. *The Community General Hospital*. New York: The MacMillan Co., 1967.

26. Darling vs. Charlestown Community Memorial Hospital, 33 Ill. 2d 326, 211 NE. 2d 253, 1965.

27. Jacobs, C.M., T.W. Christoffel and N. Dixon. *Measuring the Quality of Patient Care: The Rationale for Outcome Audit*. Cambridge, MA: Ballinger Publishing Co., 1976.

28. Strauss, A., L. Schatzman, D. Ehrlich, R. Rucher and M. Sabshin. The hospital and the negotiated order. In E. Freidson (ed.). *The Hospital in Modern Society*. New York: Free Press of Glencoe, 1963.

29. Mechanic, D. *The Growth of Bureaucratic Medicine: An Inquiry into the Dynamics of Patient Behavior and the Organization of Medical Care*. New York: John Wiley and Sons, 1976.

30. Katz, F. *Autonomy and Organization—The Limits of Social Control*. New York: Random House, 1968.

31. Kornhauser, W. (with the assistance of W.O. Hagstrom). *Scientists in Industry—Conflict and Accommodation*. Berkeley and Los Angeles: University of California Press, 1962.

32. Cohen, P.S. *Modern Social Theory*. London: Heinemann Educational Books Ltd., 1968.

33. Goode, W.J. Community within a community: the professions. *American Sociological Review* 22:194, 1960.

34. Parsons, T. *Essays in Sociological Theory*. London; Glencoe, IL: The Free Press, 1949.

35. Blum, J.D., P.M. Gertman, and J. Rabinow, *PSROs and the Law*. Germantown, MD: Aspen Systems Corp., 1977.

36. Freidson, E. *The Profession of Medicine: A Study of the Sociology of Applied Knowledge*. New York: Dodd, Mead and Co., 1970.

37. Phelps, C.E. Benefit/cost analysis of quality assurance programs. In R.H. Egdahl and P.M. Gertman (eds.), *Quality Assurance in Health Care*. Germantown, MD: Aspen Systems Corp., 1976.
38. *Professional Standards Review Organization 1978 Program Evaluation*. Department of Health, Education and Welfare; Office of Research, Demonstrations and Statistics. Washington, DC: HEW Publication No. (HCFA) 03003, 1979.
39. Hage, J. An axiomatic theory of organizations. *Administrative Science Quarterly* 10:289, 1965.
40. Arrow, K.J. *Limits of Organization*. 1st Annual Fels Lectures on Public Policy Analysis. Cambridge, MA: Harvard University, Dept. of Economics, 1973.
41. Simon, H. *Administrative Behavior*. Second edition. Glencoe, IL: The Free Press, 1957.
42. Shortell, S.M. Countdown to 1984: Managerial models. *Hospital Progress* 58, 10:64, 1977.
43. Roemer, M.I. and J. Friedman. *Doctors in Hospitals: Medical Staff Organization and Hospital Performance*. Baltimore: Johns Hopkins Press, 1971.
44. Scott, W.R., A.B. Flood, and W. Ewy. Organizational determinants of services, quality and cost of care in hospitals. *Milbank Memorial Fund Quarterly/Health and Society* 57, 2:234, 1979.

6. Professional Power and Professional Effectiveness: The Power of the Surgical Staff and the Quality of Surgical Care in Hospitals*

ANN BARRY FLOOD and W. RICHARD SCOTT

Reprinted with permission from *Journal of Health and Social Behavior* 19. Copyright © 1978, The American Sociological Association, 240-254.

A recent critical survey of the literature conducted by the Committee on Professional Organization and Control of the Medical Sociology Section of the American Sociology Association concludes that after more than two decades of research on professional work in medical settings, we still know very little about "the effect of variations in the organization (including financial arrangements) of physicians and their work setting on the technical and social quality of the medical care provided" (Goss et al., 1977). This study deals with this neglected area. We examine the effect of selected structural characteristics of hospitals—in particular, the distribution of power among professional role groups and the power exercised

*The overall design and data collection reported here were carried out under Contract PH 42-63-65 with the National Center for Health Services Research, Health Resources Administration, DHEW, through the National Academy of Sciences-National Research Council under subcontract MS-46-72-12. The analyses were carried out under contract HRA 230-75-0173 with the Health Resources Administration, DHEW.

We are indebted for assistance to all our colleagues at the Stanford Center for Health Care Research. We especially acknowledge the help of the Director of the Center, William H. Forrest, Jr., M.D., who supplied medical expertise to the project; Wayne Ewy and Byron Wm. Brown, Jr., biostatisticians, who contributed greatly to statistical aspects of the research and the overall design; and Betty Maxwell, coordinator and administrative assistant, who provided innumerable support services critical to the success of this effort. Several fellow sociologists assisted in the initial formulation of the study design and in the construction of data-gathering instruments. We acknowledge, with thanks, the contributions of Joan R. Bloom, Donald E. Comstock, Thomas G. Rundall, and Claudia Bird Schoonhoven. The Commission on Professional and Hospital Activities (CPHA) of Ann Arbor, Michigan, collaborated with the Stanford Center for Health Care Research to provide data for this study. When reference is made to CPHA/PAS data in this report, these data were supplied by CPHA only at the request and upon the authorization of the hospital whose data were used. Any analysis, interpretation, or conclusion based on these data is solely that of the authors, and CPHA specifically disclaims any responsibility for any such analysis, interpretations, or conclusions.

An earlier version of this paper was read at the Annual Meetings of the Pacific Sociological Association in Sacramento, California, April 22, 1977.

by the surgical staff over its own members—on medical outcomes experienced by patients undergoing surgery. We relate detailed measures of hospital characteristics to equally detailed measures of quality of care. Unlike most other studies of quality of care, we rely on outcome rather than process measures of quality in the belief that it is important to attempt to focus on results achieved rather than effort expended or conformity to standards of unknown efficacy. Great effort is expended to adjust medical outcome measures—morbidity and mortality—to take into account medically relevant differences among patients.

THE THEORETICAL APPROACH

In his influential paper on the professions, Goode (1957) argues that professional communities are able to secure a measure of autonomy from the larger society by organizing themselves to exercise control over their own members. Such controls are often presumed to be exercised by professional associations that set certification standards, promulgate codes of ethics, and administer sanctions to deviant members. The evidence attesting to the efficacy of these control attempts is, at best, mixed (Editors of Yale Law Journal, 1954; Cohen, 1973). Perhaps in response to these deficiencies, the locus of control appears increasingly to be shifting from the professional community to the professional organization, as Etzioni (1964) has noted.

To assert that organizational controls are exercised over professional work is not necessarily to suggest that the organizational control mechanisms are of the conventional hierarchical type. Indeed, a number of descriptive studies have shown that professional organizations tend to develop somewhat distinctive control arrangements that offer considerable autonomy to individual workers and place heavy reliance on collegial processes of control (see Goss, 1961; Hind et al., 1974; Freidson, 1975). The extent to which such distinctive arrangements develop depends largely on the power exercised by professional participants in the organization (Scott, 1972). These groups organize themselves—as a medical staff in hospitals, as a senate or assembly within universities—in order (1) to secure and protect an arena of professional decision-making and activity and (2) to promote fidelity to professional standards by careful selection, control, and continuing education of staff members. Professional groups strongly contend that the performance of these two functions—the securing of autonomy for the group, coupled with the regulation of the individual practitioner—is conducive to effective performance.

Our approach can be clarified by briefly describing four classes of variables: the two sets of independent variables measuring professional power, the dependent variables measuring effectiveness of performance, and a set of control variables whose effects must be considered.

The Power of Professionals in Hospitals

Under the assumption that professionals in organizations need to be able to define and defend an arena of professional autonomy, the first class of variables relates to the relative power of physicians, nurses, and hospital administrators in hospitals. Power is defined as the ability of members occupying positions in the organization to affect the outcome of organizational decisions. We expect such power to vary depending on the type of decision at issue; such differentiation is the hallmark of organizations, and is especially characteristic of professional organizations where there is likely to be a clear demarcation of "professional" from "administrative" spheres (Smith, 1955; Goss, 1961). Further, power is viewed in non-zero sum terms so that high power for some role groups on an issue does not preclude the possibility for high power for other groups on the same issue.

In general, we argue that, for optimal functioning, professional groups must be in a position to exercise a large amount of power, relative to other groups, over decisions within their sphere of competence. Conversely, effectiveness will not be served if professionals exercise a large amount of power over decisions outside their sphere of competence. We distinguish, therefore, between "within-domain" power and "encroachment." We expect effectiveness to relate positively to the exercise of power by a role group within its domain, and negatively to encroachment by one role group on another's territory.

The Power of the Surgical Staff Over the Surgeon

Having held claim to a sphere of autonomous functioning, the professional staff is expected to police the conduct of its own members within that realm. Generally speaking, we would not expect professional groups to exercise detailed control over the activities of their members. Such practices are inconsistent with professional norms (Goss, 1961). Freidson's study of control processes among physicians in a group-practice clinic (Freidson and Rhea, 1963; Freidson, 1975) concludes that collegial attempts to regulate performance were rare and usually ineffectual. However, hospital settings may be more conducive to the exercise of control than ambulatory settings. Hospitals tend to be larger and more formalized. Accreditation requirements mandate the operation of a number of quality-review committees under the auspices of the medical staff. In particular, surgical performance is more subject to colleague surveillance and regulation. Among the most fateful decisions made by every hospital staff is the setting of conditions under which additions to the staff are made and membership privileges withdrawn. Roemer and Friedman (1971) have argued that hospitals vary significantly in the amount of power the medical/surgical staff exercises over its own members and that the greater this power, the more effective the hospital is in its delivery of quality medical care. Studies by Neuhauser (1971), by Shortell et al. (1976), and by Rhee (1977) report some supporting evidence. We expect that greater surgical staff power over individual surgeon-practitioners will be associated with more effective performance.

Effectiveness of Performance

It is widely recognized that the assessment of professional performance is at best a complex and hazardous business. The complexity of the work, the incompleteness of knowledge, the variety of individual cases—all these factors converge to prevent consistent success. Because "good" performances can sometimes result in "poor" outcomes, professionals emphasize process measures of effectiveness—were the proper procedures correctly performed?—rather than outcome measures—did the desired effect occur? However, process measures evaluate conformity to a given standard of performance but do not evaluate the adequacy of the standards themselves and assume that it is known what activities are required to insure effectiveness. Such assumptions are always problematic when the work involved is complex and uncertain, as is the case with surgical care. We prefer outcome measures of effectiveness, agreeing with Donabedian (1966:169) that "outcomes, by and large, remain the ultimate validators of the effectiveness and quality of medical care" (cf. Suchman, 1967; Scott et al., 1976). Our study employs measures of patient mortality and morbidity, adjusted for differences in patient characteristics, as indicators of quality of surgical care.

Control Variables

Clearly, a great many other factors may potentially influence the outcomes experienced by patients following surgery. The factors selected as control variables—"control" in the statistical sense—include various characteristics of patients, surgeons, and hospitals.[1] We focus on those factors which may influence patient outcomes and are believed to vary systematically by hospital.

PROCEDURES

Data Sources and Size of Samples

The data were collected as part of a larger investigation of factors affecting the quality of surgical care in hospitals conducted by the Stanford Center for Health Care Research.[2] Seventeen hospitals were surveyed for the original study, but only 15 are included in the major portions of this analysis due to missing data on two hospitals. Sixteen of the original study hospitals were selected randomly from a stratified sample of all short-term voluntary hospitals participating in the Professional Activity Study (PAS), a widely used hospital chart abstracting system;[3] the seventeenth, administratively linked to one of the 16, agreed to participate at its own expense.

The 15 hospitals examined in this study are not completely representative of all short-term, acute-care hospitals, being somewhat larger than the average for this type (289 vs. 164 average number of beds) and somewhat more likely to have an active house staff (graduate training) program. Five of the study hospitals, or 33 percent, had such a program compared to 28 percent of comparable hospitals. The average costs of care within the 15 hospitals were quite similar to the national average ($113 average costs per patient day for our sample compared to $115 for comparable U.S. hospitals). Moreover, the goal of obtaining substantial variance within the sample along these important dimensions was achieved: for the sample, size varied from 99 to 585 beds, and average costs from $78 to $154 per patient day. Nine states and all but one major geographic region within the continental United States were represented.

Data on individual patients were collected prospectively on those undergoing one of 15 selected surgical procedures.[4] We attempted to select procedures associated with a large number of deaths and complications (undesirable outcomes) whether due to high risk or high frequency, to focus on clearly defined diagnostic categories amenable to the staging of surgical disease, and to include procedures involving a variety of organ systems, surgical subspecialties, and types of patients. Data relating to the patient's condition, both before and after surgery, were obtained by a technician trained by the Center and stationed in each study hospital. Data from all 17 hospitals were employed in adjusting outcome measures for differences in patient condition as described below. Among the 10,565 patients qualifying for study during the 10-month study period, about 80 percent (8,593) were included. Losses were due primarily to patient refusal (56% of patients dropped), surgeon refusal (19%), and lack of critical information (11%). The study patients represented approximately eight percent of admissions to the 17 hospitals during this period, and 16 percent of those undergoing surgery.

Information on organizational characteristics, relating both to hospital context and to the organization of the medical/surgical staff, was obtained primarily through interviews conducted by Center staff with key hospital personnel who acted as expert informants describing the structure and operation of their units. Additional information was obtained by questionnaire from staff nurses on surgical wards (with an N of 2,494, and a return rate of roughly 75%).

Data on the characteristics of individual surgeons came from three sources. First, working with a number code to insure anonymity of surgeons, information on education and board certification was obtained from either the records of the American Medical Association (AMA) or those of the study hospital for virtually all (98%) of the surgeons treating study patients. Second, the hospital technician gathered selected information from most (90%) of these surgeons. And third, PAS patient records for 1973 were utilized to develop for each surgeon measures of the total number of operations and the proportion of specialized operations performed during the study period. Altogether, 553 surgeons were identified as treating study patients in the 15 hospitals, and at least some of the types of information just described was available for 98 percent of them.[5]

In the analyses reported here, the primary focus is the effect of organizational power on patient outcomes. Before making these comparisons, it is important to take into account other major factors which can influence the outcomes of patient care. To accomplish this, the analyses have been performed at the individual patient level, matching the patient's outcome with the data describing his or her health at the time of surgery, the characteristics of his or her specific surgeon, and features of the larger hospital structure in which the treatment occurred. Examining the association among these variables at the level of the individual patient enables us to avoid the possible biases which arise when relationships presumed to operate at one level are aggregated for analysis at a higher level (cf. Hannan, 1971; Hannan et al., 1976). Consistent with this patient-level approach, the characteristics for each physician and hospital are associated with each patient, which has the effect of weighting them by the number of patients treated. All means and correlations reported are based on these weighted observations.

Measuring and Adjusting Surgical Outcomes

Surgical outcomes were measured both by mortality experience—obtained at the 40th day postoperatively—and by the extent of morbidity assessed at the 7th day postoperatively, or at the date of patient discharge, if earlier. Data for both measures were gathered by the Center's technician. Scores were assigned to reflect the relative undesirability of various types of outcomes. Three scoring systems were employed: one placing relatively greater weight on mortality, one placing relatively greater weight on morbidity, and an intermediate scale. In general, the weighting schemes did not strongly influence the results, and most of the analyses reported here are based on the intermediate scale. An indirect standardization procedure was employed to adjust these scores to take into account differences attributable to patient characteristics. In effect, quality-of-care measures were constructed to reflect the difference between a patient's observed outcome score and his or her expected score calculated on the basis of that patient's characteristics. A more detailed discussion of the outcome measures and adjustment procedures used appears in the Appendix.

Measuring Relative Power of Professional Groups and Power of the Surgical Staff over Surgeons

In order to determine the relative power of the medical staff in influencing various types of decisions in hospitals, we followed the approach of Tannenbaum

(1968) and asked a set of informants in each hospital to rate, on a five-point scale, the amount of influence exercised by a given position on a specified type of decision. Responses were obtained by interview or questionnaire from the following types of informants: hospital administrators, chiefs of surgery, chiefs of anesthesia, directors of nursing, ward supervisors, head nurses, and ward nurses. The positions rated included the hospital administrator, the chief of surgery, the director of nursing services, and physicians as a group. Eight decisions were selected as representing differing types of issues as well as differing levels, ranging from routine administration to policy determination (see Table 6-1). Because all organizational respondents cannot be presumed to be equally knowledgeable (Aiken and Hage, 1968; Scott, 1972), greater weight was given to respondents occupying positions higher in the hierarchical structure. Thus, responses for each occupant of a position were combined into a single "position" score, and then scores for all positions were combined to provide an average score

Table 6-1 Indices of Relative Power of Professional Groups

	Measures of Power					
	Within Domain			Encroachment		
Types of Decisions*	HA	NA	SA	P on HA	P on NA	HA on SA
1. To hire a replacement staff nurse for patient-care unit		X				
2. To increase size of a ward staff by adding new staff-nurse position		X				
3. On the best disciplinary action for nurse committing a serious medication error		X				
4. To purchase contract services, e.g., laundry	X			X		
5. To change the nursing-care system, e.g., to adopt team nursing throughout the hospital		X			X	
6. To add a clinical service, e.g., an intensive-care unit			X			X
7. To add an ear-nose-throat specialty room in the operating suite			X			X
8. To terminate a major department head, e.g., the operating-suite nursing director			X			X

HA—hospital administration; NA—nursing administration; SA—surgical administration (chief of surgery); and P—physicians as a group.
*Decision items employed in constructing the six measures of power

for each hospital. The effect was to give greater weight to the judgments of those persons who were in positions with no or few other occupants. While theoretically justified, this procedure had little effect on the results because of the high level of agreement exhibited by informants on the distribution of influence.

Combining the data from all hospitals, the distribution of influence by position was observed, as expected, to vary greatly by type of issue (Comstock, 1975). Based on these profiles as well as on the content of the decision items, we distinguished between the "within-domain" influence of a role group and its "encroachment" into the decision terrain of other role groups. Table 6-1 indicates the questions used for determining each of these conditions for the role groups of interest. As already noted, our expectations are that higher quality care will be associated with the exercise of greater influence by role groups within their respective domains, and, conversely, with less encroachment by one role group on another's turf.

The second set of power measures was designed to indicate the extent of power exercised by the surgical staff as a corporate body over individual surgeons. Three measures were developed. The first measured the degree of centralization of decision-making within the surgical staff by comparing the perceived influence of the chief of surgery to that of physicians as a group on the decisions to add a clinical service and a specialty room in the operating suite (decision items 6 and 7). Two other measures were based on interview responses by the chief of surgery regarding the strictness of admission requirements for new members of the surgical staff. The former measure was based on information on length of probationary period, differentiation by specialty, and number of review bodies; the latter considered extent of restrictions on surgical privileges, use of written procedures in reviewing surgical privileges, number of years for which privileges were granted, and rules defining who could serve as first assistant during surgery. Items were standard Z-scored and combined into an index for each measure. While not all forms of control by the surgical staff over its members would be expected to increase the quality of medical care, this is our prediction for the three measures just described.

The left side of Table 6-2 reports the intercorrelations among the nine measures of power. Note that for the hospitals surveyed, the within-domain influence of the surgical administration was inconsistent with encroachment by hospital administrators on surgical administration ($-.852$); but the within-domain influence of the hospital administration was associated with the presence of encroachment on their decision terrain by the surgical administration (.600). Such patterns are consistent with a non-zero sum view of power. Note also that the two measures of surgical-staff control over individual surgeons are uncorrelated and that each related differently to the distribution of influence measures. More stringent admissions requirements for new surgeons were associated with greater encroachment by the surgical administration on the domain of the hospital administration; but greater

Table 6-2 Correlations Among the Power Measures and with Hospital Context†

	Inter-Item Correlations									Hospital Context		
	1	2	3	4	5	6	7	8	9	Size	Expenditure	Teaching
1. Within-domain influence of surgical administration	—	.342	-.311	.192	.327	-.852*	.119	.065	.161	.377*	.129	.648*
2. Within-domain influence of hospital administration		—	.353	.600*	.419*	.076	-.054	-.035	.425*	.319	-.640*	.385*
3. Within-domain influence of nursing administration			—	.056	.236	.580*	-.422*	-.336	-.076	-.361*	-.360*	.090
4. Encroachment by physicians on hospital administration				—	-.108	.035	.208	.442*	-.682*	-.451*	-.159	.364*
5. Encroachment by physicians on nursing administration					—	.026	-.315	-.419*	-.215	.027	-.441*	.192
6. Encroachment by hospital administration on surgical administration						—	-.140	-.197	-.046	.358*	-.453*	-.602*
7. Centralization of decision-making within surgical staff							—	.287	.284	.160	.247	-.049
8. Admission requirements for new members of surgical staff								—	-.066	.095	.473*	.037
9. Power of surgical staff over tenured surgeons									—	-.125	-.233	.101

†Pearson product-moment correlations on per-patient data for 15 organizations and 14 medical staffs.
*Significant at the .1 level or better.

surgical-staff control over tenured surgeons was related to less encroachment on this same measure and was related to greater influence of hospital administrators within their own domain.

Measuring the Control Variables

As already discussed, additional factors were thought likely to have some effect on quality of surgical care. Since these factors were not of primary interest for this analysis, they are introduced in order to determine whether they will need to be controlled. The types of factors considered are patient, physician, and hospital characteristics.

Patient Variables

In addition to the patient characteristics employed to adjust surgical outcomes, five other characteristics were measured: ethnicity and marital status were treated as dichotomous variables, while education and income were each coded into seven labels. Finally, a measure of social stress based on selected items from the Holmes and Rahe (1967) instrument was employed.[6]

Physician Variables

A measure of surgeon specialization based on the distribution of operations across 12 categories was constructed based on information from PAS records reflecting all the surgery performed by the surgeon in the study hospital during 1973. Three different measures of surgeon's qualifications were employed: board certification, number of residencies, and years of practice after completion of any residency training. To assess the extent of each surgeon's commitment to the study hospital, we noted the percent of each surgeon's practice conducted at the study hospital. A higher percent of practice was associated with less surgical specialization ($-.139$) and with fewer residencies completed ($-.245$). Greater surgical specialization was related to shorter length of practice ($-.171$) and to fewer residencies ($-.150$). All of these intercorrelations were significant at the .001 level.

Hospital Variables

Three measures were employed to assess hospital context: size was measured by a product of the number of beds and the average occupancy rate for each hospital; expenditures on patient care was measured by dividing the total annual hospital expenditures by the number of patient days; and the teaching status of the hospital was assessed by the presence of an active residency program. Among these three hospital context variables, only teaching status and expenses per patient day were significantly correlated (.532). The right side of Table 6-2 reports the intercorrelations among the nine measures of power and three variables assessing hospital context.

RESULTS

In examining the effect of surgical power on adjusted patient outcomes, we first wished to take into account the impact of any control variables affecting these outcomes. Therefore, we regressed outcomes on each set of control variables to determine the presence of any significant relationships. Among the patient control variables, only income was significantly related: patients with higher incomes tended to experience better surgical outcomes. The other patient measures—ethnicity, marital status, education, and social stress—did not have a significant relation to quality of care. Among the three hospital-control variables, only expenditures were found to be significantly associated with surgical outcomes. Neither size nor teaching status was significantly related to quality of care. And among the five physician variables, the only measure significantly related to adjusted surgical outcomes was the percent of each surgeon's practice carried on at the study hospital. The greater the percent of practice within the study hospital, the better the quality of care experienced by patients. To our surprise, the other measures of surgeon's characteristics—extent of specialization, board certification, number of residencies, and years of experience—were not related significantly to quality of care (see Flood, 1976; and Flood et al., 1977).

Given these preliminary results, we retained only the three control variables revealed to have a significant effect on surgical outcomes: patient income, hospital expenditures, and percent of surgeon's practice in the study hospital. These three control variables were forced into the regression equation at step 1; then the measures of professional power were introduced into the equation. This approach is conservative in the sense that it permits the measures of patient, hospital, and surgeon characteristics to account for all of the variance in surgical outcomes that each measure can before examining the impact of the professional-power measures on patient outcomes.

Table 6-3 reports the results of a regression analysis of the effects of the distribution of power among role groups within hospitals on the quality of surgical care, after taking into account the effects of selected control variables. Of the three control variables forced into the equation at step 1, only two—hospital expenditures and patient income—had a significant impact on surgical outcomes. Turning to the three measures of the influence of role groups within their own domain, we note that two of them were significantly related to quality of surgical care: the power of hospital administrators to influence decisions within their domain was related to surgical outcomes in the expected direction—the greater

Table 6-3 Effect of Within-Domain and Encroaching Influence on Adjusted Surgical Outcomes (Using Intermediate Scale and Selected Control Variables)

Variable[a]	Standardized Reg. Coeff. (β)	Unstandardized Reg. Coeff. (B)	Standard Error B	F-ratio	Predicted Direction[b]
Control Variables					
Surgeon's percent of practice conducted at study hospital	−.010	−.036	.047	.577	
Hospital expenditures	−.085	−.004	.001	16.970†	yes
Patient's income	−.028	−.013	.005	5.901	yes
Power Variables					
Within-domain influence of hospital administration	−.133	−.224	.048	23.417†	yes
Encroachment by physicians on nursing administration	.034	.063	.036	3.110	
Within-domain influence of nursing administration	.307	.173	.083	4.307§	no
Encroachment by physicians on hospital administration	.028	.054	.038	1.987	
Within-domain influence of surgical administration	.082	.187	.109	2.929	
Encroachment by hospital administration on surgical administration	.051	.099	.098	1.028	

Multiple R = .090; R^2 = .008
Overall F at final step = 7.115†; F for incremental change from control variables to final step = 6.654†

†Significant at .001 level   §Significant at .05 level
[a]The control variables have all been forced into the regression in the first step; the power variables are listed in the stepwise order in which they entered the regression.
[b]Since a higher score for adjusted surgical outcomes reflects a more severe outcome than expected, a negative coefficient connotes an association with better quality care.

their power, the better the quality of care. The power of the nursing administration to influence decisions within their domain was also significantly related to surgical outcomes, but not in the predicted direction: the higher the influence of nurses on decisions within their own domain, the poorer was the quality of care observed. The influence of the surgical administration on decisions within their own domain was not significantly related to the quality of surgical care. None of the three encroachment measures was significantly related to quality of surgical care. The overall F-ratio of 7.115 was significant at the .001 level; the F representing the change in the sum of squares for the power measures beyond that attributed to the three control variables was 6.654—also significant at the .001 level. The total amount of explained variance was quite small; only 0.8 percent of the variance in patient outcomes was explained.

The results reported in Table 6-3 were based on the intermediate scaling of outcome measures. When we examined a parallel regression employing the scale emphasizing mortality, a similar pattern of results was observed except that the only power measure reaching significance was the influence of the hospital administration on decisions within its own domain, which was related to high-quality care. The overall F for this regression was 4.344, significant at the .001 level. The incremental F representing the change in the sum of squares related to the power measures alone was 3.371, significant at the .05 level. For the outcome scale emphasizing morbidity and regressing this measure on the same independent variables, we observed the same general pattern of relationships, but a higher proportion of them reached statistical significance. As was the case for both the intermediate scale and the scale emphasizing mortality, the influence of the hospital administration within its own domain was related to better quality of care (significant at the .001 level). Also, as predicted, two measures of encroachment—that of the medical staff on nursing and that of the administration on the medical staff—were related to poorer quality of care (significant at the .01 level). Finally, unlike the results reported in Table 6-3, the influence of the nursing staff on nursing decisions was not significantly associated with surgical outcomes. The overall F was 13.272; the incremental F was 16.006. Both were significant at the .001 level. The amount of patient variance explained by this set of variables was 1.4 percent.

In summary, these analyses suggest that among the various measures of the power of role groups considered, the perceived ability of the hospital administrators to influence decisions within their own domain was the factor most strongly and consistently related to better quality surgical care. The relative power of the surgical administration to influence decisions within its own domain showed no effect on quality of care; and the relative power of the nursing administration within its own domain was seen to relate to poorer quality of care when the intermediate scale of outcomes was used. The encroachment of one role group on another's decision domain was revealed to be associated with poorer quality care when the scale of outcomes emphasizing morbidity was used.

In Table 6-4, we turn attention to those variables measuring the regulation of individual surgeons by the surgical staff. As in the previous analyses, we first introduce the three control variables and then allow the surgical-staff variables to enter in a step-wise fashion. The results reported in Table 6-4 are based on the intermediate scaling of outcomes.

Beginning with the control variables, we note that two of them—greater hospital expenditures and higher patient income—were significantly related to better quality of care. Percent of surgeon's practice in the study hospital was not significantly associated with surgical outcomes. Two of the three measures of surgical-staff control over surgeons were significantly associated with quality of care. Both were in the predicted direction. The more strict the admissions requirements for new members of the surgical staff and the greater the power of the surgical staff over tenured surgeons, the higher the quality of surgical care. Centralization of decision-making within the surgical staff was not significantly

Table 6-4 Effect of Surgical Staff Power Over Its Own Members on Adjusted Surgical Outcomes (Using Intermediate Scale and Selected Control Variables)

Variable[a]	Standardized Reg Coeff. (β)	Unstandardized Reg. Coeff. (B)	Standard Error B	F-ratio	Predicted Direction[b]
Control Variables					
Surgeon's percent of practice at study hospital	−.016	−.061	.046	1.784	
Hospital expenditures	−.032	−.002	.001	5.408§	yes
Patient's income	−.023	−.011	.005	4.238§	yes
Surgical Staff Power over Members					
Power of the surgical staff over tenured surgeons	−.047	−.026	.007	13.654†	yes
Admission requirements for new members of the surgical staff	−.042	−.033	.010	10.469*	yes
Centralization of decision-making within the surgical staff	−.010	−.022	.029	.553	

Multiple R = .085; R^2 = .007
F at final step = 9.641†; F for increment from control variables to final step = 11.249†

†Significant at .001 level   *Significant at .01 level   §Significant at .05 level
[a]See Note a, Table 6-3.   [b]See Note b, Table 6-3.

associated with quality of care. The overall F of 9.641 was significant at the .001 level, as was the incremental F of 11.249 measuring the change in sum of squares from the control variables to the final step. The amount of explained patient variance for this set of variables was 0.7 percent.

As before, the results observed using the intermediate scale were basically similar to those which were observed using the other two outcome scales. With the scale emphasizing mortality the same pattern of results was observed, except that only two variables—patient income and strictness of admissions requirements—reached significance. The overall F for this equation was 4.977, and the incremental F was 3.669 (significant at the .05 level). Regression of the scale emphasizing morbidity on the same set of independent variables produced the same pattern of findings reported in Table 6-4. The only differences observed were that the association between patient's income and surgical outcome did not quite reach significance, and both relations involving the measures of surgical-staff regulation were significant at the .001 level. The overall F was 19.006, and the incremental F was 30.208; both were significant at the .001 level.

In sum, these analyses show strong support for our expectation that greater regulation of the work of individual surgeons by the surgical staff organization is associated with higher quality of surgical care in hospitals.

SUMMARY AND DISCUSSION

This reading has examined the relation between professional power and professional effectiveness as reflected in the organization and work of surgeons in a sample of short-term acute-care hospitals. The power of surgeons, hospital and nursing administrators was assessed by asking respondents to describe their perceptions of the influence of each role group on a set of hypothetical decisions. In addition, the power of the surgical staff to regulate the work of individual surgeons was examined by determining the degree of centralization of influence within the surgical staff and the stringency of requirements governing admission to the staff and the awarding of surgical privileges to staff physicians. Patient outcomes—the actual effects of the surgical treatments as reflected in the health status of patients following surgery—were used as indicators of professional effectiveness. For such measures to be valid indicators of the quality of care received, they must be adjusted to take into account differences in patient condition prior to treatment. Such an adjusted outcome measure was developed using linear regression techniques. Factors other than the power measures thought likely to affect quality of outcomes were also identified and measured and their effect on adjusted outcomes was taken into account. Those observed to have an effect on patient outcomes and, hence, controlled in this analysis, were patient's income, hospital expenditures per patient, and extent of surgeon's practice in the study hospital. Surprisingly, several measures of the extent of specialized training and experience of surgeons were not significantly associated with quality of surgical care.

Among the various measures of the relative power of the three role groups to influence organizational decisions, the strongest and most consistent factor related to quality of care was the power of the hospital administrators to influence decisions within their own domain. While in general we expected the influence of each role group within their own domain to be associated with better quality care, we had expected the most important factor to be the power of the surgical group to influence decisions within its own domain. However, no significant effects on quality of surgical care were observed for our indicator of surgical power. The influence of nursing administration on nursing decisions was observed to be associated with poorer quality of care, although this unexpected relation was not consistently observed across the three outcome scales. While the strong association of the power of the hospital administration with the quality of surgical care was somewhat unexpected, it is consistent with the arguments of both Perrow (1961) and Georgopoulos and Mann (1962), who view the administrator as providing coherence and coordination in a work situation fraught with fragmentation and overspecialization.

Encroachment—the exercise of power by one role group in the domain of another—was not related significantly to quality of care except when the outcome scale emphasizing morbidity was used to assess quality of care. In this circumstance, both the encroachment of the medical/surgical staff on the area of nursing influence and the encroachment of hospital administration on the arena of the medical/surgical staff were seen to be associated with poorer quality care.

The power of the surgical staff over its own members was found to relate to quality of surgical care: the more extensive the regulations imposed on individual surgeons by the surgical staff, the higher the quality of surgical care. This finding is consistent with the arguments and results of Roemer and Friedman (1971), who place great emphasis on the importance of medical/surgical staff organization and the quality of medical services. It is important to recognize that these are controls exercised *by* professionals over professionals. It does not follow from the findings that any and all attempts to regulate the performance of individual practitioners will result in greater effectiveness.

More generally, the number of significant results as well as the level at which results were significant was related to the outcome scale used. While the direction of results was basically consistent across the three scales, the number of statistically significant variables and the extent of significance increased with the increase in weight placed on morbidity for each of the scales. This increase is expected, in part on a purely statistical basis[7] and in part for substantive reasons. Analyses of these data reported elsewhere (Flood et al., 1977) present unbiased estimates of the surgeon and hospital effects on patient variance for each of the three outcome scales. These estimates increased substantially across the three scales. This would suggest that there are real differences among surgeons and among hospitals in their effects on morbidity and mortality of patients. It may be the case that the types of independent variables examined have a stronger effect on patient morbidity than they do on patient mortality. We emphasize, however, that differences in the results observed across the three scales cannot wholly separate the substantive causes from the statistical causes.

Finally we wish to comment on the small amount of variance in patient outcomes explained by all the measures of professional power examined. The analysis described here has been conducted at a patient level and therefore the amount of explained variance reported in Tables 6-3 and 6-4 (i.e., the R^2) is the variation in outcomes of *patients* which can be attributed to the measures of professional power. The variations in patients' outcomes, even after taking into account the patient's health characteristics, are not expected to be largely due to features of the hospital or its medical-staff organization. What should be noted is that a statistically significant portion of this variation was associated with these features of organization. In particular it is important to note that the R^2 reported should not be interpreted as an expression of the amount of variation accounted for in hospital-level performance. We must also recognize that we have focused attention on one set of factors in a most complex setting which bears at best a remote connection to the selected indicators of quality of care. The causal processes that link relative decision-making power in the organization, or even extensiveness of staff regulations over practitioners, to the morbidity and mortality of individual patients is a complex one, and we should not expect to observe powerful associations. To have discovered some consistent and statistically significant relations under these circumstances is encouraging.

NOTES

1. The question as to how much variance in outcome is due to the characteristics of patients or surgeons, or to hospitals, after taking into account variance attributed to the first two sources, is addressed in another paper (see Flood et al., 1977).

2. More extensive descriptions of the data collected and procedures employed are contained in Staff of the Stanford Center for Health Care Research (1974, 1976); Scott et al. (1976); and Flood (1976).

3. PAS refers to the Professional Activity Study conducted by the Commission on Professional and Hospital Activities (CPHA). This organization collects and summarizes selected information on all patient discharges from its member hospitals. At the time of our study, 1377 hospitals participated in this system.

4. The surgical categories included were: gastric surgery for ulcer, selected surgery of the biliary tract, surgery of large bowel, appendectomy, splenectomy, abdominal hysterectomy, vaginal hysterectomy, craniotomy, amputation of the lower limb (ankle to hip), repair of fractured hip, arthroplasty of the hip, lumbar laminectomy with and without fusion, pulmonary resection, prostatectomy, and selected surgery of the abdominal aorta and/or iliac arteries.

5. Since two of the hospitals shared the same surgical staff, for some analyses examining the impact of surgeon characteristics on patient outcomes, surgeons treating study patients in both hospitals were included and, in this sense, counted twice.

6. The application of this instrument to these data, as well as an analysis of the effect of social stress on recovery from surgery for selected surgical categories, is described in Rundall (1976).

7. Under the assumption that the effects of physicians and hospitals on adjusted outcomes of individual patients are multiplicative rather than additive, the expected value for statistical tests increases with an increasing mean value of the adjusted outcomes. For this statement to hold, the implied increase in means is not simply an increase in the absolute value, but an increase in the mean relative to the increase in the standard deviation. Thus, as the weights on outcomes increase from the mortality to the intermediate to the morbidity scale, the mean increases relative to the standard deviation and thus the expected value for the statistical tests increases also.

REFERENCES

Aiken, M. and J. Hage
  1968 "Organizational interdependence and intra-organizational structure." American Sociological Review 33:912-29.
Cohen, H.S.
  1973 "Professional licensure, organizational behavior, and the public interest." Milbank Memorial Fund Quarterly 51:73-88.
Comstock, D.E.
  1975 "The measurement of influence in organizations." Paper presented at the meeting of the Pacific Sociological Association, Portland, Oregon.

Donabedian, A.
1966 "Evaluating the quality of medical care." Milbank Memorial Fund Quarterly 44:166-203.
Editors of the Yale Law Journal
1954 "The American Medical Association: Power, purpose, and politics in organized medicine."
The Yale Law Journal 63:938-1022.
Etzioni, Amitai
1964 Modern Organizations. Englewood Cliffs, New Jersey: Prentice-Hall.
Flood, A.B.
1976 "Professionals and organizational performance: A study of medical staff organization and
quality of care in short term hospitals." Ph.D. dissertation, Stanford University.
Flood, A.B., W.R. Scott, W. Ewy and W.H. Forrest, Jr.
1977 "Effectiveness in professional organizations: The impact of surgeons and surgical staff
organizations on the quality of care in hospitals." Paper presented at the meeting of the
American Sociological Association, Chicago, Illinois.
Freidson, Eliot
1975 Doctoring Together: A Study of Professional Social Control. New York: Elsevier.
Freidson, E. and B. Rhea
1963 "Processes of control in a company of equals." Social Problems 11:119-31.
Georgopoulos, Basil S. and Floyd Mann
1962 The Community General Hospital. New York: Macmillan.
Goode, W.J.
1957 "Community within a community: The professions." American Sociological Review
22:194-200.
Goss, M.E.W.
1961 "Influence and authority among physicians in an outpatient clinic." American Sociological
Review 26:39-50.
1970 "Organizational goals and quality of medical care: Evidence from comparative research on
hospitals." Journal of Health and Social Behavior 11:225-68.
Goss, M.E.W., R.M. Battistella, J. Colombotos, E. Freidson and D.C. Riedel
1977 "Social organization and control in medical work: A call for research." Medical Care
15:1-10.
Hannan, Michael T.
1971 Aggregation and Disaggregation in Sociology. Lexington, Maryland: Heath-Lexington.
Hannan, M.T., J.H. Freeman and J.W. Meyer
1976 "Specification of models for organizational effectiveness." American Sociological Review
41:136-43.
Hind, R.R., S.M. Dornbusch and W. Richard Scott
1974 "A theory of evaluation applied to a university faculty." Sociology of Education 47:114-28.
Holmes, T.H. and R.H. Rahe
1967 "The social readjustment rating scale." Journal of Psychosomatic Research 11:213-18.
Neuhauser, Duncan
1971 The Relationship Between Administrative Activities and Hospital Performance. Chicago:
Center for Health Administration Studies, Research Series 28.
Perrow, C.
1961 "The analysis of goals in complex organizations." American Sociological Review
26:854-66.
Rhee, S.
1977 "Relative importance of physicians' personal and situational characteristics for the quality of
patient care." Journal of Health and Social Behavior 17:10-15.

Roemer, Milton I. and Jay W. Friedman
  1971 Doctors in Hospitals: Medical Staff Organization and Hospital Performance. Baltimore: Johns Hopkins Press.
Rundall, T.G.
  1976 "Life changes and recovery from surgery." Ph.D. dissertation, Stanford University.
Scott, W.R.
  1972 "Professionals in hospitals: Technology and the organization of work." Pp. 139-58 in B.S. Georgopoulos (ed.), Organization Research on Health Institutions. Ann Arbor: Institute for Social Research, University of Michigan.
Scott, W.R., A.B. Flood, W. Ewy, W.H. Forrest, Jr. and B.W. Brown, Jr.
  1976 "Utilizing outcomes to assess the quality of surgical care." Paper presented at meeting of the American Institute for Decision Sciences, San Francisco.
Scott, W.R., W.H. Forrest, Jr. and B.W. Brown, Jr.
  1976 "Hospital structure and postoperative mortality and morbidity." Pp. 72-89 in S.M. Shortell and M. Brown (eds.), Organizational Research in Hospitals. Chicago: Inquiry Book, Blue Cross Association.
Shortell, S.M., S.W. Becker and D. Neuhauser
  1976 "The effects of management practices on hospital efficiency and quality of care." Pp. 90-107 in S.M. Shortell and M. Brown (eds.), Organizational Research in Hospitals. Chicago: Inquiry Book, Blue Cross Association.
Smith, H.L.
  1955 "Two lines of authority are one too many." Modern Hospital 84:59-64.
Staff of the Stanford Center for Health Care Research
  1974 The Study of Institutional Differences in Postoperative Mortality. A report to the National Academy of Sciences-National Research Council. Springfield, Virginia: National Technical Information Service.
  1976 "Comparison of hospitals with regard to outcomes of surgery." Health Services Research 11:112-27.
Suchman, Edward A.
  1967 Evaluative Research. New York: Russell Sage Foundation.
Tannenbaum, Arnold S.
  1968 Control in Organization. New York: McGraw-Hill.

Appendix

Surgical outcomes were measured both by mortality and morbidity experience. Mortality status, assessed at the 40th day post-operation, was not limited to in-hospital deaths. Morbidity, assessed at the 7th day post-operation, was based on judgments made by the ward nurse with responses grouped into three categories. Under the assumption that these several types of outcomes were strongly ordered and that scores could be assigned to them representing their increasing undesirability, the following weights were assigned to each outcome: mortality within 40 days of surgery = 9; severe morbidity at 7 days post-surgery = 5; moderate morbidity at 7 days post-surgery = 2; little or no morbidity at 7 days post-surgery = 0. In addition to this "intermediate" weighting scheme, two other scales were used—one placing greater weight on mortality, using weights of 9, 2, 1 and 0, and the other placing greater weight on morbidity, using weights of 9, 7, 5 and 0—in order to determine the effect of the results of the weighting system used.

To adjusted observed outcomes to take into account differences that should be attributed to patient characteristics, data were gathered by the Center's technician for each patient on physical status, stage of surgical disease, demographic characteristics, and emergency status at the time of the surgical procedure. Physical status refers to the patient's general health apart from the specific condition to be treated surgically. Information on physical status was supplied by the patient's anesthetist, using a rating scale devised by the American Society of Anesthesiologists and supplemented by a rating for cardiovascular disease developed by the American Heart Association (Staff of the Stanford Center for Health Care Research, 1974:444). Stage of surgical disease refers to the severity and/or extent of surgical disease at the time of surgery. The type of information needed to assess disease stage was determined by Center staff in broad consultation with surgeons and anesthesiologists, and varied by surgical category. Data were supplied by the patient's surgeon, who completed a short form concerning preoperative and intraoperative findings following surgery, and from chart review. Information on the patient's age and sex was obtained by patient interview; and the patient's anesthetist was asked to record the urgency of the procedure as a measure of emergency status.

The method employed to adjust surgical outcomes was a standardization procedure which involved the computation of the expected outcome for each patient. To estimate the expected outcome, all patients in a surgical category were combined, disregarding hospital. Then the patient's observed outcome scores were regressed on his health-related characteristics. The patient characteristics used to predict outcome were: age, sex, physical status, cardiovascular status, emergency status, and stage of disease. Separate linear regressions were carried out for each of the three scalings of outcome. The explanatory power of these regression equations varied greatly by type of operation (see Flood, 1976).

To arrive at adjusted surgical-outcome scores for each patient, all variables—both patient characteristics and outcomes—were standard Z-scored to remove the effect of unequal variables and the differences in outcomes associated with type of operation. Standardized regression coefficients expressed the effect of each type of patient characteristic/surgical category for each of the three outcome scales. Standardized values for each patient on these characteristics were multiplied by the appropriate regression coefficient and then summed to arrive at an expected outcome. As a final step, adjusted outcome measures for each patient were obtained by subtracting the expected outcome scores from the observed scores.

7. Hospital Medical Staff Organization and Quality of Care: Results for Myocardial Infarction and Appendectomy*

STEPHEN M. SHORTELL and JAMES P. LoGERFO

Reprinted with permission from *Medical Care* 19. Copyright © 1981, J.P. Lippincott Company, 1041-1055.

The relationship of hospital medical staff characteristics and organization to costs and quality of care is receiving increasing attention.[1-6] Factors found to be associated with quality of hospital care include hospital structural characteristics such as bed size and teaching status; individual physician characteristics such as specialty and board-certification status; and medical staff organization characteristics such as degree of staff participation in hospital decision making and coordination and control exerted through committees. Unfortunately, most studies have failed to consider all three sets of factors (hospital structure, physician characteristics, medical staff organization) simultaneously in order to examine the relative influence of each.[7] The issue is important because while overall hospital structure and individual physician attributes are relatively difficult to change, medical staff organization processes are much more susceptible to interventions which might improve the quality and efficiency of hospital care.

The purpose of the present study is to examine simultaneously the relationships of hospital, physician and medical staff variables for two conditions: acute myocardial infarction (AMI) and appendicitis. Of particular interest is the examination of whether the medical staff organization variables exert an independ-

From the Center for Health Services Research, Department of Health Services and Department of Medicine, University of Washington, Seattle, Washington.

*This research was supported by the National Center for Health Services Research under Contract Grant #HS 01978 to the Center for Health Services, University of Washington, and also supported by the Office of Research Affairs, American Hospital Association and by Group Health Cooperative of Puget Sound. Appreciation is expressed to Walt Wood, Commission on Professional and Hospital Activities (CPHA), Ann Arbor, Michigan, for his assistance in expediting provision of the data for analysis. Appreciation is also expressed to Ray Brasto and Paul Haley for the computer programming work associated with these analyses. The analysis, interpretations, and conclusions are the sole responsibility of the authors.

ent association net of the hospital and physician variables. The existence of such an independent association would suggest that medical staff organization plays an important role as the interface between the hospital and the physician in relation to the quality of care provided. The lack of such an independent association would suggest that the hospital and physician variables are adequately reflecting medical staff organization factors, at least in relation to the quality of care provided for the two conditions under study. If this were the case, it would suggest that little attention needs to be given to medical staff organization itself and that more attention ought to be given to the types of physicians granted staff privileges and the structural characteristics of hospitals granting such privileges.

The above central relationships are examined, taking into account other factors which might be associated with differences in the quality of care provided for the two conditions under study. These include the volume of procedures performed, the degree to which physicians concentrate their work at one hospital, the degree of hospital commitment to quality assurance activities and, in the case of AMIs, the impact of treating patients in a coronary care unit.

The study is primarily exploratory but is guided by a number of propositions suggested in the literature. Given the current state of knowledge, no differential predictions are made for AMI versus appendicitis. Specifically, it is hypothesized that bed size, number of interns and residents per bed and presence of a director of medical education will each be positively associated with higher quality of care. This is based on the assumption that, other things being equal, larger hospitals and those involved in teaching activities have more resources to provide higher quality of care. Board certification as a proxy measure for physician competence is also expected to be associated with higher quality of care. For AMIs it is expected that a higher ratio of internists to family practitioners will be positively associated with higher quality of care. This is based on the assumption that, on the average, internists receive more extensive training in cardiology than family practitioners. Similarly, for appendectomies it is expected that a higher ratio of surgeons to family practitioners will be associated with higher quality of care, assuming that surgeons have more extensive training in surgery than family practitioners. However, in both the AMI and appendectomy cases, physicians' *experience over time with the condition* may offset differences in training.

Based primarily on the findings of Luft et al.,[8] it is also expected that greater volume of procedures performed will be associated with higher quality of care. Given conflicting evidence in the literature,[9-12] no specific prediction is made regarding the effect of treating patients in a coronary care unit, but the available data will enable this relationship to be examined while controlling for a greater number of competing variables and explanations than is presently the case.

The percentage of active staff physicians on contract is hypothesized to be positively associated with higher quality of care, based on the assumption that such a measure at least partially reflects a greater structuring of medical staff organization. Roemer and Friedman[4] have previously found such structuring to be associated with higher quality of care. Concentration of professional activity at one hospital is also felt to be positively associated with higher quality of care on the assumption that such a situation provides more opportunity for peer review, sharing of information among physicians and systematic quality assurance activities. Flood and Scott,[1] for example, have found that the greater the percentage of a surgeon's practice that is concentrated in a given hospital, the better the quality of care.

Physician participation in hospitalwide decision making, measured by such variables as having the medical staff president vote on the governing board and physician participation in the governing board executive committee activities, has also been suggested to be positively associated with higher quality of care.[6,13] The assumption is that such involvement increases the opportunity for awareness and feedback regarding physician practices and provides the opportunity for physicians, administrators and board members to discuss patient care quality issues. Similarly, greater communication via committee meetings among medical staff members is expected to be associated with higher performance. This is because such meetings provide opportunity for learning and peer reinforcement for taking corrective action. Finally, the degree of a hospital's commitment to quality assurance activities is also expected to be positively associated with higher quality of care. Whether or not the hospitals subscribed to an additional medical audit program of the Commission on Professional and Hospital Activities (CPHA) was used as a proxy behavioral indicator of such additional commitment.

DATA AND METHODS

Sample Selection

A 35 per cent proportionately stratified random sample of all hospitals in the East North Central Region (Illinois, Indiana, Michigan, Ohio and Wisconsin) who subscribe to the Commission on Professional and Hospital Activities (CPHA) was selected for study. The East North Central Region was selected because it represents the area of the country within which the highest percentage of hospitals (approximately 45 per cent) subscribe to CPHA. The sample was stratified by bed size, ownership and teaching status, using the following categories: <100 beds, 100-399 beds, and ≥400 beds; short-term voluntary general versus governmentally owned hospitals; teaching hospitals (defined as being affiliated with a medical school or having a residency or internship program) versus nonteaching hospitals. These categories were used in combination to create 12 potential strata. In fact, no hospitals existed in the stratum of less than 100 beds, short-term voluntary general and teaching, nor in the stratum of ≥400 beds, governmental and nonteaching. Of the 131 hospitals sampled, 96 (73.3 per cent) agreed to release their CPHA data for analysis. There was a somewhat higher nonresponse rate for hospitals under 100 beds but little difference by teaching status or ownership.

Data

Given the problems involved in an attempt to measure the overall quality of hospital care, particularly in regard to adjusting for differences in case mix severity, we chose a *condition specific* approach, examining coronary conditions involving myocardial infarction, ischemic heart disease or disorders of heart rhythm (H-ICDA 410.0-416.9) and conditions involving primary appendectomy (H-ICDA 47.0). Of 54,904 coronary care condition patients, 3,745 were excluded due to missing or misrecorded information, leaving 51,159 records available for analysis.

In order to correct for the fact that some patients who were discharged in a few days may have been miscoded as having an AMI, we excluded those patients discharged alive with approval in five or less days. We note that currently some patients with documented AMI might be discharged as early as the fifth day, but very few such patients would have been discharged this early in 1973, the relevant year of study. These exclusions represented three per cent of all AMI patients.

The remaining group is referred to as the "filtered AMI patients" and represents 97 per cent of the total AMI patients in the study. In order to adjust the expected mortality for each hospital according to case severity on admission, these patients were stratified based on admission systolic blood pressure level and age, two variables which have strong correlation with mortality and which were available from the CPHA data set.[14-16] The six categories based on age and systolic blood pressure readings upon admission to the hospital were as follows: 1) <65 years old and <90 mmHg; 2) ≥65 and <90 mmHg; 3) <65 and 90-99 mmHg; 4) ≥65 and <90-99mmHg; 5) <65 and ≥100mmHg; and 6) ≥65 and ≥100mmHg. The number of patients and the number of deaths within each of the six groups were calculated for each hospital, and a standardized mortality ratio (SMR) was developed, indicating the number of expected versus actual deaths for each hospital based on each hospital's number of patients falling into the respective age and systolic blood pressure categories (see technical appendix for calculation).

For the primary appendectomy study, information on 8,695 patients was originally collected for analysis, but 512 patients were excluded due to missing or misrecorded information, leaving 8,183 patients available for analysis. Since we were interested in the pathologic state of the appendix at operation, we stratified patients based on age and sex, as these characteristics are known to be correlated with the probability of the appendix being normal or perforated.[17] Accordingly, the patients were stratified into the following four groups: 1) males ≤5 years old and ≥65; 2) males 6-64; 3) females ≤5 years old and ≥65; and 4) females 6-64 years of age. For each hospital, information was available on the total number of patients, number of deaths, number of patients with diagnosis of acute appendicitis with peritonitis (H-ICDA code 540.1) and number of patients with tissue result of no abnormality. We chose to focus on the proportion of normals removed rather than of perforations because removal of a normal is an act that can be avoided without necessarily increasing perforation rates. Furthermore, there are major pitfalls in using case rates of perforation, rather than population-at-risk rates, as an indicator of quality.[18] Thus, a standardized normal tissue removed (SNTR) ratio was computed for each hospital in a fashion similar to that of the standardized mortality ratio for AMI patients. (See appendix.) Thus, the quality-of-care indicators for both the AMI patients and the appendectomy patients have been adjusted for differences in case mix severity and standardized against the experience of other hospitals in the sample.

The hospital, physician and medical staff data are derived from a 1973 national survey of hospital medical staff organization conducted by the American Hospital Association. This survey gathered a variety of data on specialty composition, board-certification status, contractual relationships between physicians and hospitals, governance, decision making, committee structure and related items. For 1973, this information was linked with the CPHA data described previously for the sample of East North Central hospitals to conduct the analyses described below.

Methods

The relative effects of the hospital, physician and medical staff characteristics on the AMI standardized mortality ratio and the standardized per cent normal tissue removed were assessed using multiple-regression analysis. In addition to assessing the effects of the individual variables, indexes of "resource capability," "participation in decision making" and "local staff orientation" were constructed based on previous research and factor analysis of the present data.[6] The variables composing each factor are presented in the appendix. In brief, the resource capability factor represents primarily the ability of the hospital to attract qualified staff and is heavily influenced by hospital bed size and teaching capability. Consistent with previous predictions, it was hypothesized that this factor would be positively associated with better outcomes. Participation in decision making includes measures of physician involvement in hospital wide decision-making bodies and is predicted to be positively associated with better outcomes. Local staff orientation primarily reflects smaller hospitals with fewer physicians per bed and fewer physician members per committee and is hypothesized to be associated with poorer quality of care.

Results are presented for 95 of the 96 hospitals, since data on the SMR were not available for one hospital. In addition, for approximately 12 hospitals, data on the percentage of active staff board certified were estimated using the overall sample mean for per cent of physicians board certified. This substitution yielded results virtually identical to those obtained from deleting these hospitals from analysis. Thus, the substitution results in no bias for the sample overall, and the findings presented below are based on all 95 hospitals.

RESULTS

Acute Myocardial Infarction Results

Table 7-1 shows the AMI mortality ratios within each of the six age/systolic blood pressure categories. The data indicate significant independent effects of age and systolic blood pressure as well as a strong joint effect. Briefly, controlling for systolic blood pressure on admission, those 65 and over are two to three times more likely to experience death from AMI. Controlling for age, those with systolic blood pressure ≤89 mmHG are approximately three to four times more likely to experience death from AMI than are patients with systolic blood pressure ≥100 mmHg. Looking at the age and systolic blood pressure in combination, patients 65 and over with systolic blood pressure ≤89 mmHG are more than eight times as likely to experience death than those under 65 with systolic blood pressure ≥ 100 mmHg.

Table 7-2 presents the descriptive statistics for all variables examined; the results of the AMI regressions are presented in Table 7-3. Most of the associations among the variables were in the range of 0.10 to 0.30, with the exception of the correlation between hospital bed size and per cent of active staff physicians board certified ($r = 0.41$) and the association between bed size and existence of a director of medical education ($r = 0.53$). As shown, the volume of AMI patients per internist and family practitioner, having the president of the medical staff on the hospital governing board and hospital size are most strongly associated with lower AMI standardized mortality ratios. The unstandardized regression coefficients indicate that a one-unit increase in volume of AMI patients per physician is

---

Table 7-1 Mortality Ratios for Filtered AMI Patients Based on Age and Systolic Blood Pressure for 96 Hospitals in East North Central Region

Systolic Blood Pressure	Age	
	< 65 Years	≥ 65 Years
≤ 89 mmHg	0.470	0.828
90-99 mmHG	0.282	0.641
≥ 100 mmHG	0.096	0.334

Table 7-2 Descriptive Statistics for Study Variables

Variable	Mean or %	Standard Deviation	N
Standardized AMI mortality ratio	1.06	0.31	95
Standardized per cent normal tissue (appendectomy) removed ratio	1.00	0.68	96
Hospital bed size	242	171.3	96
Number of interns and residents per bed	2.1/100	5.2/100	96
Director of medical education	25.8%	44%	96
Ratio of internists to family practitioners	1.05:1	2.00:1	96
Ratio of surgeons to family practitioners	1.6:1	2.2:1	96
Number of AMI patients per internist and family practitioner*	5.43	4.51	96
Number of appendectomies per surgeon and family practitioner	2.83	2.10	92
Per cent active staff board certified	43.5%	24.4%	84
Per cent active staff on contract	16.8%	11.8%	96
Per cent staff with major professional activity at this hospital	85.4%	24.0%	96
Physicians on executive committee of the hospital governing board	22.1%	41.7%	96
President of Medical Staff on hospital governing board	38.5%	48.9%	96
Number of meetings per medical staff committee per year	11.64	3.52	96
Resource Capability factor†	0.082	3.39	96
Participation in decision making factor†	0.001	2.08	96
Local staff orientation factor†	0.091	4.45	96
Hospital reports having a coronary care unit	63.2%	48.5%	96
Hospital also subscribes to CPHA medical audit program	76.0%	42.9%	96

*This is computed by dividing the total number of AMI patients by the total number of internists and family practitioners on the active staff. Ideally data specific to each internist and family practitioner treating AMI patients are desired but were not available from the existing data. The same is true for number of appendectomies per surgeon and per famlily practitioner.
   †See appendix for further description.

associated with a 0.014 decrease in the SMR, controlling for or holding constant the other variables in the analysis.

Further analysis also revealed that hospitals seeing 60 or fewer filtered AMI patients per year had a standardized mortality ratio of 1.17, as compared with 1.00 for those seeing more than 60 patients per year (F = 7.06, p ≤ 0.009).

The results also indicate that hospitals having their medical staff president on the governing board experienced standardized mortality ratios 0.108 lower than those of hospitals whose staff president was not on the board, again controlling for

Table 7-3 Individual Variable-Regression Results for AMI Standardized Mortality Ratios

Independent Variable	Unstandardized Coefficient (Standard Error)	Standardized Coefficient*
Volume of acute AMI patients per family practitioner and internist	− 0.0136† (0.007)	−0.200
President of Medical Staff is on Hospital Governing Board	− 0.108‡ (0.063)	−0.171
Hospital bed size	− 0.0003‡ (0.0002)	−0.170
Physicians concentrate most of their professional activity at one hospital	0.0017 (0.0014)	0.123
Hospital has a coronary care unit	− 0.092 (0.071)	−0.144
Per cent board-certified physicians	− 0.0016 (0.0016)	−0.121
R^2 = 0.174	F = 3.10, p ≤ 0.008	

$\overline{R}^2$ = 0.12

(Adjusted R^2)

*The standardized regression coefficients place all variables on equivalent units of measurement based on the standard deviations involved. The magnitude of these coefficients is one way of reflecting the relative importance of the variables in the analysis.
† p ≤ 0.05
‡ p ≤ 0.10

other variables in the analysis. Presence of a coronary care unit and per cent of physicians board certified were also associated with a lower AMI standardized mortality ratio, but these relationships were not statistically significant. The per cent of physicians concentrating their activity at one hospital was not found to be significantly associated with lower AMI standardized mortality ratios. Whether or not the hospital subscribed to CPHA's additional medical audit program and the ratio of internists to family practitioners were not associated with the AMI standardized mortality ratio. Overall, the above variables explained 17 per cent of the variability in the AMI standardized mortality ratios (F = 3.10; p ≤ 0.008). The amount of variation explained by each variable is largely unaffected by the order in which it entered the equation. The exception is board certification, which when entered last in the equation explained only an additional 0.008 per cent but which in the stepwise regression explained 8 per cent of the variation. The magnitude of the standardized regression coefficients indicates the relative importance of the variables, suggesting that volume, followed by president of staff on governing board and bed size, are the most important predictors.

The impact of the overall factors, shown in Table 7-4, reveals a moderately strong effect of physician participation in hospital decision making on AMI standardized mortality ratios. The unstandardized regression coefficient indicates that a one-unit increase in this factor is associated with a 0.033 decrease in the AMI standardized mortality ratio. Similarly, a one-unit increase in the volume of AMI patients per internist and family practitioner is associated with a 0.013 decrease in the standardized mortality ratio, and the presence of a coronary care unit is associated with a 0.116 lower AMI standardized mortality ratio. The local staff orientation factor was associated with a higher SMR as predicted, but was not statistically significant. Resource capability was not related to the AMI standardized mortality ratio, nor did it make any difference whether or not the hospital subscribed to CPHA's additional medical audit program. None of the other variables of interest were significantly related. Overall, 18 per cent of the variability in AMI standardized mortality ratio was explained by the above variables ($F = 4.17$; $p \leqslant 0.004$).

When the participation in decision-making factor was forced into the equation first, it explained 7 per cent of the variation in standardized mortality ratios. When it was forced into the equation last, after allowing the other variables to explain as much of the variation as possible, the participation in decision-making factors still explained an additional 5 per cent of the variation. An interaction term involving volume times presence or absence of a coronary care unit was also examined but was not significantly related to the standardized mortality ratio.

Table 7-4 Composite Factor Regression Results for AMI Standardized Mortality Ratios

Independent Variable	Unstandardized Coefficient (Standard Error)	Standardized Coefficient
Physician participation in hospital decision-making factor	−0.033* (0.015)	−0.225
Volume of acute MI patients per family practitioner and internist	−0.013† (0.007)	−0.187
Hospital has a Coronary Care Unit	−0.116‡ (0.077)	−0.183
Local staff orientation factor	0.010 (0.0085)	0.147

$R^2 = 0.176$ $F = 4.17, p \leqslant 0.004$

$\bar{R}^2 = 0.134$

*p $\leqslant$ 0.025.
† p $\leqslant$ 0.05.
‡ p $\leqslant$ 0.10.

Appendectomy Results

Table 7-5 shows the per cent of normal tissue removed within each of the age/sex categories. As indicated, age makes no difference for males, but females between the ages of 6 and 64 are more than twice as likely to have normal tissue removed as females 5 years or younger and 65 or older. The per cent of females between the ages of 6 and 64 with normal tissue removed is approximately twice that of males 6 to 64. The higher rate for females 6 to 64 is primarily due to the number of female conditions, such as ovarian cyst and pelvic inflammatory disease, whose symptoms may be closely related to those of acute appendicitis.

The results shown in Table 7-6 are based on 92 hospitals, due to missing data on the variable volume of appendectomies per surgeon and family practitioner. The findings also exclude an "outlier" hospital,† which performed nearly twice as many appendectomies per surgeon and family practitioner per year than other hospitals in the study (21.67 vs. 12.83) and had a standardized per cent normal tissue removed ratio of 3.13, as compared with 2.61 for the next-highest hospital. As shown, the frequency of medical staff committee meetings, the degree to which physicians concentrated most of their activity at the hospital under study, the per cent of physicians on contract and the presence of a director of medical education are each significantly associated with a lower standardized per cent of normal tissue removed. The unstandardized regression coefficients indicate that a one-unit increase in the frequency of staff committee meetings is associated with a 0.057 decrease in the SMR; a one-unit increase in per cent of physicians concentrating their activity at one hospital is associated with a 0.0068 decrease in the SMR; a one-unit increase in the per cent of active staff physicians on contract is associated with a 0.013 decrease in the SMR; and the presence of a director of medical education is associated with a 0.246 decrease in the SMR. Whether or not the hospital subscribed to CHPA's additional medical audit program, the ratio of surgeons to family practitioners, number of appendectomies performed per sur-

---

†A 322-bed voluntary community general hospital with no interns and residents.

Table 7-5 Per Cent Normal Tissue Removed by Age and Sex for 96 Hospitals in East North Central Region

Age	Male	Female
≤ 5 and ≥ 65	0.088	0.067
6-64	0.083	0.145*

*The increased rate for females is primarily due to the number of female conditions, such as ovarian cyst or pelvic inflammatory disease, whose symptoms may be closely related to those of acute appendicitis.

Table 7-6 Regression Results for Standardized Per Cent Normal Tissue Removed

Independent Variable	Unstandardized Coefficient (Standard Error)	Standardized Coefficient
Frequency of medical staff committee meetings	−0.057* (0.021)	−0.280
Physicians concentrate most of their professional activity at one hospital	−0.0068* (0.003)	−0.240
Percentage of active staff physicians on contract	−0.013† (0.006)	−0.222
Hospital has a director of medical education	−0.246‡ (0.162)	−0.155
Volume of appendectomies per family practitioner and surgeon	0.028 (0.037)	0.088
R^2 = 0.17		F = 3.56; p ≤ 0.006
$\overline{R}^2$ = 0.12		

*p ≤ 0.005.
†p ≤ 0.025.
‡p ≤ 0.10.

geon and family practitioner, per cent of physicians board certified and other variables included in the analysis were not associated with the standardized per cent normal tissue removed ratio. The lack of a volume/quality relationship for appendectomies confirms the results of Luft et al.[8] Overall, frequency of committee meetings, concentration of professional activity at one hospital, per cent of physicians on contract and presence of a director of medical education explained 17 per cent of the variability in the per cent standardized normal tissue removed ratio (F = 3.56; p ≤ 0.006).

It should be noted that the variables were not sensitive to the order in which they entered the equation. For example, whether forced in first or last, volume explained none of the variation in per cent standardized normal tissue removed. In contrast, frequency of committee meetings explained 7 per cent of the variance even when forced in last and also explained 7 per cent when forced into the equation first.

Analysis of the overall factors involving resource capability, medical staff participation in decision making and local staff orientation revealed no significant associations. The only variable that continued to be significantly associated with a lower standardized per cent normal tissue removed ratio was concentration of major professional activity at the hospital under study. The higher the percentage of physicians indicating that they concentrated their activity at one hospital, the lower the per cent standardized normal tissue removed ratio.

DISCUSSION

Differences in mortality in coronary care units are well documented.[19-21] Less well documented are the factors that might be associated with these differences. Bloom and Peterson found that coronary care units with full-time medical directors experienced better performance.[19] Stross et al.[21] found that units seeing fewer than 60 AMIs a year experienced *twice* the mortality of those seeing 60 or more per year. Others have identified the critical elements in treating CCU patients, including the positive impact of educating CCU nurses in problem recognition and response.[22,23] Policy changes permitting nurses to intervene immediately have also been associated with declines in mortality.[24] On a different level, the very effectiveness of CCUs in treating AMI patients has been questioned relative to at-home treatment and treatment in regular hospital beds.[9-12]

The present results suggest that the presence of a CCU does make a difference in the standardized mortality ratios of AMI patients. Hospitals with a CCU had lower standardized mortality ratios than those without a CCU, even after controlling for hospital size, volume and related variables. However, for those hospitals with a CCU, it was not possible to analyze whether those patients in the CCU did better than those treated in private or semiprivate rooms.

Further, the results suggest that volume of AMI patients treated is, indeed, a significant factor, with those treating 60 or fewer AMI patients a year experiencing a 17 per cent greater standardized mortality ratio than those treating more than 60 a year. More relevant is the fact that number of AMI patients treated *per* internist and family practitioner is significantly related to lower standardized mortality ratios, even after taking other variables into account. This finding suggests that recent research linking volume of surgical operations to postoperative mortality may also be part of a more generalized phenomenon in which the amount of clinical experience with a given condition within a given year plays an important role in nonsurgical cases as well.[8] If supported by other studies, the results suggest some important implications for grouping or clustering CCU services around those hospitals with sufficient volume to maintain high performance outcomes. Under the guidance of health systems agencies and faced with other external pressures, hospitals are already beginning to group or cluster their obstetric and pediatric services. However, treatment of AMI patients raises a somewhat more difficult set of issues in terms of travel time to receive treatment factors. Thus, a policy of reducing the number of individual hospitals with CCUs would also depend in part on the availability of competent emergency medical transport services available, particularly in rural and semirural areas. The question also arises as to whether volume or the existence of a CCU is the more important factor. Results from Table 7-4 suggest that both are about equally important in terms of their association with standardized mortality ratios. However, analysis of covariance involving only volume, presence or absence of a CCU and standardized mortality ratios revealed a stronger effect of volume ($F = 7.91; p \leq 0.006$) than of presence or absence of a CCU. ($F = 2.70; p \leq 0.104$.)

The present results involving AMI standardized mortality ratios also suggest the important role played by medical staff organization, particularly in regard to participation in hospital decision making. Whether or not the president of the medical staff was on the hospital governing board and an overall measure of participation, which included also whether or not other medical staff officers were on the governing board, and whether there were physicians on the governing board executive committee, were significantly related to lower standardized mortality ratios, taking into account other possible explanatory factors. In fact, the present results suggest that the overall medical staff participation in decision making factor is the single most important variable associated with lower standardized mortality ratios, more significant than either the volume of AMI patients per internist and family practitioner or the presence or absence of a coronary care unit. Other variables commonly believed to be associated with better performance, such as hospital bed size, degree of teaching activity and per cent board-certified physicians, were not as significantly associated with lower standardized mortality ratios when the above variables were taken into account. Each of them, however, was in the expected direction.

The literature suggests wide variation in the removal of histologically normal appendices.[25-28] Yet, again, there is little documentation of the factors that might be associated with the amount of normal tissue removed. Neutra's research suggests that with a more careful history and exam and close observation for several hours, hospitals can reduce the rate of normal tissue removed without any increase in the rate of perforation.[25] The present analysis suggests some medical staff organization factors which may be associated with and may facilitate the kinds of behavior suggested by Neutra. Specifically, frequency of medical staff committee meetings, concentration of physician activity around one hospital, per cent of active staff physicians on contract, and presence of a director of medical education are each associated with a lower standardized per cent normal tissue removed ratio. Frequent medical staff committee meetings promote communication and exchange of information among staff members, increasing the probability of implementing changes in treatment practices, which may improve the process and/or outcomes of care. Lending support to this notion, Morlock et al. recently found a significant association between frequency of medical staff committee meetings and lower overall hospital death rates after adjusting for patient diagnostic mix.[29]

Concentration of professional activity at one hospital offers greater opportunity for peer review and establishment of new practice habits and patterns. For example, in early quality-of-care research, Morehead found that those physicians who spent most of their time (greater than 75 per cent) treating Health Insurance Plan (HIP) of Greater New York patients provided a higher quality of care than those scattered throughout several locations or those seeing HIP patients only part-time.[30] Flood and Scott have found that the greater the percentage of a surgeon's practice that is concentrated in a given hospital, the better the quality of patient care.[1]

Having a greater percentage of physicians on contract also affords the opportunity for closer physician involvement in hospital treatment practices and facilitates the opportunity to initiate and implement improvements in care. The present results in this regard are also supported by previous work which found positive associations between measures of physicians on contract and a variety of quality-of-care measures.[4] Finally, the presence of a director of medical education may provide the kind of systematic leadership and direction which, when combined with the greater emphasis on teaching implied by such a position, may stimulate better treatment practices.

The above findings and interpretations are only suggestive. Variables associated with differences in outcomes for AMI were not the same as those associated with differences in outcomes for appendicitis, although both sets of variables contained measures of medical staff organization concepts. Findings for these conditions should be replicated. Subsequent research should also examine other conditions as well as hospitalwide measures of quality in order to extend present results. Further specification of volume-quality relationships with regard to concentration of admissions and operations around smaller numbers of physicians would be a useful avenue of inquiry. Particularly useful would be studies of the impact of planned changes in medical staff organization and hospital-physician relationships on quality of care that would include data from hospitals not introducing such changes. Variations in implementation of quality assurance programs might be a source for such studies. The impact of regulation (rate review, certificate of need, and so on) on physician-hospital relationships and medical staff organization in relation to both cost and quality considerations is also a fertile area for study. Finally, it is of interest to note that the relatively aggregate measures used in the present research explained approximately 15 per cent of the variation in quality of care. Thus, examination of medical staff and hospital organization at a less aggregate or more micro level (such as the actual organization and staffing of coronary care units) would be likely to add to the explanation of differences in quality of care across hospitals.

While inferences drawn from the above results can, in a strict sense, only be generalized to other CPHA-subscribing hospitals in the East North Central Region of the country, the findings are suggestive of some important medical staff influences which may hold implications for many U.S. hospitals. Of particular interest is the fact that, for the conditions and hospitals studied, neither hospital structural characteristics such as bed size and degree of teaching involvement nor individual physician characteristics such as specialty composition were strongly related to better performance. Rather, medical staff organization characteristics, such as degree of physician participation in hospital decision making, frequency of committee meetings, concentration of activity in one hospital and percentage of physicians on contract, were found to be more strongly associated with superior performance, although not consistently so for both conditions. In addition, for AMI patients, the presence of a coronary care unit and the volume of AMI patients per internist and family practitioner were related to superior performance. It appears that simply having "good" people (e.g., well-trained, board-certified physicians) and having these people affiliate with "good" hospitals (e.g., large-size, teaching-oriented hospitals) is not sufficient to guarantee superior results. Rather, the actual organization of the medical staff itself, as reflected partly by participation in hospitalwide decision-making bodies and communication through committee meetings, appears to be most strongly associated with the quality of care provided. Thus, activities aimed at changing medical staff organization and articulating its relationship and involvement with the overall hospital organization and decision-making process can be a key factor in improving the quality of hospital care.

REFERENCES

1. Flood A, Scott WR. Professional power and professional effectiveness: the power of the surgical staff and the quality of surgical care in hospitals. J Health Soc Behav 1978;19:240.

2. Pauly MV. Medical staff characteristics and hospital costs. J Hum Resour 1978;13(Suppl):77.

3. Rhee SO. Factors determining the quality of physician performance and patient care. Med Care 1976:14:733.

4. Roemer M, Friedman J. Doctors and hospitals: medical staff organization and hospital performance. Baltimore: John Hopkins Press, 1971.

5. Shortell SM, Becker S, Neuhauser D. The effects of management practices on hospital efficiency and quality of care. In: Shortell SM, Brown M, eds. Organizational research in hospitals. Chicago: Blue Cross Association, 1976:90-107.

6. Shortell SM, Getzen T. Measuring hospital medical staff organizational structure. Health Serv Res 1979;14:97.

7. Palmer RH, Rielly MC. Individual and institutional variables which may serve as indicators of quality of medical care. Med Care 1979:17:693.

8. Luft H, Bunker JP, Enthoven AC. Should operations be regionalized? The empirical relation between surgical volume and mortality. N Engl J Med 1979;388:1364.

9. Mather HG, Pearson NG, Reed KLQ, et al. Acute myocardial infarction. Home and hospital treatment. Br Med J 1971;3:334.

10. Dellipiani AW, Kolling WA, Donaldson RJ, et al. Teesside Coronary Survey: fatality and comparative severity of patients treated at home, in the hospital ward, and in the coronary care unit after myocardial infarction. Br Heart J 1977;39:1172.

11. Hill JC, Hampton JR, Mitchell JRA. A randomized trial of home versus hospital management for patients with suspected myocardial infarction. Lancet 1978;i:837.

12. Astvad K, Fabricius-Bjerre N, Kjaerulff J, et al. Mortality from acute myocardial infarction before and after establishment of a coronary care unit. Br Med J 1974;1:567.

13. Shortell SM, Evashwick C. The structural figuration of U.S. hospital medical staffs. Med Care 1981;19:419.

14. Helmers C. Short and long term prognostic indices in acute myocardial infarction. ACTA Med Stand (Suppl SSS), 1973.

15. Schor S, Shani M, Madar B. Factors affecting immediate mortality of patients with acute myocardial infarction: a nationwide study. Chest 1975;68:217.

16. Peterson DR, Thompson DV, Chinn N. Ischemic heart disease prognosis: a community-wide assessment. JAMA 1972;219:1423.

17. Gilmore OJA, Browett JP, Griffin PH, et al. Appendicitis and mimicky conditions. Lancet 1975;ii:421.

18. LoGerfo JP, Brook RH. Evaluation of services and care, Chapter 13, In: Williams SJ, Torrens PR. Introduction to health services. New York: John Wiley and Sons, 1980:361-363.

19. Bloom BS, Peterson OL. End result, cost and productivity of coronary care units. N Engl J Med 1973;288:72.

20. Klaus AP, Sarachek MS, Greenberg D, et al. Evaluating coronary care units, Am Heart J 1970;79:471.

21. Stross JK, Willis PW, Reynold EW Jr., et al. Effectiveness of coronary care units in small community hospitals. Ann Intern Med 1976;85:709.

22. Clipson CW, Wehrer JJ. Planning for cardiac care: a guide to the planning and design of cardiac care facilities. Ann Arbor: The Health Administration Press, 1973.

23. Stross JK, Bellfy LC. Health Lung 1979;8:318.

24. Killip T, Kamball JT. Myocardial infarction in a coronary care unit: a two year experience with 250 patients. Am J Cardiol 1976;20:474.

25. Neutra RR. Appendicitis: decreasing normal removals without increasing perforations. Med Care 1978;16:956.

26. Lichtner S, Pflanz M. Appendectomy in the Federal Republic of Germany: epidemiology in medical care patterns. Med Care 1971;9:311.

27. Thomas EJ, Mueller CB. Appendectomy: Diagnostic criteria and hospital performance. Hosp Pract 1969;4(4):72.

28. Wennberg J. Gittelsohn A. Small area variations in health care delivery. Science 1973;182:1102.

29. Morlock L, Nathanson CA, Horne SD. Organizational factors associated with quality of care in 17 general acute care hospitals. Paper presented at the annual meeting of the Association of University Programs in Health Administration, Toronto, Canada, May 6, 1979.

30. Morehead MA. Quality of medical care provided by family physicians as related to their education, training and methods practice. New York: HIP of New York, 1958.

Appendix

A. Calculation of Standard Mortality Ratio (SMR) for AMI Patients and Standardized Normal Tissue Removed Ratio (SNTR) for Appendectomy Patients.

1. Standardized Mortality Ratio (SMR) =

$$\frac{\sum\limits_{i=1}^{6} d_i}{\sum\limits_{i=1}^{6} n_i (P_i)}$$

where:

d_i = each hospital's number of AMI deaths in each age, systolic blood pressure category

n_i = each hospital's number of filtered AMI patients in each age, systolic blood pressure category

P_i = total number of deaths in each age, systolic blood pressure category for *all* study hospitals *divided by* the total number of patients in each age, systolic blood pressure category for *all* study hospitals.

2. Standardized Normal Tissue Removed Ratio (SNTR) =

$$\frac{\sum\limits_{i=1}^{4} t_i}{\sum\limits_{i=1}^{4} n_i (P_i)}$$

123

where:

t_i = each hospital's number of patients with normal tissue removed in each age, sex category

n_i = each hospital's number of appendectomy patients in each age, sex category

P_i = total number of patients with normal tissue removed in each age, sex category for *all* study hospitals *divided by* total number of appendectomy patients in each age, sex category for *all* study hospitals.

B. Factor Analysis Results

1. Resource Capability Factor

Variables	Factor Loadings	Communality
Hospital bed size	0.82	0.82
Existence of a director of medical education	0.67	0.55
Number of services and benefits provided to medical staff	0.51	0.51
Per cent of active staff board certified	0.45	0.63
Number of interns and residents/bed	0.36	0.77
Per cent of active staff who are radiologists and pathologists	−0.41	0.81

Eigenvalue = 4.96
Per cent of variance explained = 30.3 per cent.

2. Participation in Decision Making Factor

Variables	Factor Loadings	Communality
Other medical staff officers are on governing board	0.84	0.81
Physicians are on executive committee of governing board	0.44	0.37
President of medical staff is on hospital governing board	0.29	0.41

Eigenvalue = 1.39.
Per cent of variance explained = 8.5 per cent.

3. Local Staff Orientation Factor

Variables	Factor Loadings	Communality
Per cent of active staff who are radiologists and pathologists	0.82	0.81
Per cent of active staff who are generalists (i.e., family practitioners and pediatricians)	0.32	0.29
Number of active staff physicians per bed	−0.31	0.90
Per cent of active staff board certified	−0.36	0.63
Number of medical staff members per committee	−0.36	0.64
President of medical staff is elected by the staff	−0.43	0.30

Eigenvalue = 1.60.
Per cent of variance explained = 9.8 per cent.

8. Organizational Determinants of Medical Care Quality: A Review of the Literature

SANG-O RHEE

INTRODUCTION: OBJECTIVES AND SCOPE

While concern over the quality of health care is not new, the expansion of regulatory and legal constraints on health institutions is shifting the locus of concern to the organizational level in an effort to ensure that quality care is being provided. This new emphasis becomes more appropriate as (1) the structure of delivery shifts from the rather personal doctor-patient relationship to a process increasingly conducted within the complex organizational settings of hospitals, clinics, physician groups, and emergency rooms; (2) the methods of payment shift from the dyadic exchange between provider and client to more complex structures involving the interventions of third (private and governmental insurance programs) and fourth (employers and union) parties; and (3) the pressures of malpractice join the legal interests of individual practitioners and delivery organizations.

The implications of this shift for the state of the art in quality assurance are significant. No longer can quality assurance efforts be viewed primarily as process measurement and assessment. To be sure, the problems in defining, measuring, and assessing quality are far from easy to solve. However, the state of the art must develop beyond such "technical" concerns to address the organizational problem of assuring that quality is improved once problems are identified. The changing environment in health care thus necessitates a better understanding of the internal and external dynamics that affect the quality as well as the cost of care.

This chapter identifies, through a review of the literature, various organizational factors that have been linked with the quality of medical care. In this review, the main focus will be on the organizational aspects of institutional settings, with primary emphasis on hospital settings.

ORGANIZATIONAL DETERMINANTS OF THE QUALITY OF MEDICAL CARE

Throughout the 1960s organizational researchers were mainly concerned with identifying the determinants of organizational structures.[1-4] In the decade of the 1970s, the relation of organizational structure to the performance of organizations became a major interest.[5-8] Among these efforts were several studies that examined the relation of hospital structure to hospital performance.[2,9] From such studies, as well as others, one can identify numerous organizational variables that may be expected to influence organizational effectiveness in general and the quality of hospital care in particular.* Shortell and Brown, after reviewing 19 comparative empirical studies of hospitals, classified organizational variables into six major categories: (1) environment, (2) goals, (3) technology, (4) decision-making structure, (5) reward system, and (6) modes of coordination.[35] Starfield hypothesized that the following five variables facilitate the health outcomes of patient care in hospitals: (1) personnel, (2) facilities and equipment, (3) organization (leadership, politics, planning and goals, organizational control, consumer involvement), (4) information flow, and (5) finance.[36]

In this chapter the discussion will focus on a consideration of selected research findings concerned with the following organizational attributes:

- goals
- technologies
- size of organization
- volume of services
- specialization
- formalization
- decision-making structure
- coordination, control and integration
- visibility of consequences
- medical staff organization.

---

*Discussions of the specific definition and measurement of medical care quality and their theoretical and practical implications are already extensively provided elsewhere and will not be included in this chapter.[10-21] The general definitional and measurement issues relating to organizational effectiveness have also been discussed elsewhere.[7,22-34] A general consensus on the definition or organizational effectiveness has yet to be reached.[6] However, since this is a concept not much discussed elsewhere in this book, we offer the definition developed by Steers: "an organization's ability to successfully integrate technology, structure, personal and social factors into a congruent goal-oriented entity."[8]

Goals

According to the rational model of organizational behavior, organizations may be viewed as goal-seeking entities with goal-directed activities. Organizational goals provide direction for managers in their attempts to acquire and use organizational resources and also to serve as a rationale for the structures and functions of their institutions.

Most frequently mentioned hospital goals include patient care, education, teaching and research, and non-profit-making in addition to the provision of high quality care. Goss provided early evidence of the association between the goal of teaching and quality of care in her systematic review of the hospital literature.[37] From this review and other evidence, it would appear that a formal hospital commitment to the teaching goal facilitates a higher quality of care than does commitment to patient care service alone. Goss also observed that hospital specialization, involvement in research activities, and other hospital activities may contribute positively to better quality of care. When the extent of commitment to the teaching goal is differentiated between medical school affiliation and internship and/or residency program alone, there is evidence that the more extensive the hospital commitment to medical education, the better is the quality of care provided.[38-41] Another view on the relationship between teaching activities and quality of care was provided by the Stanford Center for Health Care Research. The researchers at the center found that the teaching status of a hospital is not related to the quality of care, as measured by the results of surgical care in hospitals— mortality and morbidity rates adjusted for differences in patient characteristics.[32-34] More studies are needed to confirm the relationship between the presence of teaching and quality of care in her systematic review of the hospital literature.[37]

Absence of profit-making as a hospital goal is sometimes posited to be associated with the quality of care. Several earlier studies found that a higher percentage of pelvic surgery with an incorrect diagnosis was positively associated with the proprietary status of hospitals.[42,43] In another study in which differences in case mix were controlled, little difference was found between proprietary and nonproprietary hospitals in the quality of care.[44,45] It is critical that such studies introduce appropriate controls in their analyses, since ownership is confounded with differences in size, teaching status, case mix, and many other variables that could be related to the measured quality of care.[46]

Technology

Technology as used in organization literature generally refers to the nature of the work being carried out and is concerned with the complexity (the extent of intricacy) and uncertainty (lack of predictability) of task activities.[47] While medical science has made great advances in the knowledge and technology used for diagnosing and treating disease, hospitals differ widely in the extent to which they have incorporated these new technologies. This may be an important discriminating variable in terms of relative quality, since it is generally assumed that those institutions that employ high medical technology provide a higher quality of care than those that do not.[48] Several technology-related hypotheses have been proposed by various researchers[47,49] including, for example: with high complexity of technology, the greater the differentiation of structure, the better the quality of care; with high complexity of technology, the higher the staff qualifications, the better the quality of care; and with high uncertainty of technology, the greater the formalization of procedures, the poorer the quality of care. However, the empirical relationship of technology to the quality of patient care has received little attention in the research literature. Studies have examined the effect of the scope of services on the quality of care, but no definitive study has determined the impact of technology per se on the quality of care. (For an examination of the impact of technology on quality at the macro level, see Orloff.[50])

Size of Organization

The size of an organization is frequently viewed as a determinant of various aspects of organizational effectiveness. For example, increased organizational size is expected to enhance organizations by maintaining orderly managerial succession, reduced labor costs, economies (or diseconomies) of scale, and improved environmental control. It is also expected to be inversely related to employee attachment to an organization. In general, it would appear that the effect of organization size on the quality of care provided in hospitals is not clearly established.

Several studies have found that large hospitals tend to provide a higher quality of care.[51,52] Others have found no correlation between size and validated reputational measures of quality of care.[9] In a more extensive, highly controlled analysis, size was not found to have an independent and direct influence on the quality of care.[23,49] One problem with such studies is that size tends to be associated with other powerful correlates of quality, such as medical school affiliation, highly specialized physicians, advanced technology, and greater service volumes in specific types of conditions and diseases, thus making it difficult to separate out the unique effect of size on quality. Since size is easily measured, it has often been used as a catchall variable, as a surrogate composite indicator of organizational structure.

Related to the size of the entire organization is the size of work groups within organizations.[8] Larger work group sizes have generally been found to be positively associated with lower job satisfaction, lower attendance and retention rates, and more labor disputes and inversely related to the ability of group members to become better acquainted, develop closer friendships, and build stronger group cohesion. The improved organizational attachments of smaller work groups can be expected to lead to improvements in the effectiveness of the members' performance in organizations. No studies, however, were found that examined the direct effect of work unit size on the quality of care.

Volume of Services

The volume of service in specific types or conditions of diseases has been considered to be a very important variable in predicting the quality of care. A key assumption here is that it is essential to have a minimum caseload if the proficiency of staff is to be maintained. For practical and economic reasons, an adequate volume of patients of specific types is necessary for a hospital to support specialized facilities, services, skills, and necessary staff.

A number of studies have provided evidence that volume is directly related to quality, including: severity-adjusted case-fatality rates for cancer of the cervix,[53] mortality rates for myocardial infarction,[54] and neonatal mortality rates adjusted for birth weight.[55] Luft, Bunker, and Enthoven examined mortality rates for 12 surgical procedures of varying complexity in 1,498 hospitals.[56] They reported that as the volume of operations increased, the mortality rates from open heart surgery, vascular surgery, transurethral resection of the prostate, and coronary bypass decreased significantly. Hospitals with 200 or more operations in a given diagnosis annually had case mix-adjusted death rates that were 25 to 41 percent lower than those with lower volumes. Further, the authors support the value of regionalization for improving the quality of certain operations.

Indirect evidence of the low-volume problem is found in the study of Rhee and associates of within and outside domain practice. In their study of physician performance in Hawaii, they found that when specialist physicians treated patients whose diagnoses could be considered to have been outside the domain of their usual practice (as reflected by their specialties), the relative quality of care provided by them declined. It could be hypothesized that the important reason for this is that the specialists are not as "practiced" in outside domain work as they are in their within-domain practice.[57]

It is important to point out that the impact of an excess volume on the quality of care has not been determined. On the other hand, the eagerness of hospitals to add sophisticated units and services for which there is often insufficient volume to assure efficient use and high quality care makes the concern over excess volume less problematical than the problem of quality care in relation to low utilization.*

---

*While a high volume of patients is a necessary condition for the maintenance of proficiency of a hospital staff, there is a lack of consensus concerning the appropriate volumes for selected services. The Joint Commission on Accreditation of Hospitals (JCAH), Veterans Administration (VA), and Social Security Administration (SSA) have promulgated minimum volumes for selected procedures. However, the adequacy and validity of such suggested volumes should be tested in relation to quality of medical care.[29]

Specialization

Specialization refers to the degree of division of work within an organization. The need for specialized knowledge and skills encourages employees to acquire expertise in a particular area in order to maximize their contributions to goal-directed activities. Increased specialization appears to have both functional and dysfunctional impacts on organizational performance. Unless effective coordinating mechanisms are established, specialization alone may not lead to improved organizational performance.

Mosley and Grimes examined the relationship between what they called "functional" and "role" specialization and patient care quality as measured broadly by expert evaluation.[58] A sample of 32 Houston hospitals of varying sizes was chosen for study. Functional specialization was measured by asking the question: Do you have at least one full-time person performing certain identified functions? Role specialization was measured by counting the number of different types of full-time employees existing within the organization. Hospital effectiveness was determined by 28 experts in hospital administration and medical care and was evaluated by a combined measure of quality obtained from medical audit, autopsy rate, adjusted death rate, and other data. In their study, Mosley and Grimes found that all high performing hospitals showed a greater tendency than did other hospitals to assign particular tasks to specific individuals and to make certain that the task was the only one performed by that individual.

A number of studies have examined the relative performance of specialist and generalist physicians. Rhee and associates, in the study noted earlier, found that after adjusting for a number of physician background and practice setting characteristics, as well as for the mix of patients treated, specialist physicians tended to receive significantly higher performance scores than did generalist-trained physicians.[57] These results provide suggestive evidence of the generally assumed greater performance of physicians who specialize and practice within their chosen specialties.

Formalization

Formalization refers to the extent to which employee work activities are specified by official rules, regulations, and procedures.[59] Various theoretical orientations have made important contributions in this area. While a hierarchical approach in classical management theory has emphasized the importance of highly specified procedures, an open systems model from the human relations school tends to deemphasize standardization of procedures.[2,60-62] A number of contingency theorists have found that there is no one best way of managing all organizations.[22,63]

Instead, management structure is conceived as a function of the interaction between the environment (internal as well as external) and the tasks to be performed. When environment and technology are relatively constant, higher degrees of formalization may be achieved; but in an unstable or unknown environment, less formalized organizational design may be more appropriate.[22,64,65]

Hospitals are likely to be operating in an environment characterized by a high degree of complexity, diversity, instability, and uncertainty. The complexity of tasks performed by hospital personnel also varies. While the tasks carried out by employees in the pharmacy and laundry departments are rather routine, certain, and predictable, the tasks conducted by medical practitioners tend to be more complex, nonroutine, uncertain, and unpredictable.

Hospital structures typically incorporate at least two different levels of operating procedure specification (the concept of organizational coupling): high specification for low complexity task environments (low complexity hierarchical control) and low specification for high complexity task environments, as in the case of the professional component (high complexity collegial control).[22]

Becker and Neuhauser studied the impact of the specification of procedures on hospital effectiveness and quality of care.[22] Using data from 30 medium-sized (100 to 300 beds) short-term general, not-for-profit community hospitals in the greater Chicago area, they tested the influence of the specification of procedures on hospital efficiency for both low complexity nonmedical divisions and high complexity medical divisions. When there were more specified procedures for nonmedical divisions, such as use of the budget by the hospital, use of position control, use of salary control systems, and use of worker job descriptions, results indicated that the hospitals tended to have higher cost efficiency, lower manhour use, better JCAH evaluations and higher occupancies. For the medical division, the finding was quite the opposite. When there were less specified production procedures, the quality of care was relatively higher. In other words, they found that when hospitals limited the range of drugs to be prescribed by their medical staffs, when hospital administrators were willing to invoke suspensions of admissions, and when physicians had less influence because of their being burdened by high volumes of specified procedures, the quality of care tended to suffer. Such hospitals experienced lower expert evaluations of hospital quality, lower JCAH evaluation scores, and higher death rates adjusted for case mix. Their findings generally suggest that the more procedures are specified in the highly complex medical components, the lower is the quality of care.*

---

*This finding has implications for the design of quality assurance programs as mandated by the JCAH. Hospitals should be made aware of the potential negative and positive effects of developing highly structured control mechanisms in medical and nursing areas of practice.

Decision-making Structure

Centralization-decentralization of power and authority in organizational decision making is thought to affect organizational effectiveness. For example, decisions are expected to be more effective if they are made closer to their information sources. While corporate control over major policy matters should be centralized, decentralization of operational and production decisions is expected to enhance open communications and feedback and to increase rank and file employee participation in organizations. In other words, participative management is generally expected to improve employee satisfaction and attachment to an organization.

Power in decision making, its location, legitimacy, and encroachment, is thus expected to affect the behavior and performance of organizational members. With respect to the health care field, a very limited literature is available on the impact of the relative power of physicians, nurses, hospital administrators, and boards of trustees on hospital performance in general and quality of care in particular.

Hospital Administration

Flood and Scott examined the influence of hospital administrators on the quality of medical care. When hospital administrators exercised greater power within domain areas such as purchasing contract services (e.g., laundry), the better was the quality of surgical care. Higher power exercised by hospital administrators was the factor most strongly associated with the quality of surgical care.[23] This finding could imply that hospital administrators provide coherence and coordination in a work situation fraught with fragmentation and overspecialization. However, a later study by these researchers revealed hospital administrator's influence to be positively associated with poorer quality outcomes.[31] Further studies are clearly needed to clarify this relationship.

Surgical Administration

Flood and Scott also examined the relationship between the legitimate power of surgical staff and the quality of care. Centralization of decision making within the surgical staff was not found to be related to the quality of care. In fact, the limited relationship was observed to be in the opposite direction from expectations.[23]

Nursing Administration

When examining the power of nursing administration within its own area of expertise, Flood and Scott did not find the expected relationship. The higher the influence of nurses on decisions within their own domain (such as hiring and firing of nursing staff and making changes in the nursing care system) the poorer was the measured quality of care.[31]

Trustee Power

Morlock and associates at Johns Hopkins University examined the relationship between the power of the board of trustees and the quality of care rendered in hospitals. Their preliminary findings suggest a strong positive relationship between the influence of trustees in hospital decision making and the quality of care as measured by severity-adjusted mortality. Hospitals with influential boards of trustees may be more likely to produce frequent internal statistical monitoring of, for example, the percentage of normal tissue removed and the number of anesthesia deaths.[66] Possible theoretical implications of monitoring will be discussed later in the section on the visibility of consequences of practice.

With respect to the domain of power and authority, Flood and Scott have suggested that any professional group must be in a position to exercise a great deal of power relative to other groups over decisions within their sphere of competence (within domain).[23] Conversely, effectiveness will not be served if professionals exercise a large amount of power over decisions outside their sphere of expertise (encroachment).

While it is not certain how the location of power is related to the quality of care, it is quite interesting to find that "encroachment" is related to poorer quality of care. Flood and Scott report that the quality of care as measured by surgical outcome is poorer when there is encroachment by physicians on nursing or hospital administration and by hospital administration on surgical administration.[23] When the power of role groups is considered, the perceived ability of hospital administrators and the monitoring activities of trustees are found to be strongly and consistently related to better care. On the other hand, the relative power of the surgical administration over its own domain areas was related to poorer quality. This finding may indirectly confirm the expectation that a highly complex task cannot be easily standardized and controlled.

Coordination, Control, and Integration

Organizational differentiation and specialization require integrative mechanisms to bring the production procedures together if organizational goals are to be achieved.[65] In their early study of community general hospitals, Georgopolous and Mann conceptualized four types of coordination: (1) corrective, (2) preventive, (3) regulatory, and (4) promotive.[9] Longest further refined these concepts and tested them in hospitals.[67] The combined findings of these two studies indicate that high use of *corrective* coordination (coordinative activities that rectify an error or correct a dysfunction in the system after it has occurred) is negatively related to efficiency and to the quality of care; high use of *preventive* coordination (coordination aimed at preventing the occurrence of anticipated problems) is positively related to efficiency and to the quality of care; the use of *promotive* coordination (coordination that attempts to improve the articulation of the parts of the system or to improve the existing organizational arrangements without regard for specific problems) is positively related to the quality of care; and the use of *regulatory* coordination (coordinative activities that are aimed at the maintenance of existing structural and functional arrangements in the organization) is positively related to efficiency but negatively related to the quality of care. Georgopolous and Mann also determined that preventive and promotive coordination were positively related to attitudinal measures of quality of care.[9] However, their assessment of regulatory coordination produced mixed findings.

The positive impact of promotive coordination also appears to be supported in the Shortell, Becker, and Neuhauser study. They found that in those hospitals in which nursing engaged in a high degree of regularly scheduled meetings with other key departments, medical/surgical death rates were generally lower.[48] Mosley and Grimes also reported that high performing hospitals tended to employ formal mechanisms such as full-time coordinators and standing committees in order to ensure that the various components and factions worked closely together.[58]

Thus, while research on the effects of the decision-making structures produced contradictory results, research into the coordination and control structures has produced some interesting consistencies in the results. The quality of care provided in hospitals was generally found to be positively related to specific types of coordinative activities within hospitals, especially those focused on assuring the quality of care.

Visibility of Consequences

In their discussion of organizational efficiency, Becker and Neuhauser introduced "visibility of consequences" as an important determinant of the quality of care and hospital efficiency.[22] Gordon and Becker defined visibility of consequences as the degree to which owners/administrators of organizations can and do evaluate the costs of obtaining a given level of goal attainment from a procedure or resource allocation.[22] If owners' objectives are to be realized and unintended consequences minimized, they must be aware of the effects of their actions. When the visibility of consequences is high, owners/administrators tend to specify procedures that maximize efficiency and eliminate inappropriate procedures. High visibility of consequences is therefore likely to produce optimal organizational structure and functioning.

Becker and Neuhauser, for example, observed that when administrators and chairmen of the board were more aware of the actual standing of their hospitals (relative to other hospitals) in terms of the quality of care, the higher was their hospitals' quality of care.[22] Shortell, Becker, and Neuhauser, in their study of hospitals in Massachusetts, reported a less coherent relationship.[48] They used as a measure of "procedures" to increase the visibility of consequences the percentage of reports actually sent to the board of trustees among those that actually could have been sent. The "actual" visibility of consequences was measured by the percentage of operating statistics that the administration and the president of the medical staff could not themselves estimate and the percentage of operating statistics on which they could not themselves compare their hospitals to other similar hospitals in their areas. They found that the visibility of consequences thus measured was not significantly related to medical/surgical death rates. Thus, while the visibility of consequences would seem to be an important factor in controlling the quality of care, the research evidence (at least with respect to the hospital literature) is too limited to draw meaningful inferences.

Medical Staff Organization

Finally, a number of studies have examined the relationship between medical staff organization and the quality of care. It is generally hypothesized that physicians affiliated with active medical staff organizations will provide a higher quality of care than those affiliated with less active medical staff organizations. The level of activity of a medical staff is measured by a number of variables, including the control of physician behavior through the use of contractual agreements, rigorous staff appointment procedures, review of privileges, peer review and ongoing education, and the like.

Roemer and Shain, in their early study, provided some evidence of the association between medical staff organization and the quality of care.[52] They assumed that the higher the percentage of salaried physicians, the more structured was a given medical staff organization. From an extensive sample of U.S. hospitals, they found that the percentage of full-time equivalent salaried physicians on hospital medical staffs was positively associated with accreditation, facilities, and services, all of which were assumed to reflect indirectly the quality of care.

Roemer and Friedman identified seven dimensions of medical staff organization: (1) staff composition, (2) appointment process, (3) commitment, (4) departmentalization, (5) control committees, (6) documentation, and (7) informal dynamics. In an analysis of ten sample hospitals, they found that the more active or structured the medical staff, the better was the quality of care, as measured by hospital case mix-adjusted mortality rates.[68]

Flood and Scott also provide evidence of a positive relationship between medical staff organization and the quality of care. The power of the surgical staff over its own members was found to be related to the quality of surgical care: the more extensive the regulations imposed on individual surgeons, the higher was the quality of surgical care. It should be pointed out, however, that, as discussed earlier, they used several variables to represent different aspects of medical and nursing staff organization, not all of which were found to be consistent with the hypothesized positive association between greater staff organization and the quality of care.[23]

Shortell and associates, using data based on the 1973 nationwide survey of hospital medical staffs conducted by the American Hospital Association, factored out six relatively independent dimensions of medical staff organization and examined patterns and interrelationships among the factors.[69,70] These included (1) resource capability, (2) generalist physician contractual orientation, (3) communication control, (4) local staff orientation, (5) participation in decision making, and (6) hospital-based physician contractual orientation. Although they did not test them directly, the authors advanced a number of important hypotheses relating to the subject of this paper: hospitals with medical staffs scoring high on the resource capability dimension would have both higher costs and higher quality, and the coordination and control dimensions (i.e., communication) would be associated with lower costs but higher quality.

In general, the literature suggests that medical staff organization is a very important facilitator of high quality care.

A summary of the various findings relating to the impact of organizational structure on the quality of care is presented in Table 8-1.

FUTURE DIRECTIONS

While we have over the past 10 to 15 years been injecting increasing amounts of health care dollars into quality control, we have not observed the expected improvement in medical care quality. This reading began with the premise that perhaps one important reason for this is a failure to address the organizational variables that directly and indirectly influence the behavior of organizational members. Its purpose was to review and to identify some of the various organizational factors that determine or are associated with the quality of care. The scope of the review was limited to hospital organizational variables.

While it is recognized that a wide variety of conceptual and methodological limitations constrain the generalizability of specific studies, the overall view of the research findings is that organizational factors play an influential role in determining individual and group behavior and, consequently, the quality of care. Examination of the relationship between organizational factors and the quality of care reveals the need for research to resolve a number of key questions and methodological issues.

Although there are numerous methodological concerns one could discuss, perhaps most important in this particular area of research is the problem of sample size. In most of the studies reviewed, the samples tended to be very small, hence limiting the generalizability of study findings. Future studies should thus be supported that use a sufficient number of hospitals and/or individual practitioners such that resultant findings can be readily generalized.

Table 8-1 Studies on the Organizational Determinants of the Quality of Medical Care

Organizational Measures		Theory/Prediction	Relationships to the Quality of Care		
Variables	Operationalization		Overall Findings	Studies Findings	Source
Goals	Teaching/research	Positive	Mixed	Positive Positive Positive Positive No relation No relation	Goss (1970) Lee (1957) Morehead (1958) Rosenfeld (1957) Stanford (1974) Stanford (1976)
	Profit (absence of)	Positive	Mixed	Positive Positive No relation	Morehead (1964) Trussell (1962) Roemer (1959)
	Specialization (for example, cancer hospital, children's hospital)	Positive	Positive	Positive	Graham/Paloucek (1963)
Technology	Scope of services	Positive	Yet to be determined	Positive	Orloff (1978)
Size	Bed size or discharges or product of both	Positive	Mixed	Positive Positive No relation No relation	Rhee (1976) Roemer (1959) Flood (1978) Scott et al. (1976)
Volume	Types or conditions of diseases	Positive	Positive	Positive Positive Positive	Bloom (1973) Graham (1963) Yankauer (1958) Luft et al. (1979)

Table 8-1 continued

Organizational Measures			Relationships to the Quality of Care		
Variables	Operationalization	Theory/Prediction	Overall Findings	Studies Findings	Source
Specialization: functions and roles	Functional specialization Division of labor	Positive	Positive	Positive	Mosley/Grimes (1976)
	Role specialization Structure within division	Positive	Positive	Positive	Mosley/Grimes (1976)
Formalization: specification of procedures					
Nonmedical component	Production procedures Use of budget Use of positive control Use of salary control Use of job description	Positive	Positive (higher efficiency)	Positive	Becker/Neuhauser (1975)
Medical component	Production procedures Restrictions on prescription range Restrictions on admissions privilege Limited medical staff influence	Negative	Negative	Negative	Becker/Neuhauser (1975)
Decision-making structure:					
Hospital administration	Centralization of decision making: within domain—general administration	Positive	Mixed	Positive Negative	Flood/Scott (1978) Scott et al. (1979)

Surgical administration	Centralization of decision making: legitimate power of surgical staff*	Positive	Negative	Negative	Flood/Scott (1978)
Nursing administration	Hiring/firing of nursing staffs; change in nursing care systems; legitimate power of nursing staff	Positive	Negative	Negative	Flood/Scott (1978)
Trustee power	Frequent internal monitoring: statistics on tissue removals, autopsy, anesthesia deaths	Positive	Positive	Positive	Morlock et al. (1979)
Within domain power	Use of legitimate authority: performed task corresponds with expertise	Positive	Mixed	Mixed	Flood/Scott (1978)
Encroachment	Use of illegitimate authority: performed task does not correspond with expertise	Negative	Negative	Negative	Flood/Scott (1978)
Coordination, control, and integration	Preventive coordination	Positive	Positive	Positive	Georgopolous/Mann (1962) Longest (1974)
	Promotive coordination	Positive	Positive	Positive	Georgopolous/Mann (1962) Longest (1974)
	Regulatory coordination	Positive	Mixed	Negative Negative Positive	Longest (1974) Neuhauser (1971) Georgopolous/Mann (1962)

*The total power shared among the surgical staff organization is associated with higher quality of surgical care: the higher the total amount of perceived control by the surgical staff, the more efficient and effective the organization.

Table 8-1 continued

Organizational Measures		*Relationships to the Quality of Care*			
Variables	*Operationalization*	*Theory/Prediction*	*Overall Findings*	*Studies Findings*	*Source*
Visibility of consequences	Corrective coordination	Positive	Negative	Negative	Longest (1974)
	Procedures to improve the visibility of consequences: frequency of statistical reports on medical staff activities	Positive	Positive	Positive	Becker/Neuhauser (1975)
	Awareness of the consequences of hospital activities by administration, boards, and medical staff president	Positive	Mixed	Positive	Becker/Neuhauser (1975)
Medical staff organization	Staff composition Appointment process Commitment Departmentalization Control committees Documentation Informal dynamics	Positive	Positive	Positive Positive Positive Positive	Flood (1978) Roemer (1960) Roemer (1971) Shortell (1979)

Second, future hospital research may need a conceptual framework to develop research agenda and priorities. Several external and internal factors influence not only hospital organization but also hospital performance, including the regulation environment, the structure of administrative authority, and the organization of work. It is essential that valid and reliable measures for such variables be developed and that their individual and joint effects on the quality of medical care be assessed. In view of the many rapid changes that are occurring in the system for delivering health services, particular attention, we suggest, should be given to two areas of development: (1) efforts to control the costs of health care and (2) the significant growth in multihospital systems.

It is generally assumed that higher hospital costs are positively related to the quality of patient care. However, a study cited earlier demonstrated that high cost is positively associated with surgical complications and mortality rates. The compatibility between cost and quality is critical in an environment of intense regulation and competitive behavior and hence should be examined in much greater detail.

Also, the rapid growth in multihospital systems is likely to be accompanied by significant organizational change. Given the important effect organizational factors appear to have on quality, studies of the determinants of performance should focus on the unique effects of multisystem organization.

In summary, the research reviewed in this reading represents an important beginning in the assessment of the effects of organizational factors on the quality of care. The need for further research, however, is very apparent, since many gaps remain in our understanding of the determinants of performance. The existence of such gaps becomes all the more critical as the system changes and the pressures for assuring organizational accountability increase.

REFERENCES

1. Blau PM, Schoenherr R: *The Structure of Organizations.* New York, Basic Books, 1971.
2. Heydebrand W: *Hospital Bureaucracy: A Comparative Study of Organizations.* New York, Dunellen Publishing Co, 1973.
3. Pugh DS, Hickson DJ, Hininges DR, et al: Dimensions of organization structures. *Adm Sci Q* 1968; 13:65-105.
4. Pugh DS, Hickson DJ, Hininges DR, et al: The context of organization structures. *Adm Sci Q* 1969; 14:91-114.
5. Child J: Managerial and organizational factors associated with company performance: I and II. *J Manage Stud* 1974; 11:175-189; 1975; 12:12-27.
6. Goodman PS, Pennings JM et al (eds): *New Perspectives on Organizational Effectiveness.* San Francisco, Jossey-Bass Inc, 1977.
7. Price JL: The study of organizational effectiveness. *Sociol Q* 1972; 13(Winter):3-15.
8. Steers RM: *Organizational Effectiveness: A Behavioral View.* Pacific Palisades, Calif, Goodyear Publishing Co, 1977.

9. Georgopoulos BS, Mann FC: *The Community General Hospital.* New York, Macmillan Publishing Co, 1962.

10. Brook RH, Williams KN, Avery RD: Quality assurance in the 20th century: Will it lead to improved health in the 21st? in Egdahl RH, Gertman RM (eds): *Quality Assurance in Health Care.* Rockville, Md, Aspen Systems Corp, 1976, pp 111-131.

11. Donabedian A: Evaluating the quality of medical care. *Milbank Memorial Fund Q* 1966; 44:166-203.

12. Donabedian A: Measuring and evaluating hospital and medical care. *Bull NY Acad Med* 1976; 43:51-59.

13. Donabedian A: *Needed Research in the Assessment and Monitoring of the Quality of Medical Care.* US Dept of Health, Education, and Welfare, publication No. (PHS) 78-3219. National Center for Health Services Research, 1978.

14. Donabedian A: The quality of medical care: A conceptive search of a definition. *J Fam Pract* 1979; 9:227-284.

15. Donabedian A: *The Definition of Quality and Approaches to its Assessment.* Ann Arbor, Mich, Health Administration Press, 1980.

16. Greenfield S, Lewis CE, Kaplan SK, et al: Peer review by criteria mapping: Criteria for diabetes mellitus—the use of decision making in chart audit. *Ann Intern Med* 1975; 83:761-770.

17. McAuliffe WE: Studies of process outcome correlations in medical care evaluation: A critique. *Medical Care* 1978; 16:907-930.

18. Williamson JW: Evaluating quality of patient care: A strategy relating outcome and process assessment. *JAMA* 1971; 218:564-569.

19. Williamson JW: *Assessing and Improving Health Care Outcomes: The Health Accounting Approach to Quality Assurance.* Cambridge, Mass, Ballinger Publishing Co, 1978.

20. Griffiths JR: *Measuring Hospital Performance, An Inquiry Book.* Chicago, Blue Cross Association, 1978.

21. Doll R: Surveillance and monitoring. *Int J Epidemiol* 1974; 3:305-314.

22. Becker S, Neuhauser D: *The Efficient Organization.* New York, Elsevier Press, 1975.

23. Flood AB, Scott WR: Professional power and professional effectiveness: The power of the surgical staff and quality of surgical care in hospitals. *J Health Social Behavior* 1978; 19:240-254.

24. Flood AB, Ewy W, Scott WR, et al: The Relationship Between Intensity and Duration of Medical Services and Outcomes for Hospitalized Patients. *Medical Care* 1979; 17:pp 1008-1102.

25. Flood AB, Scott WR, Ewy W, et al: Effectiveness in Professional Organizations: The Impact of Surgeons and Surgical Staff Organizations on the Quality of Care in Hospitals. Dept of Sociology and Dept of Anesthesia, Stanford University, revised 1979. Read before the American Sociological Association, Chicago, Ill, 1977.

26. Steers RM, "Problems in the Measurement of Organizational Effectiveness," Administrative Science Quarterly, 1975; 20:546-58.

27. Morse EV, Gordon G, Moch M: Hospital costs and quality of care: An organizational perspective. *Milbank Mem Fund Q* 1974; Summer:27, 315-346.

28. Neuhauser D, Andersen R: Structural comparative studies of hospitals, in Georgopoulos BS (ed): *Organization Research on Health Institutions.* Ann Arbor, University of Michigan Institute for Social Research, 1972, pp 83-136.

29. Palmer RH, Reilly MC: Individual and institutional variables which may serve as indicators of quality of medical care. *Medical Care* 1979; 17:693-717.

30. Scott WR: Effectiveness of organizational effectiveness studies, in Goodman PS, Pennings JM, et al (eds): *New Perspectives on Organizational Effectiveness.* San Francisco, Jossey-Bass Inc, 1977, pp 63-95.

31. Scott WR, Flood AB, Ewy W: Organizational determinants of services, quality and cost of care in hospitals. *Millbank Mem Fund Q* 1979; 57:234-264.

32. Stanford Center for Health Care Research: Study of Institutional Differences in Post Operative Mortality. 1974. A report to the National Academy of Sciences, DHEW, Springfield, VA; National Technical Information Services, P.B. 250 940.

33. Stanford Center for Health Care Research: Comparison of hospitals with regard to outcomes of surgery. *Health Serv Res* 1976; 11:112-127.

34. Stanford Center for Health Care Research: The hospital as a factor in the quality of surgical care in surgery in the United States: A report on the study of surgical services for the United States (SOSSUS). American College of Surgeons and the American Surgical Association, 1976, vol 3.

35. Shortell SM: Organization theory and health services delivery, in Shortell SM, Brown M (eds): *Organizational Research in Hospitals.* Chicago, Blue Cross Association, 1976, pp 1-12.

36. Starfield B: Health services research: A working model. *New Engl J Med* 1973; 289:132-136.

37. Goss MEW: Organizational goals and quality of medical care: Evidence from comparative research and hospitals. *J Health Soc Behav* 1970; 11:255-268.

38. Lee JAH, Morrison SL, Morris JN: Fatality from three common surgical conditions in teaching and non-teaching hospitals. Lancet 1957; 2:785-791.

39. Morehead MA: *Quality of Medical Care Provided by Family Physicians as Related to their Education, Training, and Methods of Practice.* New York, Health Insurance Plan of New York, 1958.

40. Rosenfeld LS: Qualify of medical care in hospitals. *Am J Public Health* 1957; 47:856-868.

41. Garrell M, Jekel JF: A comparison of quality of care on a teaching and non-teaching service in a university affiliated community hospital. *Conn Med* 1979; 43:659-663.

42. Morehead MA, Donaldson R: *A Study of the Quality of Hospital Care Secured by a Sample of Teamster Family Members of New York City.* New York, Columbia University School of Public Health and Administrative Medicine, 1964.

43. Trussell RE, Morehead MA, Ehrlich J: *The Quantity, Quality and Costs of Medical and Hospital Care Secured by a Sample of Teamster Families in the New York Area.* New York, Columbia University School of Public Health and Administrative Medicine, 1962.

44. Roemer MI: Is surgery safer in larger hospitals? *Hospital Manager* 1959; 87:35-101.

45. Roemer MI, Moustafa AT, Hopkins CE: A proposed hospital quality index: Hospital death rates adjusted for case severity. *Health Services Research* 1968; Summer: 96-118.

46. Bays CW: Case mix differences between non-profit and for-profit hospitals. *Inquiry* 1977; 14:17-21.

47. Schoonhoven CB, Scott WR, Flood AB, et al: Measuring the complexity and uncertainty of surgery and postsurgical care. *Medical Care* 1980; 18:893-915.

48. Shortell SM, Becker S, Neuhauser D: The effects of management practices on hospital efficiency and quality of care, in Shortell SM, Brown M (eds.): *Organizational Research in Hospitals.* Chicago, Blue Cross Association, 1976, pp 90-107.

49. Scott WR, Forrest JR, Brown BW Jr: Hospital structure and post operative mortality and morbidity, in Shortell SM, Brown M (eds): *Organizational Research in Hospitals.* Chicago, Blue Cross Association, 1976, pp 72-89.

50. Orloff MJ: Contributions of research in surgical technology to health care, in Egdahl RH, Gertman PM (eds): *Technology and the Quality of Health Care*, Germantown, Md, Aspen Systems Corp, 1978, pp 71-104.

51. Rhee S: Factors determining the quality of physician performance in patient care. *Medical Care* 1976; 14:733-750.

52. Roemer MI, Shain M: Contractual physicians in general hospitals: A pilot study. *Hospitals* 1960; May:34 38-43.

53. Graham JB, Paloucek FP: Where should cancer of the cervix be treated? *Am J Obstet Gynecol* 1963; 87:405-409.

54. Bloom BS, Peterson OL: End results, costs, and productivity of coronary care units. *N Engl J Med* 1973; 288:72-78.

55. Yankauer A, Allaway NC: An analysis of hospital neonatal mortality rates in New York State. *Am J Dis Child* 1958; 95:240-244.

56. Luft HS, Bunker JP, Enthoven AC: Should operations be rationalized? The Empirical Relation Between Surgical Volume and Mortality. *N Engl J Med* 1979; 301:1364-1369.

57. Rhee S, Luke RD, Lyons TD, et al: Domain of practice and the quality of physician performance. *Medical Care* 1981; 19:14-23.

58. Moseley SK, Grimes RM: The organization of effective hospitals. *Health Care Manage Rev* 1976; 1:13-23.

59. Hall RH: *Organizations: Structure and Process*. Englewood Cliffs, NJ, Prentice Hall Inc, 1972.

60. Weber M: The essentials of bureaucratic organization: An ideal-type construction, in Morton R, Gray A, Hockey B, et al (eds): *Reader in Bureaucracy*. Glencoe, Ill, Free Press, 1952.

61. Thompson J: *Organizations in Action*. New York, McGraw-Hill Book Co, 1967.

62. Likert R: *New Patterns of Management*. New York, McGraw-Hill Book Co, 1961.

63. Lawrence PR, Lorsch JW: *Organization and Environment: Managing Differentiation and Integration*. Homewood, Ill, Richard D Irwin Inc, 1969.

64. Burns T, Stalker GM: *The Management of Innovation*. London, Tavistock, 1961.

65. Lawrence PR, Lorsch JW: *Organization and Environment*. Cambridge, Mass, Harvard University Division of Research, Graduate School of Business Administration, 1967.

66. Morlock L, Nathanson C, Horn S, et al: Organizational Factors Associated with Quality of Care in 17 General Acute Hospitals. Presented at the Annual Meeting of the Association of University Programs in Health Administration (AUPHA), Toronto, Canada, 1979.

67. Longest B: Relationships between coordination, efficiency and quality of care in general hospitals. *Hosp Administration* 1974; 19:65-86.

68. Roemer MI, Friedman J: *Doctors in Hospitals: Medical Staff Organization and Hospital Performance*. Baltimore, Johns Hopkins Press, 1971.

69. Shortell SM, Getzen TE: Measuring Hospital Medical Staff Organization Structure. *Health Serv Res* 1979; 14:97-109.

70. Shortell SM, Evashwick C: The structural configuration of U.S. hospital medical staffs. *Medical Care* 1981; 19:419-430.

9. Barriers Limiting the Implementation of Quality Assurance Programs

ROICE D. LUKE and R. WAYNE BOSS

Reprinted with permission from *Health Services Research* 16(3). Copyright © 1981, 305-314.

Since the early work of Codman [1], the implementation of quality assurance programs in health institutions has come to be identified with three major barriers: the conceptualization, the measurement, and the assessment of the quality of care. The major conceptual problem is simply to determine what quality is. It is now almost axiomatic that any thoughtful discussion of quality assurance will question what constitutes quality and how it should be defined. There is, of course, no right answer to the question, but as many answers as there are purposes motivating the question [2, 3].

Even if a satisfactory definition of quality were agreed upon, one would still have to overcome the second major barrier to quality assurance: the measurement of quality. Here one encounters a vast array of reliability and validity questions. Perhaps most important among these is the polar dilemma, originally attributed to Donabedian [4], of determining which are better, measures of process or measures of outcome. Once again, there have been no clear responses to the question, a point amply and very cogently demonstrated in the recent literature [5-7].

The ultimate barrier to quality assurance may well be the selection of an assessment strategy. In the implementation of quality assurance programs, one must select from among a number of competing approaches, including the Bicycle approach [8], the Tracer method [9], Health Accounting [10], and the Quality Assurance Monitor [11], to name a few. The appropriate strategy in quality assurance is unclear and depends upon such factors as the level and type of care provided (e.g., acute inpatient versus ambulatory), the resources or information system base, and the purpose of the assessment.

Given these formidable barriers, it was not surprising to read of the finding reported by Saywell et al. in *Health Services Research* 16:3 (Fall 1981) that a number of independent measures of physician performance are relatively unassociated. Their findings raise the question whether there is or should be a strong correlation between measures of physician clinical performance and utilization behavior.

One could conclude, as do Saywell et al., that the results imply that no one measure of performance should be "relied upon to provide a totally accurate measure of a physician's performance." A more important conclusion to be drawn from this and other such studies [5, 12-14] is the inaccuracy of the assumption that quality assurance programs must be implemented after the development of detailed and highly sophisticated measurement and assessment techniques. In other words, if the weight of quality assurance rests on the resolution of highly technical matters of data acquisition and analysis, it is bound to continue to be both costly and highly ineffective.

The real question in quality assurance is not whether such technical problems can be resolved, but whether it is appropriate to assume that providing people or organizations with data will change their behavior. The demonstrated effectiveness of quality assurance systems founded on the medical audit and centered in complex information systems is, to say the least, underwhelming [15-17]. And this, we suggest, is due not only to an excessive emphasis on highly technical measurement and assessment strategies, but also to a failure to conceptualize quality assurance primarily as a problem of organizational and behavioral change. This reasoning is consistent with the JCAH decision of April 1979 to approve its new standard on quality assurance [18]. By dropping its numerical requirements for medical *audit* and adding the requirement that hospitals establish effective *programs* in quality assurance, the JCAH appeared to shift the focus of quality assurance from technical to organizational/behavioral considerations.

It will most certainly be argued that traditional approaches to the management of change may not be applicable to hospitals [19]. There is, however, little direct empirical support for this argument, whereas there is a substantial literature that demonstrates the general applicability of such approaches in a variety of both public and private institutional settings. For example, positive results are reported for public utilities [20], health services [21], education [22], criminal justice agencies [23], and in government at the local [24], state [25] and federal levels [26]. Successful change efforts have also taken place in the private sector, as illustrated by reports from a banking system [27], the Corning Glass Works Corporation [28], a hotel chain [29], a heavy metal production plant [30], and others whose business purposes remain unspecified [31].

It is true that there is relatively little direct evidence of the applicability of change strategies to hospitals, and in particular to the work of health professionals in hospitals. This, however, points up only the lack of serious attempts at such application. We suggest, therefore, that the real barriers to quality assurance are not the impediments to data acquisition and analysis but the points of resistance to change within health institutions. Without an understanding of the organizational and human barriers to change, and a clear set of strategies to overcome them, little effectiveness in quality assurance can realistically be expected.

There are a number of potential barriers [32] that may substantially inhibit the implementation of quality assurance programs; we suggest that these become the focus of quality assurance research in the future.

TEN BARRIERS TO CHANGE IN HEALTH INSTITUTIONS

Autonomy Expectations of Health Professionals

Perhaps the most important barrier to implementing quality assurance programs is health professionals' expectation of autonomy [33, 34]. Because of the importance of the work performed by health professionals (i.e., it is highly personal and deals often with critical matters of life, death, and human suffering) as well as the complex technology and knowledge base required for diagnosis and treatment, health professionals have traditionally been afforded high levels of functional independence [34]. The autonomy expectations of health professionals thus not only serve to minimize observation of their work but, more importantly, constitute a formidable source of resistance to the imposition of formal approaches to assuring the quality of care. Simply put, quality assurance programs cannot be implemented without the cooperation and support of physicians, nurses, and other key actors in health institutions. It is quite possible that because of this barrier, quality assurance has been deflected into the technical domain of measurement and assessment and away from traditional approaches to organizational and behavioral change.

Collective Benefits of Stability

People in organizations, particularly health institutions, tend to develop regularities of behavior. These include routines, standard operating procedures, prescribed behavior, and mandatory ways of communicating. For example, hospitals tend to rely upon specific admissions procedures regardless of whether all the steps in these procedures are appropriate or even essential. Such regularities are perceived by the organization as functional and often as absolutely essential for its survival. Thus they constitute important barriers to change that must be addressed in quality assurance programs.

The resistance attributable to such barriers is universal. As the Declaration of Independence states, "All experience hath shown that mankind are more disposed to suffer, while evils are sufferable, than to right themselves by abolishing the forms to which they are accustomed." Thus, though there may be collective benefits of stability, more often than not the collective wisdom merely favors the status quo for its own sake, resulting in a general predisposition against change.

Calculated Opposition to Change

Change efforts in quality assurance encounter organized resistance from individuals and groups both within and outside of organizations. These resistance maneuvers carry a number of titles and their supporters have logical reasons for their behavior. But each presents a clear set of obstacles that must be overcome if change is to be achieved. Here are three examples:

- *A Loss of Prevailing Advantage.* Effective quality assurance activities are likely to lead to changes that go beyond specific practice patterns of physicians and nurses. For example, quality assurance programs could affect the roles and communication patterns of all health care professionals, particularly if change is required in the organizational structure. Some individuals or groups will be affected more than others. Some will lose power, influence, or status; others will have to learn new skills, change certain behavior patterns, work in different environments, associate with different people, experience changes in titles, supervise fewer people, or have less resources available to them. And those who see the change as depriving them of their prevailing advantage will certainly resist the change effort. Such resistance may be particularly forceful if it means changes in the relative power of competing groups such as physicians and nurses.

- *Protection of Quality.* Change, even if pursued in the name of quality, is often resisted on the grounds that it would *impair* the quality of care provided. This is a common point of resistance outside of the health care arena. Examples include the resistance of professors to open enrollment or the elimination of grades in universities, the reluctance of judges to let the accused present defenses themselves, and the opposition of airline pilots to a wide variety of cost saving strategies of the airlines for which they work. In each case, the professionals' concern for safeguarding the public is clear. However, a fine line often divides concern for the public welfare and concern for private interest. And the "protection of quality" argument [34] is often an effective vehicle for preventing change that would, in the long run, improve the overall quality and, perhaps, even the cost-effectiveness of care provided in health institutions.

- *Psychic Cost of Change.* To engage in any change activity requires effort. And the greater the ambiguity associated with the change effort—the greater the movement away from the secure and the familiar—the greater the psychological energy needed to implement the change. Further, psychological energy is one of the most expensive forms of human energy. In addition, the psychic risks associated with change are substantial, as illustrated by the embarrassment and loss of influence resulting from a change that is adopted and subsequently fails, or the inevitable abuse from critics who misinterpret the behavior and misjudge the intentions of the change agents. Members of health institutions may therefore be inclined to approach any change with caution, at best.

Programmed Behavior

Regularities of behavior in organizations tend to be programmed into the members. Some of this programming is inadvertent and results from imitation and observation. A great deal, however, is deliberate, particularly in health institutions. This is not to say that programmed behavior is always negative. On the contrary, health institutions could not function without it. What is being argued here, however, is that programmed behavior often prevents innovation.

Programming is done in a variety of ways. Methods of programming are often related to division of labor (where behavior and job responsibilities are clearly defined in detail), recruitment and selection practices (where future employees are screened on skills, aptitudes, attitudes, and personality traits), reward structures (where desirable behaviors are rewarded both financially and with promotion, while misfits are expelled during probationary periods), training programs (which clearly emphasize both the organization's values and its way of doing things), and the use of symbolic activities to increase cohesiveness and strengthen solidarity and organizational commitment (such as staff retreats, the functioning of a vast array of nursing and medical staff committees, social gatherings, etc.). In each case, the desired behaviors tend to become a way of life, to the point where they are perceived as expressions of personal as well as organizational preference.

Tunnel Vision

Often the daily problems that absorb health professionals take on such a disproportionate level of importance that the resulting behavior may appear "petty" to outside observers. The result is that people may tend to lose perspective on a problem, to the point where small hills resemble huge mountains. The division of labor into specific tasks often produces such results, so that meticulous observance of institutional rules becomes a life-and-death matter, and those involved in small tasks lose perspective on how their activities relate to the objectives of the organization. To such people, attempts to improve quality may appear highly threatening and disruptive, whether those changes include opportunities for implementing modern management approaches to team delivery or the possibility of implementing technological improvements such as the use of computers in clinical problem solving. Such resistance is not caused by a lack of intelligence or good intentions. Rather, people become so concentrated on their specialized functions that they tend to lose sight of the broader implications of innovation and change.

Resource Limitations

Another increasingly important barrier in health institutions is the scarcity of resources. With sufficient resources, some organizations or individuals would eagerly change their structure or behavior. However, the law of scarcity is a stark reality: wants are unlimited, but means are not. Some resources are rendered inadequate by the social environment, as in the case of institutions located in states that are heavily committed to regulation, are experiencing declining markets, or have inadequate physical facilities. Thus resource limitations tend to bind organizations or individuals to established behaviors and render them powerless to change, even though quality assurance activities may suggest the wisdom of such change.

Sunk Costs

Another systemic barrier to change is the amount of assets committed to sunk costs, in the form of things and modes of behavior, whether they be capital investments or the acquisition of knowledge, skills, or specialized experience. Simply put, a sunk cost is any investment that is not convertible. Affluent health institutions and highly trained health professionals experience this as a barrier more often than do others. The paralysis caused by sunk costs is a function of the relationship between available resources and the size of the investment in question. To purchase some new reporting forms is one thing; to change a hospital's entire information system is quite another. In order to remain competitive, new capital investments are often required. But if resources are currently tied up in nonconvertible assets, the end result is that organizations tend to become trapped in their own wealth.

Accumulations of Official Constraints on Behavior

Health institutions or the individuals who work within them often find it difficult to change because statutes, regulations, and internal policies form explicit sources of constraint. It is even possible that traditional approaches to quality assurance, in which explicit criteria for assessment are established, will themselves become barriers to change. Such constraints often serve positive functions, in that they reduce the injustice caused by inconsistent applications of general rules. Thus we see the creation of formal policies, departmental rules, operating manuals, and detailed specifications clearly defining organizational behavior.

Another source of official constraints on behavior results from the "knowledge explosion" and our subsequent reliance upon health care specialists of various types and levels of training. Each collection of specialists becomes the custodian of its part of the health institution, generating still more sets of specifications that govern the action of its members.

Unofficial and Unplanned Constraints on Behavior

The costs are often substantial to health institutions attempting to implement changes that generate internal opposition. The informal organizations within health institutions wield significant power, particularly when comprised of high-status health professionals, i.e., physicians. These informal organizations can thwart change by a variety of subtle, though effective, actions. It is quite possible, for example, that the implementation of PSRO programs may have been hampered at the institutional level through a general, though informal, withholding of support by members of the hospital medical staffs.

Interorganizational Agreements

Agreements between organizations obviously place limitations on their members. Indeed, change may be more successfully prevented by interorganizational understandings than by internal obstacles. Labor contracts constitute a classic example. But others, of increasing importance to the health care field, are also important; they include sharing arrangements, mergers, and joint medical staffs. Quality assurance programs should reflect the interdependent aspects of system design if they are to avoid unnecessary entanglements at the interorganizational level.

Certainly these are formidable barriers to change, elements of which are found in most large-scale health institutions. Even if only some of these barriers are present, the impediments to innovative quality assurance may be significant. Since the effectiveness of quality assurance can only be measured by its impact, it would seem that an emphasis on the technical aspects of measurement and assessment is misplaced, especially if needed change is not produced.

Little is known, however, about how to bring about needed change in health institutions. This problem is quite obviously not new, though it is becoming more and more troublesome as health institutions respond to an increasing array of external threats. These include the pressures of malpractice suits, a growing structure of state and federal regulations, and the evolving requirements of the JCAH. Future research in quality assurance should, therefore, address at least the following five key topics: (1) the organizational determinants of clinical performance; (2) specific barriers to change, particularly as they may restrict change on the part of health professionals; (3) strategies for implementing change in health institutions with emphasis on health professionals; (4) determinants of quality assurance program design and function, with emphasis on the response of hospitals to the new JCAH standard on quality assurance; and (5) the relationship between the structure and function of quality assurance programs and clinical performance.

Continued research on the technical aspects of quality assurance should flow from a demonstrated need for such research, based upon evidence that without it, improvements in quality cannot otherwise be achieved. Such evidence, though rarely documented, unfortunately is generally assumed to exist. In sum, if the important barriers to quality assurance are to be overcome, research attention should shift away from the technical considerations of data acquisition and analysis and toward the organizational and behavioral aspects of bringing about needed change.

REFERENCES

1. Codman, E.A. *A Study in Hospital Efficiency: The First Five Years*. Boston: Thomas Todd Co., 1916.
2. Donabedian, A. *The Definition of Quality and Approaches to its Assessment*. Ann Arbor, Health Administration Press, 1980.
3. Luke, R. and R. Modrow. An Accountability Framework for the Measurement of Quality. In E.J. Hinman (ed.), *Advanced Medical Systems: Health Decisions Systems*. Chicago: Year Book Medical Publishers, 1980.
4. Donabedian, A. Evaluating the quality of medical care. *Milbank Memorial Fund Quarterly* 44 (Part 2): 166, July 1966.
5. Brook, R.H. Quality of care assessment: Choosing a method for peer review. *New England Journal of Medicine* 288:1323, June 1973.
6. McAuliff, W.E. Studies of process-outcome correlations in medical care evaluations—A critique. *Medical Care* 16:907, November 1978.
7. McAuliff, W.E. Measuring the quality of medical care: Process versus outcome. *Milbank Memorial Fund Quarterly* 57:118, Winter 1979.
8. Brown, C.R. and S.H.M. Uhl. Mandatory continuing education: Sense or nonsense? *Journal of the American Medical Association* 213:1660, 1970.
9. Kessner, D.M., C.E. Kalk, and J. Singer. Assessing health quality—The case for tracers. *New England Journal of Medicine* 288:189, 1973.
10. Williamson, J.W. *Assessing and Improving Health Care Outcomes*. Cambridge, MA: Ballinger Publishing Co., 1978.
11. Lowe, J.A. PASport. *Quality Review Bulletin* 3:20, August 1977.
12. Given, B., C.W. Given, and L.E. Simons. Relationships of processes of care to patient outcomes. *Nursing Research* 28:85, March-April 1979.
13. Lyons, T.F. and B.C. Payne. Interdiagnosis relationships of physician performance measures. *Medical Care* 12:369, 1974.
14. Rhee, S., T.F. Lyons, and B.C. Payne. Interrelationships of physician performance—Technical quality and utilization and implications for quality and utilization controls. *Medical Care* 16:496, 1978.
15. Anderson, O.W. and M. Shields. Quality measurement and control in physician decision making: State of the art. *Health Services Research* 17:125-155, 1982.
16. Health Services Administration, Office of Planning, Evaluation, and Legislation (OPEL). *PSRO: An Initial Evaluation of the Professional Standards Review Organization*. Vol. 1, February 1978.

17. Ginsburg, P.B. and D.M. Karetz. *The Effect of PSROs on Health Care Costs: Current Findings and Future Evaluations.* The Congress of the United States, Congressional Budget Office, June 1979.

18. New Quality Assurance Standard Approved. *Perspectives on Accreditation* (3):1, May-June 1979.

19. Weisbord, M. Why organization development hasn't worked (so far) in medical centers. *Health Care Management Review* 18:17, Spring 1976.

20. Golembiewski, R.T. and A. Keipper. Marta: Toward an effective, open giant. *Public Administration Review* 36:46, January-February 1976.

21. Beckhard, R. ABS in health care systems. *Journal of Applied Behavioral Science* 10:93, 1974.

22. Schmuck, R.A. and M. Miles. *Organization Development in Schools.* Palo Alto, CA: National Press Books, 1971.

23. Boss, R.W. It doesn't matter if you win or lose, unless you're losing: Organizational change in a law enforcement agency. *Journal of Applied Behavioral Science* 15:98, 1979.

24. Eddy, W.B. and T. Murphy. Applying Behavioral Science to Urban Management. In C.H. Levine (ed.), *Managing Human Resources.* Beverly Hills, CA: West Publishing Co., 1976.

25. Freedman, A.M. Organization Development in a State Mental Health Setting. In J.J. Partin (ed.), *Current Perspectives in Organization Development.* Reading, MA: Addison-Wesley, 1973.

26. Manley, R. and C.W. McNichols. OD at a major government research laboratory. *Public Personnel Management* 6:51, 1977.

27. Beckhard, R. and D.G. Lake. Short- and Long-Range Effects of a Team Development Effort. In W. French, C. Bell, and R. Zawacki (eds.), *Organization Development: Theory, Practice and Research,* pp. 458-469. Dallas, TX: Business Publications, Inc., 1978.

28. Dowling, W.F. The Corning approach to organization development. *Organization Dynamics* 3:16, Spring 1975.

29. Beckhard, R. The confrontation meeting. *Harvard Business Review* 45:149, 1967.

30. Varney, G.H. and R.J. Hunady. Energizing commitment to change in a team building intervention: A FIRO-B approach. *Group and Organization Studies* 3:435, 1978.

31. Harvey, J.B. and C.R. Boettger. Improving communication within a managerial workgroup. *Journal of Applied Behavioral Science* 7:164, 1971.

32. Kaufman, H. *Limits of Organizational Change,* pp. 1-50. Birmingham, AL: University of Alabama Press, 1971.

33. Hetherington, R. Quality assurance and organizational effectiveness in hospitals. *Health Services Research* 17:185-201, 1982.

34. Freidson, E. *Profession of Medicine: A Study of the Sociology of Applied Knowledge.* New York: Dodd, Mead, 1973.

10. Quality Assurance—A Strategy for Planned Change

RACHELLE KAYE

Quality assurance in medical care involves three processes: (1) monitoring, (2) assessment, and (3) improvement or change. Of the three, the most critical and least effectively implemented is the change process. This chapter thus focuses on change and is predicated on the thesis that quality assurance is a change process and thus involves the selection of change strategies that are consistent in their structure and operation with the basic principles of change theory. The theories and applications of change will be explored for the purpose of providing those who are concerned with quality assurance with a framework of knowledge that has practical implications for the design and operation of quality assurance programs.

CHANGE IN HUMAN BEHAVIOR

There are essentially three major bodies of knowledge that address change in human behavior: (1) psychotherapy and attitude change, (2) organizational development, and (3) diffusion of innovation. All address Lewin's three stages of the change process: (1) unfreezing, (2) changing, and (3) refreezing. As described by Edgar Schein, unfreezing involves the upsetting of the existing status quo:

> Any change in behavior or attitudes . . . tends to be emotionally resisted because even the possibility of change implies that previous behavior and attitudes were somehow wrong or inadequate, a conclusion which the change target would be motivated to reject. If change is to occur, therefore, it must be preceded by an alteration of the present stable equilibrium which supports the present behavior and attitudes.[1]

157

Changing is the "process of seeking out, processing and the utilization of information for the purpose of achieving new perceptions, attitudes and behaviors." And refreezing is "the process of integrating new responses into the ongoing personality and into key emotional relationships, (leading) ultimately to changes which may be considered stable."[1]

In quality assurance the process of explicating group values, achieving group consensus on a set of criteria and standards for patient care, and identifying discrepancies between values and behaviors is, in effect, the process of unfreezing. Feedback of a discrepancy to individual practitioners is the first step in the change process. Any other actions following the feedback, such as acknowledgement by the involved practitioners that the discrepancy constitutes a problem in behavior that should be changed, or a change in policies and procedures for the health care facility staff are also part of the change process. Reassessment results that indicate that change has occurred and persisted over time are indicative of the refreezing process. These three concepts thus provide the focus for discussing the three bodies of change literature mentioned above.

PSYCHOTHERAPY AND ATTITUDE CHANGE

Psychotherapeutic and *psychoanalytic* theories tend to address all three stages of change, although the focus tends to be on the intervention of the therapist or analyst and the effects of therapy on the patient. Wheelis, for example, describes three concepts that are similar to the stages of unfreezing, changing, and refreezing. These are (1) conflict and suffering, awareness; (2) insight and action; and (3) sustained action.

Conflict and suffering "all lead us to look again at ourselves, to look more carefully, in great detail to find what we have missed, to understand a mystery; and all this extends awareness." Awareness thus leads to insight, which Wheelis suggests "is instrumental to change; often an essential part of the process, but does not directly change it."[2] Therefore, insight must be followed by action. According to Wheelis, personality change follows change in behavior. "Since we are what we do, if we want to change what we are, we must begin by changing what we do, we must undertake a new mode of action."[2] Finally, the new mode of action must become a part of our personality. "Change will occur only if such action is maintained over a long period of time."[2]

Urban and Ford have described the change process in psychotherapeutic terms. They do this by utilizing Dewey's five phases of reflective thinking. A *problem identification* phase is viewed as the first in "a succession of very critical steps in the psychotherapeutic process," which entails a particularization of the concrete behaviors that are considered to be at fault, or the behaviors that are not taking place.[3] This phase includes the definition and specification of a difficulty. Recognition of a difficulty, in this case, may be a tension state, a condition of frustration, or a lack of drive satisfaction and may motivate an individual to enter into the psychotherapeutic process.[3] *Analysis* of the *problem,* the second phase, involves the identification of deficiencies in organization or individual behaviors (that is, "behavioral dysfunctions"). (Many general categories of dysfunction have been identified. For example, Smith specified ten different models of human behavior, ranging from the Pavlovian model to the sociogenic model.[4])

The third phase involved *objectives* and *therapy,* which begins with a conception of developmental or therapeutic alternatives.[3] Which specific therapeutic strategy is to be implemented, of course, is contingent upon the form of behavior that is to be changed.[3] Nevertheless, five general modes of intervention for effecting change can be identified: (1) intervention into the physical structures upon which behavior depends (e.g., surgical units); (2) intervention into the ongoing function of the behavioral organizations themselves (for example, electrochemical interventions); (3) verbal interventions; (4) tactics that seek to operate upon the patterns of overt action that a person emits; and (5) modification or control of the situational circumstances that surround the person and that, in turn, govern the occurrence of his or her behavior.[3]

Implementation of the *problem solution* is the fourth phase and is equated with therapy itself. The fifth phase is *evaluation* or the monitoring of performance and comparing performance against a standard. This process leads to corrective or terminating actions.[3]

The first two phases, problem recognition and analysis of the problem, are analogous to Schein's unfreezing stage; selection of goals and the therapy itself are the changing phase; and the evaluation stage is where the refreezing occurs.

The above concepts are relevant to the quality assurance process in that the fundamental change that must occur is likely to be a response to feedback of a discrepancy between values and behavior. Recognition of such a discrepancy should also create a tension state. Particularization of the concrete behaviors considered to be at fault is thus an inherent part of the change process, which should lead health care providers to the conclusion that given variations from a standard are unjustified. This requires an identification of whether the practitioner failed to perform a specific procedure or failed to document his/her activity in the patient record. Feedback is the major step in the intervention phase and is analogous to Urban and Ford's "verbal interventions." This may be reinforced by the fifth mode of intervention, that is, modification or control of the circumstances that surround a person and that, in turn, govern his behavior. In the medical care setting the latter might involve a change in hospital procedures or structures that govern or at least influence a practitioner's behavior. Finally, the evaluation phase is the remeasurement of current practitioner performance and comparison of that performance against a standard.

Closely related to psychotherapy are the theories and research on *attitude change.* Although they will not be developed in any detail here, it is important to note that there are a number of theoretical perspectives that fall under this heading, including, for example: affective-cognitive coexisting theory,[5] attitude change,[4,6-9] structural change,[10-12] congruity theory,[13] balance theory,[14-21] dissonance theory,[22-24] attribution theory,[22,25-27] assimilation-contrary theory,[28] and inoculation theory.[29] Such theories as these and their supporting research address the important questions of how and why attitude change occurs.

Perhaps the most comprehensive of the attitude theories is Rokeach's theory of cognitive inconsistency, which is both a summation of most of the other theories of human behavior change and an alternative to them. Rokeach's basic hypothesis is that self-dissatisfaction is a fundamental determinant of change. The self-conception of an individual is the focal area of concern; and an awareness of the contradiction between an attitude, value, or behavior and a self-conception is that which produces a state of dissatisfaction. Cognitive and behavioral change can occur most easily when the state of self-dissatisfaction is highly specific, which occurs when the individual is able to identify the values that are inconsistent with his or her self-conceptions.[30]

In the case of quality assurance, we assume that the behavior of an individual practitioner results from a given attitude or set of cognitions. When feedback to a health care practitioner of an inconsistency between behavior and a value occurs, it is important to be sure that the standards used represent "good medical or nursing practice" as would be provided by a "good" or competent health care practitioner. By so doing, the standard is tied closely to the practitioner's professional self-concept. The purpose of feedback of a discrepancy is thus to create self-dissatisfaction on the part of the practitioner. The assumption is that self-dissatisfaction is a fundamental determinant of change.

All of the attitude theorists focus on an induced or existing inconsistency between attitudes and behaviors, cognitions, attitudes of significant others, values, or self-conceptions. This is the mechanism for Schein's "alteration of the present stable equilibrium," which occurs in the "unfreezing" stage and which motivates individuals to change some aspect of their understanding, their perceptions, their attitudes, or their personalities to achieve a new equilibrium. Wheelis calls this incongruity conflict and suffering; and psychotherapists talk of tension states and frustration. Fundamentally, all of these theories are consistent with one another. Change occurs when things are out of balance and uncomfortable. Change will occur in the direction of reachieving the most comfortable balance.

ORGANIZATIONAL DEVELOPMENT

The concept that change occurs due to a perceived imbalance and occurs in the direction of reachieving balance also appears in the organizational development literature. Again, Schein's concepts of unfreezing, changing, and refreezing are a part of this literature. The basic thrust of the organizational literature, however, is not internal motivations of individuals; but, rather, it is the facilitation of planned change within human organizations by using various strategies. This makes this literature particularly relevant to quality assurance since a substantial proportion of medical care is delivered in an organizational setting, such as a hospital. And, it is in the organizational setting that formal quality assurance programs are generally developed.

Assessing the quality of care is frequently the responsibility of subgroups within an institution (for example, the medical staff, nursing staff). Thus to focus on subgroups is a strategy that can be used to create awareness of inconsistencies between values and behaviors on the part of the individuals within a group. But, in many cases, the problem is a group problem, that is, the discrepancy is consistent for an entire subgroup or for the organization as a whole. When such is the case, concern is focused on the facilitation of change at an organizational level.

Walton describes two strategies of organizational change: (1) a *power strategy*, in which a basis of negotiation is established and probable outcomes are improved by virtue of one group increasing its power over another, and (2) an *attitude change strategy*, which involves increasing the level of attraction and trust between two groups—minimizing perceived differences between goals and between group members' characteristics.[31] Of the two, the power strategy is the least likely to be used in health care settings, given the general ability of professional groups to resist the use of power exerted by individuals either within or without their professional subgroups.

Bennis conceives of what is called planned change as a situation where a change agent is brought in to "help" a client system that perceives the need for change. He also expands the list of change strategies to include indoctrination change, coercive change, technocratic change, interactional change, socialization change, emulative change, and natural change.[32] Coercive change, for example, is change that occurs through mutual and deliberate goal setting but under unilateral power (a category similar to Walton's power strategy), while natural change is, in a sense, accidental. Quality assurance methodologies may be viewed as structured strategies for planned change. That is, mutually established goals, based on criteria and standards, are established to represent efficiency and effectiveness expectations. An identified discrepancy or problem is thus resolved by applying "valid" knowledge to the problem.

Other theorists emphasize the "how to" of change.[33-35] Greiner, for example, describes a series of approaches to change in organizations, including: the decree approach, the replacement approach, the structural approach, the group decision approach, the data discussion approach, the group problem solving approach, and the T-group approach.[36] Of these approaches, three appear most commonly in quality assurance activities in health institutions: the group decision, data discussion, and problem solving. The group decision approach involves participation by group members in alternatives specified by them, while the data discussion approach involves the presentation and feedback of relevant data to the client system by a change catalyst or a change agent within the organization. The group problem-solving approach elicits change through problem identification and problem solving. Thus, in hospital quality assurance programs we see staff meetings in which results are simply fed back orally by an individual to a group; assessment results are presented and followed by problem identification and analysis, leading to decisions to change policies or procedures.

Still others focus on the factors that increase or decrease resistance to change within organizations. As described by Huse, factors increasing resistance to change include the perception that change is threatening or that change is imposed by others. He notes that the "magnitude of opposition to change will be a direct reflection on the magnitude of change."[37] Factors that decrease resistance to change include perception of personal benefit to be gained, the prestige of the leader, a shared perception in a group of the need for change and participation by the affected group(s) in the plan for change.[37] Unfortunately, such factors as these are not always taken into account by those responsible for operating quality assurance programs, a problem that must be corrected if quality assurance activities are to have any chance of being effective.

The difference between the psychotherapeutic and attitude concepts and the organization approach is thus not so much a difference in theory about how change occurs as it is a matter of perspective. Psychotherapists and attitude change theorists are concerned with the dynamics of change at the individual or personal level. Organizational theorists are concerned with the dynamics of change in groups of individuals. The structure is the same: a stable equilibrium is altered, the process of change is initiated, and the desired outcome is a new equilibrium. The difference is one of level and strategy.

DIFFUSION OF INNOVATION RESEARCH

Diffusion of innovation research shares the same general theoretical base as the other perspectives already discussed. Diffusion of innovation is probably most similar to the concept of planned change in that innovations are introduced into a social system and the process of change is viewed as a process of adopting the innovation. While diffusion of innovation theory focuses on individual change, it is also concerned with the characteristics of social systems that are more or less amenable to change. Further, it is the introduction of the innovation itself that is the source of the altered equilibrium, the conflict, or the dissonance between values and behaviors.

Feedback of a discrepancy between medical practice and standards of care often involves the introduction of an idea, a procedure, or an approach that is "new" to a practitioner group. Likewise, the introduction of quality assurance activities or new approaches to quality control is innovative. Hence, the diffusion of innovation perspective is relevant to quality assurance.

Rogers and Shoemaker postulate that modern social systems are more oriented and more open to change than are traditional social systems. By the same token, certain individuals are more open to change than others. Diffusion research categorizes individuals in terms of their response to an innovation. For example, they may be classified as innovators, early adopters, early majority, late majority, and laggards. Early adopters are those who tend to be more educated, less dogmatic, more favorably inclined toward change, and more cosmopolitan, have more social participation, and are more likely to belong to social systems with modern rather than traditional norms.[38] Health care practitioners are often considered to possess the qualities ascribed to early adopters and thus should, at least theoretically, be more open to change than might other categories of workers. Whether or not this is true, of course, remains to be demonstrated.

It has been pointed out that the rate of adoption of an innovation is dependent not only on the characteristics of the individuals and the social systems to which they belong but also on the characteristics of the innovation itself. Examples of such characteristics include: relative advantage of an innovation, its compatibility with existing norms, its complexity, its trialability, and its observability.[38] The concept that the compatibility of an innovation with existing norms or values increases its acceptability is consistent with theories of change described in the attitude change and psychotherapeutic literature. It is also pertinent to quality assurance since the desired change is in the direction of greater consistency between behavior and existing norms or values.

The innovation decision process, postulated in 1955 by the North Central Rural Sociology Subcommittee for the Study of Diffusion of Farm Practices, involves five basic steps: (1) awareness, (2) interest, (3) evaluation, (4) trial, and (5) adoption.[39] As suggested by this list, although there are many ways to conceptualize the steps included in the introduction of an innovation, most parallel Schein's three phases of change. For example, of four steps described by Rogers and Shoemaker—knowledge, persuasion, decision, and confirmation[38]—the first two can be considered to be part of the unfreezing process, the third as changing, and the last as the beginning of the refreezing process. These are also very clearly present in most quality assurance methodologies. Knowledge occurs through the initial assessment process. Feedback is a method of persuasion, and decision occurs following the feedback process. The occurrence of confirmation or adoption is measured by reassessing post-feedback behavior.

THE ROLE OF COMMUNICATION IN CHANGE

Just as the improvement or change component of the quality assurance process has often been overlooked, the more specific role of communication in the change

164 ORGANIZATION AND CHANGE IN HEALTH CARE QUALITY ASSURANCE

process itself has been much neglected. We generally assume that if we tell someone that change is needed, change will occur. Because talking and writing are so embedded in the daily routine of everything we do, we rarely examine how we talk or write and the role our communicative acts play in achieving our goals.

The role of communication in change is both directly and indirectly addressed in the three major bodies of literature discussed above. In the psychotherapeutic literature, the communication focus is on the acts of communication between therapist and client. In discussing alternative modes of therapy, Urban and Ford talk about the many techniques that rely on verbal intervention to effect changes in attitudes, perceptions, thoughts, or feelings. These techniques, they suggest, rest upon a set of assumptions, that is, a person's behavior is governed by his or her cognitive functions and is modified by the emotional patterns associated with them.[3] Changes in the way in which a person perceives, thinks, remembers, evaluates, judges, and recalls in effect construe and symbolize events experienced by an individual. Thus, an individual can be affected or changed if he or she can be led to verbalize such perceptions or thoughts. Once they become explicit, they become subject to modification by a therapist. Since it is assumed that a person's actions are guided by such subjective factors, it is anticipated that if the person can be brought to think, and hence, to feel differently, he or she will necessarily come to act differently as well. This is the assumption underlying the feedback approach to change. The purpose of the feedback is to bring the individual to modify his or her thinking and, perhaps, his or her feelings so that change is effected.

As an example of the research in which the role of communication in effecting change is examined, Scott found that students who were reinforced by group approval for expressing an attitude opposite their own showed a change in the direction of the expressed attitude.[40] This supports the notion that group feedback would facilitate changes in the attitudes and behaviors of group members. A number of studies[41-43] have investigated the effect of verbal reinforcement on attitude formation and change. Verbal reinforcement consisting of feedback comments such as "good," "mm'hmm," for example, were successful in providing favorable (although not unfavorable) opinion responses. The implication of these findings for quality assurance is that feedback strategies may be needed that encourage the targets of change to express their opinions about discrepancies between behaviors and values and positively reinforce those expressions that are consistent with desired attitudes.

With regard to the role of positive reinforcement in feedback, McGuire demonstrated that communication that presents desirable information prior to the presentation of undesirable information is more persuasive than communication that presents information in the reverse order. The placement of desirable information first tends to reinforce or condition attention and comprehension responses, thus enhancing the likelihood that they continue even when communication emphasizes less desirable information.[44]

Many of the studies on the role of communication in change focus on the effects of group pressure on individual change. For example, Asch conducted an experiment in which a subject was exposed to two contradictory and irreconcilable forces: (1) the evidence of his own experience as a clear perceptual fact and (2) the unanimous evidence of a group of equals. Under these conditions, Asch found a marked movement toward the majority.[45] Dittes and Kelley investigated the conformity of group members and found that perceived acceptance by the group was related to group conformity.[46]

In a related study, Deutsch and Gerard examined the effects of normative and informational social influences on individual judgments. They found that normative influence on individual judgments was greater among individuals forming a group than among those who do not compose a group.[47] Applied to quality assurance programs, these findings suggest the need to examine group structures when designing feedback mechanisms and to give priority to group over individual feedback.

The degree to which groups influence individual change, of course, is modified by many factors. MacBride, for example, found that personal confidence in judgments influenced individual susceptibility to group influence. Most importantly, MacBride found that simulated influence resulted in a significant amount of yielding toward majority opinion.[48] This suggests that in developing feedback strategies for quality assurance, the importance of personal confidence in judgments should be considered. Physicians, for example, tend to exhibit a high degree of confidence in their own or their colleagues' judgments in making patient care decisions. It is also reasonable to infer that they can be expected to require the same confidence in quality assurance decisions themselves. This expectation is also likely to be true of many other health care professional groups as well.

The key role that communication plays in effecting change is emphasized throughout the three bodies of literature reviewed earlier. Rogers and Shoemaker, for example, state emphatically that "communication is essential for social change."[38] In fact, they define diffusion as "the process by which . . . new ideas are communicated to the members of a social system. . . . Change occurs when a new idea's use or rejection has an effect. Social Change is, therefore, an effect of communication."[38] We broaden this to state that any change, deliberately planned and pursued through human dialogue, is an effect of communication.

SUMMARY

We have briefly explored the theory and research on change and have indicated how principles of change relate to quality assurance in health care. It would appear that almost all of the approaches to change support a similar model for change: the creation of a disequilibrium; the process of change, leading to a new equilibrium; and the formation and consolidation of the new equilibrium. In addition, communication is viewed as a means of initiating change as well as a mechanism for directing the change process.

In summary, we suggest a number of principles, from change theory, that have practical implications for the design of quality assurance programs in health institutions:

- Mechanisms for assessing the quality of care are keys to establishing a perception on the part of individuals or groups of practitioners of discrepancies between their professional practice and accepted standards of care.
- People change because they are uncomfortable with an existing situation and their role in it. Therefore, part of the process of quality assurance involves the heightening of dissonance and discomfort, accompanied by some clue as to how the dissonance can be reduced.
- Change involves action and the formation of new behavioral patterns. Often this requires a modification of the environment in which individuals carry out their professional behaviors.
- The prestige of the individual who communicates the need for change is of some importance. Respect for the communicator may be a key variable in achieving desired results.
- Change must often occur by stages. Since people tend to change if the advocated change is not too discrepant from their present position and beliefs, efforts should be made to emphasize the consistency between the desired change and the present positions and beliefs of the group one is trying to change.
- Self-dissatisfaction is a fundamental determinant of change. Professional self-dissatisfaction should be used as a powerful motivator in quality assurance.
- Advocated change should be presented in a supportive fashion. Perceived threat should be avoided as much as possible.
- Advocated change needs to be presented so that the participants perceive some personal or professional benefit to them.
- The extent to which an individual or a group participates in the identification of the need for change, as well as the plan for change, will substantially impact the extent to which the change takes place.
- The proposed change must be as compatible as possible with the value system of the participants.
- Change efforts should focus on issues that are important. More trivial issues will generally follow but should not be strongly emphasized.
- Positive reinforcement, both verbal and otherwise, is important in effecting change.

- Whenever possible, desirable information should be presented in the review of individual or group performance before undesirable information is discussed.
- Peer pressure is an important part of the review process. However, the concept of peer pressure in the simplistic sense has probably been overplayed. There are many forms of resistance to peer pressure. Nonetheless, it is valuable and must be an inherent part of the process.
- Assessment data should be used primarily to open the channels of communication rather than as ends in themselves.

More encompassing and perhaps more critical than the above principles is the change in perspective that emerges from this overview. Quality assurance has been viewed in the past primarily as a method for identifying and solving problems. In reality, however, quality assurance should be viewed as an approach to planned change. It enables professionals and decision makers at all levels to assess the weaknesses and strengths of their institutions, establish clear and compelling goals, and move systematically in the attainment of those goals. To do this, however, is a major challenge in that it involves one of the more difficult of organizational tasks—the bringing about of human and organizational change.

REFERENCES

1. Schein E: The mechanisms of change, in Bennis WG, Benne KD, Chin R (eds): *The Planning of Change*. New York, Holt, Rinehart & Winston Inc, 1969, p 99.
2. Wheelis A: *How People Change*. New York, Harper & Row Publishers Inc, 1973, p 116.
3. Urban H, Ford D: Some historical and conceptual perspectives, in Bergin AE, Garfield SL (eds): *The Handbook of Psychotherapy and Behavior Change, An Empirical Analysis*. New York, John Wiley & Sons Inc, 1971, p 10.
4. Smith M: Personal values as determinants of political attitude. *J Psychol* 1949; 28:477-486.
5. Rosenberg M, Abelson R: An analysis of cognitive balancing, in Hovland C, Rosenberg M (eds): *Attitude Organization and Change*. New Haven, Yale University Press, 1960, pp 112-163.
6. Rosenberg M: Cognitive structure and attitudinal affect. *J Abnorm Soc Psychol* 1956; 53:367-372.
7. Woodruff H, DiVesta F: The relationship between values, concepts and attitudes. *Educ Psychol Measure* 1948; 8:645-660.
8. Cartwright D: Some principles of mass persuasion. *Hum Relations* 1949;2:253-267.
9. Fishbein M: An investigation of the relationships between beliefs about an object and the attitude toward that object. *Hum Relations* 1963; 16:233-239.
10. Carlson E: Attitude change through modification of attitude structure. *J Abnorm Soc Psychol* 1956; 52:256-261.
11. DiVesta F, Merwin J: The effects of need-oriented communications on attitude change. *J Abnorm Soc Psychol* 1960; 60:80-85.
12. Rosenberg M: An analysis of affective-cognitive consistency, in Hovland C, Rosenberg M (eds): *Attitude Organization and Change*. New Haven, Conn, Yale University Press, 1960, pp 15-64.

13. Osgood CE, Tannenbaum PH: The principle of congruity in the prediction of attitude change. *Psychol Rev* 1955; 62:42-55.

14. Heider F: *The Psychology of Interpersonal Relations*. New York, John Wiley & Sons, 1958.

15. Newcomb TM: Individual systems of orientation, in Koch S III (ed): *Psychology: A Study of a Science*. New York: McGraw-Hill Book Co, 1959.

16. Jordan N: Behavioral forces that are a function of attitudes and of cognitive organization. *Human Relations* 1953; 6:273-287.

17. Morisette J: An experimental study of the theory of structural balance. *Human Relations* 1958; 11:239-254.

18. Price K, Harburg E, and Newcomb T: Psychological balance in situations of negative interpersonal attitudes. *J Pers Soc Psychol* 1966; 3:265-270.

19. Burdick H, Barnes A: A test of "strain toward symmetry" theories. *J Abnorm Soc Psychol* 1958; 57:367-370.

20. Sampson E, Insko C: Cognitive consistency and performance in the autokinetic situation. *J Abnorm Soc Psychol* 1964; 68:184-192.

21. McGuire W: A syllogistic analysis of cognitive relationships, in Hovland C, Rosenberg M (eds): *Attitude Organization and Change*. New Haven, Conn, Yale University Press, 1960, pp 65-111.

22. Festinger L: *A Theory of Cognitive Dissonance*. Stanford, Calif, Stanford University Press, 1957.

23. Brehm J, Cohen A: *Explorations in Cognitive Dissonance*. New York, John Wiley & Sons, 1962.

24. Kiesler CA: *The Psychology of Commitment*. New York, Academic Press, 1971.

25. Jones EE, Davis KE: From acts to dispositions, in Berkowitz L (ed): *Advances in Experimental Social Psychology*. New York, Academic Press, 1965.

26. Bem DJ: Self perception: An alternative interpretation of cognitive dissonance phenomena. *Psychol Rev* 1967; 74:183-200.

27. Kelley HH: Attribution theory in social psychology, in Levine D (ed): *Nebraska Symposium on Motivation*. Lincoln, University of Nebraska Press, 1967.

28. Sherif M, Hovland C: *Social Judgement*. New Haven, Conn, Yale University Press, 1961.

29. McGuire W: Inducing resistance to persuasion, in Berkowitz L (ed): *Advances in Experimental Psychology*. New York, Academic Press, 1964, pp 191-229.

30. Rokeach M: *The Nature of Human Values*. New York, Collier Books, 1973, p 222.

31. Walton R: Two strategies of social change and their dilemmas, in Bennis WG, Benne KD, Chin R (eds): *The Planning of Change*. New York, Holt, Rinehart & Winston Inc, 1969, p 168.

32. Bennis WG: *Changing Organizations*. New York, McGraw-Hill Book Co, 1966.

33. Beckhard R, Harris RT: *Organization Transition: Managing Complex Change*. Reading, Mass, Addison-Wesley Publishing Co Inc, 1977.

34. Drucker P: *Managing in Turbulent Times*. New York, Harper & Row Publishers Inc, 1980.

35. Guest RH, Hersey P, Blanchard K: *Organizational Change Through Effective Leadership*. Englewood Cliffs, NJ: Prentice-Hall Inc, 1977.

36. Greiner LE: *Organizational Change and Development*, dissertation. Harvard University, Cambridge, Mass, 1965.

37. Huse EF: *Organizational Development and Change*. St. Paul, Minn, West Publishing Co, 1975, p 111.

38. Rogers EM, Shoemaker FF: *Communication of Innovations: A Cross-Cultural Approach*. New York, Free Press, 1971, p 33.

39. North Central Regional Rural Sociology Committee. Subcommittee for the Study of Diffusion of Farm Practices. *How Farm People Accept New Ideas.* Ames, Iowa, Agricultural Extension Services, Iowa State College, 1955.

40. Scott W: Attitude change through reward of verbal behavior. *J Abnorm Soc Psychol* 1957; 55:72-75.

41. Hildum D, Brown R: Verbal reinforcement and interview bias. *J Abnorm Soc Psychol* 1956; 53:108-111.

42. Ekman P: *A Comparison of Verbal and Nonverbal Behaviors as Reinforcing Stimuli of Opinion Responses,* dissertation. Adelphi College, Garden City, NY, 1958.

43. Krasner L, Knowles J, Ullman L: Effects of verbal conditioning of attitudes on subsequent motor performance. *J Pers Soc Psychol* 1965; 1:407-412.

44. McGuire W: Order of presentation as a factor in "conditioning" persuasiveness, in Hovland C, Janis IL, Kelley HH (eds): *The Order of Presentation in Persuasion.* New Haven, Conn, Yale University Press, 1957, pp 94-114.

45. Asch SE: Studies of independence and conformity in small group research. in McGrath J, Altman I (eds): *Small Group Research.* New York, Holt, Rinehart & Winston Inc, 1966, pp 198-200.

46. Dittes FE, Kelley HH (eds): Effects on different conditions of acceptance upon conformity to group norms. *J Abnorm Soc Psychol* 1956; 53:100-107.

47. Deutsch M, Gerard HB: Study of normative and social influence upon individual judgment. *J Abnorm Soc Psychol* 1955; 51:629-636.

48. MacBride PD: Studies in conformity and yielding, in McGrath J, Altman I (eds): *Small Group Research.* New York, Holt, Rinehart & Winston Inc, 1966, pp 629-636.

11. Research Innovations in Nursing: Implications for Quality Assurance Programs*

JOYCE CRANE and JOANNE HORSLEY

Quality assurance and research utilization are two forces that currently dominate the field of nursing as we strive to document the contributions nursing makes to health care in the United States. These forces are inextricably linked at a conceptual level but seldom merged at an operational level. This reading will attempt to demonstrate how scientific nursing knowledge and the processes involved in using that knowledge in practice can facilitate and enhance quality assurance efforts in nursing. Specifically, how research utilization facilitates the definition of criteria and standards, the identification of means of measuring criterion variables, and the development of data recording devices will be discussed. For our purposes, research utilization consisted of the introduction and implementation of specific scientific knowledge and methods in the daily practice of registered nurses employed in in-patient settings.

BACKGROUND

The ideas embodied in this reading were developed during the conduct of a research development project.** The principal goal of the project was to develop and test a research utilization model for nursing. The model was based on the work of Havelock and included both research utilization and planned change concepts.[1] Thirty-five nursing service departments participated in the project, nursing staff teams from 16 sites actually carried out the research utilization processes to be discussed here, while the nursing staff from other sites served as controls and/or participated in another aspect of the project.[2]

*This project was supported by the Division of Nursing, DHEW, Grant #RO NU00542, and conducted under the auspices of the Michigan Nurses Association. The scientific work of the project was conducted at the University of Michigan School of Nursing, Michigan State University.

**Conduct and Utilization of Clinical Nursing Research (CURN Project) R02NU00542 funded by the Division of Nursing and carried out under the auspices of the Michigan Nurses Association.

SCIENTIFIC KNOWLEDGE FOR PRACTICE

Central to the development of scientific nursing practice is the identification of nursing research that is suitable and ready for use in clinical settings. This involves retrieving studies and selecting those that are scientifically sound, safe for use with patient populations, and within the capacity of nursing service departments to implement and evaluate.

Three sets of criteria have been developed for use in evaluating a given area of research and determining its suitability for utilization in practice settings. The first set of criteria addresses the evaluation and integration of conceptually related studies into a research base and screen for replication, scientific merit, and risk to patients. The second set leads to determination of the practice relevance of an identified research base and includes consideration of clinical merit, clinical control, feasibility in relation to implementation, and cost/benefit factors. The final set of criteria relates to an innovation's potential for evaluation in the clinical setting. In applying this set of criteria, consideration is given to the availability of valid and reliable evaluation measures that are practice relevant and available for use by clinicians.[3]

With the use of these carefully identified criteria, research-based practice protocols can be developed. A practice protocol provides a synthesis of the research base and transforms research knowledge into clinically useful knowledge that has clearly defined parameters for practice and yields an intervention with predictable patient outcomes. Its content is directed toward implementation and evaluation of the research-based practice innovation.

The research studies that form the base for each protocol produce knowledge with the following characteristics:

- The independent and dependent variables can be transformed into relatively precise nursing interventions and patient outcomes that can be evaluated in a natural clinical environment.
- A defined patient problem, nursing intervention, and patient outcome are definitively linked together.
- The relationship between the nursing intervention and patient outcome is predictable in its direction if not in absolute magnitude.

These characteristics alone offer some indication of how scientific knowledge can facilitate the operation of a quality assurance program by providing precision in the definition of criteria, valid and reliable means for the measurement of selected criteria, and a definitive and predictable relationship between process and outcome criteria. The processes involved in implementing research-based practice change also facilitate and enhance quality assurance efforts.

THE RESEARCH UTILIZATION PROCESS

Implementation of research-based innovations requires commitment on the part of the nursing service department to develop the *capacity* to base its practice on scientific knowledge. Research utilization is in part an organizational process that requires both organizational commitment and organizational change. The interest and commitment of individual practitioners alone is not sufficient. The change process to be undertaken is one of considerable scope that requires the structuring of mechanisms to carry out functions basic to research utilization and the provision of resources to maintain these functions over time. Specifically, mechanisms and resources must be provided to assure that:

- Patient care problems which need new or more effective solutions are systematically identified.
- Relevant scientific knowledge is identified, assessed, and selected for use in solving patient care problems.
- Scientifically sound practice innovations are adapted from the research base and designed to meet the particular requirements of the service agency.
- The practice innovation is initially introduced on a trial basis, which includes an evaluation of its effectiveness in solving the patient care problems.
- A reasoned decision to adopt, modify, or reject the innovation based in part on data generated during the clinical trial is made.
- Adopted innovations are diffused to other appropriate nursing units.
- The quality of the practice innovation is maintained over time.[2,4]

Although these organizational functions are proposed as being vital for clinical research utilization efforts, they can also contribute to quality assurance efforts. In the next section, each function will be discussed together with its implications for quality assurance programs.

RESEARCH UTILIZATION AND QUALITY ASSURANCE

The first organizational function to be addressed is *systematically identifying patient care problems that need solutions*. Planned change literature supports the notion that if an innovation is to be accepted it must meet a felt need on the part of those who will be affected by the change. Further, the nature of the need should be such that the costs of seeking a solution are considered worth the anticipated benefit. An early task in the research utilization process is to ascertain patient care problems needing solutions and to quantify the extent of these problems through systematic data collection procedures.

Agency staff teams participating in the project used a brief survey question-naire, the Patient Care Problem Identification Guide, to determine the nursing staff's perceptions of existing patient care problems (Exhibit 11-1).[5] In using this questionnaire, respondents were directed toward problems for which there were research-based solutions. When additional data were available, such as audit data, these were used to augment the survey data. As a result of these procedures, team members were able to make data-based decisions regarding unresolved patient care problems and to begin to match these problems with appropriate research-based practice innovations. These activities led to the selection of one or two research-based protocols for further review. A summary of the data regarding the identified patient care problems was fed back to the nursing staff.

The process involved in this particular function is also relevant to quality assurance programs if the programs are viewed as innovations for which there may or may not be a "felt need" in the broad nurse population. To the extent that the

---

Exhibit 11-1 Sample Items from the Patient Care Problem Identification Guide

The patient care problems which follow are those for which research-based solutions have been identified. For each item, check one of the answers in the left hand column. For each item marked "yes," move to the right and place an (X) in the box which best reflects the extent to which you believe it is a problem *on your nursing unit(s)*.

Patient Care Problems on My Unit	Does your unit have patients who have this problem?	Insignificant	Moderate	Relatively Large	Don't Know
		Extent of the Problem			
1. Patients are reluctant to cough and deep breathe and/or engage in post-op exercises	no ( ) yes ( )	( )	( )	( )	( )
2. Patients at high risk of developing skin breakdown	no ( ) yes ( )	( )	( )	( )	( )
3. Patients who receive tube feedings have diarrhea	no ( ) yes ( )	( )	( )	( )	( )

Source: CURN Project. *Using Research to Improve Nursing Practice: A Guide.* New York: Grune & Stratton, Inc., 1982, p. 109-116. Reprinted by permission.

general nurse population lacks understanding of or disagrees with the criteria and/or standards incorporated in a given quality assurance program, quality as defined by the program is as likely to be ignored as it is assured. The processes involved in this research utilization function can be used to determine the extent to which nursing staff agree/disagree or do not understand specific aspects of the program as it develops.

The second function, *identifying, assessing, and selecting relevant research-based knowledge to solve identified patient care problems*, leads to a decision as to what research-based innovation is to be implemented. During this stage of the process, criteria for protocol selection need to be established and considered. The criteria may address such issues as the relative importance of staff feedback regarding need, the relative importance of the extent to which nurses control the conditions necessary to manipulate and measure the patient care variables of interest, and the ability to achieve a reasonable cost/benefit ratio. Using the established criteria as a guide, one or two protocols should be selected for potential implementation. A protocol provides a synthesis of the research base and transforms research knowledge into nursing knowledge that has clearly defined parameters for use in practice. It is important at this point to consider carefully each protocol's potential for adoption in a specific hospital setting. Knowledge of the parameters of the research base as well as of characteristics and resources of the organization is fundamental to the ultimate selection of a protocol.

A Probability for Adoption Assessment Guide was developed to assist in matching an innovation with key organizational variables. The guide has two major sections: (1) factors affecting the ease of implementation and (2) cost/benefit factors (Exhibit 11-2).[5] Scoring of this guide provides an indication of probability for successful adoption of a specific innovation in a specific nursing service department.

The third organizational function focuses on *adapting and designing the nursing practice innovation*. This step in the process is needed in light of the fact that research outcomes are generated under controlled conditions for purposes of providing generalizable knowledge. New knowledge is rarely produced in a form that is immediately transferable into nursing practice activities that are applicable to a particular setting. With few exceptions it is necessary for clinicians to transform the research-based innovation into practice activities that are adapted to meet a hospital's unique needs while, at the same time, maintaining the integrity of the research base. If the parameters of the research base are violated, it can no longer be claimed that the innovation is research based. To accomplish this, it is necessary to thoroughly understand the research base underlying the innovation as well as the characteristics of the particular organizational setting in which the change is to take place.

It is important that those responsible for the research utilization effort read the original research reports comprising the base for a particular practice innovation.

Exhibit 11-2 Probability for Adoption Assessment Guide

Keeping the characteristics of your innovation in mind, answer each question and give the item a score which you record in the right hand column. When you have completed the questionnaire, total the scores and compare the total with the probability scale. This will give you a working estimate of the likelihood that your innovation can be successfully implemented in your hospital.

I. Factors Affecting Ease of Implementation   *Score*

   a. To what extent does this innovation address a relevant nursing practice problem or need in your hospital?

1	2	3	4	5
Little or no concern		Moderate concern		Great concern

   b. To what extent would this innovation fall under the control of nursing in your hospital?

1	2	3	4	5
Nursing would have no control		Control unclear		Nursing would have clear control

II. Cost/Benefit Factors   *Score*

   a. To what extent would personnel require specialized training in order to implement the innovation?

1	2	3	4	5
Extensive training required		Some training required		Little or none required

   b. How costly will it be to start this innovation?

1	2	3	4	5
Requires extra staff, costly equipment		Requires some extra staff, equipment		Requires no extra staff, equipment

Source: CURN Project. Using Research to Improve Nursing Practice: A Guide. New York: Grune & Stratton, Inc., 1982, p. 135-143. Reprinted by permission.

Although the protocol provides a useful synthesis of the research base, it is not intended to substitute for the detail included in the original research report that is needed for implementation and evaluation purposes. Further, it is important for clinicians to be able to read research reports and understand their clinical implications.

A Guide to Reading Research Critically was developed to assist nurses in reading and understanding the facets of research reports relevant to research utilization (Exhibit 11-3).

This organizational function, then, primarily required those responsible for the change to learn as much as was feasible about the research base and about their organization for the purpose of defining, very specifically, the innovative practice and the process supporting its implementation. Both the practice and the process should be written to assist in achieving specificity and to provide focus for planning activities that follow.

The second and third functions should result in the identification of a nursing intervention and patient outcome that are clearly defined and capable of being operationalized in a given nursing department. When this is the case, the intervention and patient outcome should be readily transferable into process and outcome criteria for a quality assurance program.

Exhibit 11-3 Guide to Reading Research Critically

RESEARCH ARTICLE/REPORT

    Title and Author:

    Source:

QUESTIONS TO BE CONSIDERED

1. What was the problem that was studied?

2. In what setting was the research conducted? Be specific and describe in detail. (For example, was it in a laboratory or clinical setting? What type of institution? What type of unit? Was there anything about the setting that makes you think that it is not typical of clinical settings?)

3. In what ways is your practice setting similar or different from the setting in which the research was conducted?

4. What is the independent variable that was studied? (An independent variable is the variable that comes first in time and is assumed to cause the effect that is being studied. It is often a nursing intervention, patient characteristic, or patient behavior that is studied to determine its effect.)

5. Based upon this report, can you ascertain whether or not the researcher has carried out other studies in this area? Does this study expand on prior research?

6. After reading this article, what additional information is needed to evaluate these findings?

Source: CURN Project. Using Research to Improve Nursing Practice: A Guide. New York: Grune & Stratton, Inc., 1982, p. 130-134. Reprinted by permission.

Conducting a clinical trial and evaluation of the innovation comprises the fourth function. Once an innovation has been adapted for use in a particular hospital setting, it should be tested and clinically evaluated on a small scale, preferably on one clinical unit, prior to its large scale adoption on multiple units. Planned change strategies call for a trial prior to adoption of an innovation in order to determine the merits of the new practice and to work out problems that may exist with its initial implementation. If the trial disproves the validity or merit of the new practice, reversibility to the original condition is more readily achieved without disruption to the organization as a whole. Clinical evaluation is an essential component of the research utilization process and provides an opportunity to compare the results (both process and patient outcomes) of the utilization effort with the results of the research on which it is based.

This organizational function requires the completion of two major tasks: (1) planning for the trial and its evaluation and (2) implementing the clinical trial. Planning for a trial requires a number of planned change strategies:

- projecting a time line
- identifying and securing needed resources
- developing materials
- making teaching plans for staff development
- securing sanctions and approvals
- selecting a representative trial unit
- dealing with resistance

Planning for the evaluation component of the trial is equally as complex and includes:

- developing an overall evaluation strategy
- designing forms for collecting evaluation data
- training staff who will participate in data collection
- establishing a plan for achieving inter-rater reliability where needed
- establishing procedures for ensuring consistency in collecting data

In the evaluation process, both outcomes and process data are collected at baseline and postinnovation. Dependent variables from the research base are measured to permit direct comparisons between the research outcomes and the trial outcomes. Adequate numbers of patients should be evaluated to provide confidence in the generalizability of the evaluation data. Further, it is essential that evaluation measurements are made reliably. Training for inter-rater reliability is a necessary activity within the evaluation component.

The complexities in conducting the clinical trial and its evaluation should not be underestimated. At a minimum, several months will be needed to complete this phase of the research utilization process, depending on patient availability and numerous organizational factors, many of which will be unpredictable in advance. During this time, attention is given to handling unexpected problems, monitoring progress, trouble-shooting when needed, and dealing with staff reactions to the change in routine practice. This is one point in the process when resistance can be expected, since many staff members will be involved directly with the innovation for the first time.

This function is facilitative of quality assurance efforts in several ways. First it provides an empirical look at the intervention and in doing so permits an opportunity for "debugging" it before it serves as the basis for process criterion development. Second, it results in the development of data recording devices that may later be used as part of the record for audit purposes. Third, it dictates the development of processes to ensure that data are collected and recorded adequately. Fourth, the occurrence (or lack of occurrence) of staff resistance during the clinical trial may serve as a prediction of staff response to subsequent quality assurance efforts and/or indicate the occurrence of problems that need to be solved if subsequent quality assurance expectations are to be accepted. Finally, it yields a quantitative outcome that can be transformed readily into the process and outcome standards that accompany the criteria. Such empirically based standards have an advantage over normative standards in that the data generated in the clinical trial take into account the aspects of patient care and hence patient outcomes that are unique to each nursing department and are not controlled by nursing practice.

The set of activities relating to the next function center on *using the data generated by the clinical trial in making a decision to adopt, modify, or reject the innovation.* The quality of the decision made regarding adoption or rejection of the innovation is totally dependent on the adequacy *and* accuracy of the evaluation measures carried out during the trial and on their subsequent interpretation. Following the clinical trial, the data must be organized, summarized, and interpreted for decision-making purposes. Simple descriptive statistics should be adequate for the purpose of analyzing the evaluation data.

Patient outcome data, both baseline and postintervention, are reviewed for predicted results and compared with outcome data from the research base. Process data are similarly reviewed; apparent relationships between process and outcome data are noted and interpreted. In instances when divergence occurs between the research base and trial data, careful attention should be given to potential reasons, looking at both process and outcome variables. Such divergence should be considered a serious problem that merits resolution before the full meaning of the evaluation can be determined. In addition to looking at the congruence between research base data and trial data, cost/benefit factors need to be considered in the final decision-making stages.

When the analysis of evaluation data is completed, reports are prepared to be used in the decision-making process. Issues such as to whom the data might be presented (for example, director of nursing, nursing staff, physicians, hospital administrators, hospital board, others); the purpose to be served by the report; and how to display the data to serve the intended purpose must be considered.

The activities related to this organizational function culminate in a decision to adopt the innovation as originally designed, to adopt it with modifications based on the trial experience and made within the limits of the research base, or to reject the innovation. A decision to reject an innovation terminates the research utilization process in relation to the particular innovation in question. It is hoped that the process begins again with a new patient care problem and its related research base. A decision to modify the innovation leads to returning to earlier steps in the process.

If a decision is made to adopt the innovation, it will be necessary to *develop the means to extend (or diffuse) the innovation to other appropriate units*. Patient care units appropriate for diffusion are identified, and staff representatives from these units become involved in making plans for the larger scale implementation of the innovation. Modifications made at this time should be minor and primarily directed at adapting the process to accommodate larger numbers of patients and multiple nursing units. Again, modifications are made within the parameters of the research base. The evaluation component is eliminated in the diffusion process, assuming that the outcomes of the trial may be reasonably generalized to the other units involved. Diffusion involves as much or more planning as the trial, and, in general, the complexity of this function is underestimated. At this stage there is a need to retrace many of the earlier planning steps within the context of implementing the innovation on multiple units and, now, on a permanent (or somewhat less reversible) basis. Resistance, while present earlier and expected in any change effort, is often increased as larger numbers of staff (both nurses and others) are directly and more permanently affected by the practice change. An issue not to be overlooked in the diffusion effort is the need to assist others in understanding that this is a *research-based* innovation and in beginning to distinguish the characteristics of scientifically based practice. This is important in the nursing department's efforts to improve the quality of patient care by expecting nursing staff to value and use research outcomes to guide practice.

The seventh function, and one of the most important, is *developing mechanisms to maintain the innovation over time*. An innovation, no matter how well planned and implemented, will not survive over time without institutionalizing mechanisms for its maintenance. Written procedures for the research-based practice are developed, approved through regular channels, and accepted as standard practice. Plans are made for incorporating the new practice into the staff development program for newly employed nurses. It is recognized that if maintenance of the practice change is to be assured, practitioner accountability for research-based practice is needed. At this point in the process, the relationship between research utilization and quality assurance changes direction, that is, long-term maintenance of the research-based practice is dependent on whether it has been incorporated into the ongoing quality assurance program of the institution.

The seven organizational functions outlined here underlie the research utilization process and are germane to its successful implementation. This research utilization process is intended to recycle and to be used with the introduction of future practice innovations. Recycling begins with problem identification and the subsequent review of another research base and can occur while an earlier innovation is in the process of being implemented and evaluated or diffused.

SUMMARY

Scientific knowledge, when combined with the type of utilization process discussed above, substantially supports and facilitates the operation of a quality assurance program. Bloch has described a scheme that clarifies how research contributes to quality assessment efforts. Our experience with research utilization supports Bloch's ideas. Some of the relationships between quality assurance and research utilization identified in our experiences are enumerated below and in Exhibit 11-4.

1. The research on which the protocols were based clearly establishes process-outcome relationships for each clinical problem area.
2. The relatively objective definitions of independent and dependent variables in the research bases were readily transformed into specific nursing processes and patient outcomes (criterion variables).
3. Instruments to be used in measuring the outcome variables and some of the process variables could be identified in the research bases.
4. The process involved in evaluating the trial of the innovation:

   - resulted in reliable clinical measurement by selected staff members
   - simulated the development of devices on which to record the clinical data of interest in each protocol
   - determined the extent to which both process and outcome variables for a given protocol occurred in the staff and patient population in individual clinical settings.

Although the research utilization program described in this reading was not designed as a quality assurance effort per se, the natural relationships that exist between research utilization and quality assurance made themselves apparent throughout the conduct of the project. We did not force the relationships we have identified, they simply happened as a result of the research utilization process.

Exhibit 11-4 Relationship Between Research Utilization Functions and Quality Assurance Activities

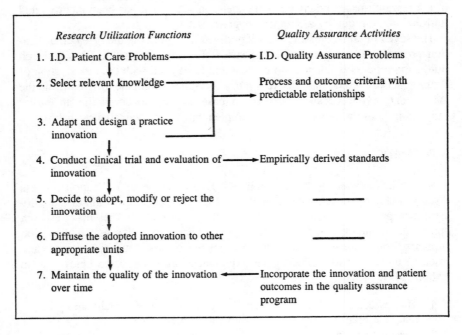

REFERENCES

1. Havelock RG: *Planning for Innovation Through Dissemination and Utilization of Knowledge*. Ann Arbor, Mich, Center for Research on Utilization of Scientific Knowledge, Institute for Social Research, The University of Michigan, 1969, pp 11-16.

2. Horsley J, Crane J, Bingle JD: Research utilization as an organizational process. *J Nurs Adm* 1978; 8(July):4.

3. Haller KB, Reynolds MA, Horsley J: Developing research-based innovation protocols: Process, criteria and issues. *Res Nurs Health* 1979; 2:45-51.

4. Crane J: Promoting Research-Based Practice Innovations. Presented at the American Nurses' Association Bienniel Convention, Houston, Texas, June 11, 1980.

5. CURN Project, Using Research to Improve Nursing Practice: A Guide, Grune & Stratton, New York: 1982.

6. Bloch D: Interrelated issues in evaluation and evaluation research: A researcher's perspective. *Nurs Res* 1980; 29(March-April):69-73.

12. Quality Assurance as a Managerial Innovation: A Research Perspective*

ARNOLD D. KALUZNY

Reprinted with permission from Health Services Research 17(3). Copyright © 1982, 253-268.

Quality assurance (QA) has been termed a major innovation in the delivery of health services within the United States [1]. Unfortunately, the relationship between existing theory and research on innovation, and quality assurance activities as an innovation, remains obscure. In some areas of quality assurance the application of innovation theory and research is extremely insightful and provides a useful research agenda to improve our understanding of how QA programs may be effectively implemented. In other areas, the application can be misleading or irrelevant. This ambiguity is a function of the nature of QA activities as well as the state of much innovation theory and research. Both areas suffer from a great deal of contradictory evidence and ideological fervor that often limit their potential for dealing with critical problems facing the health services field.

The mystique of medical care and the evolving state of management and organizational theory, particularly that branch dealing with innovation, makes imperative a clear definition of terms. For our purpose, quality assurance is defined as those activities and programs intended to assure the quality of care in a defined medical setting. Such programs or activities must include educational or other components intended to remedy identified deficiencies in quality as well as the components necessary to identify such deficiencies and assess the program's own effectiveness.

These activities involve an expanding spectrum of activities relevant to the basic services, production processes, structure, people, and policies of various types of health service organizations. For example, the introduction of quality of care review programs may be seen as directly affecting the production processes as well

---

*This paper was originally presented at the Invitational Conference on Research in Quality Assurance sponsored jointly by the University of Colorado Health Sciences Center, the Association of University Programs in Health Administration, and the Joint Commission on Accreditation of Hospitals, November 7, 1980 in Denver, Colorado.

as involving basic policy decisions of the organization. These activities are often new relative to the organization and always influence or attempt to influence the decision-making processes within the organization. These characteristics make it possible to define quality assurance as a managerial innovation: that is, any program, product, or technique which represents a significant departure from the state of the art at the time it first appears in the organization. This type of innovation tends to affect the nature, location, quality and/or quantity of information that is available in the decision-making process [2].

Following Kimberly [2], two distinct although not mutually exclusive perspectives are relevant to the study of QA activities as a managerial innovation: diffusion perspective and adoption perspective. From each perspective research questions may be generated to aid our understanding of QA programs as innovations in health care management. The purpose of this reading is to (a) examine the concept of innovation from both the diffusion and adoption perspective and identify those areas of theory and research particularly relevant to quality assurance activities and (b) identify future areas of research to facilitate the successful diffusion and implementation of QA programs.

DIFFUSION PERSPECTIVE

In the diffusion perspective the focus is on the spread of a new object, product or idea among some population of organizations or individuals. This perspective focuses on the study of the innovation itself. It is possible to assess the rate of implementation among a set of organizations or examine the type of organizations adopting various types of QA activities over time. For example, diffusion perspective may assess the rate and type of organizations incorporating cost effectiveness analysis into the PSRO hospital review mechanisms or the rate and type of organizations implementing new systems of audit like the comprehensive quality assurance system of the American Group Practice Association [3].

While the diffusion perspective has received considerable attention in the health services field in the study of specific technologies and programmatic innovations, its application to quality assurance must be approached with caution. First, while there is great potential to study the diffusion of innovative QA activities, particularly in long-term and ambulatory care facilities [5], many QA activities for inpatient facilities are mandated by the federal government or by the Joint Commission on Accreditation of Hospitals (JCAH). For inpatient QA activity, the classic diffusion perspective provides little insight since implementation is required. The acceptance by personnel and the eventual utilization of information generated by the QA activity in the overall decision-making process of the organization are major concerns of the adoption perspective and will be discussed in a subsequent section of this reading.

A second limitation of applying the diffusion perspective is the newness of the QA activity. While quality assurance may be termed an innovation, in many cases it is simply a relabeling of previous ongoing activities. Relabeling makes it extremely difficult for researchers to define the innovation operationally. Perhaps most important, relabeling reinforces the level of cynicism among organizational personnel who have lived through many so-called ''innovations.''

Despite these limitations the diffusion perspective helps identify several important areas of QA research: attributes, types of innovations, and patterns of innovations. These areas provide an opportunity to expand our understanding of QA activities and to enhance the current literature on organizations and innovations.

Attributes

A critical concept inherent in the diffusion perspective is the attribute of the innovation itself. The literature has generated an extensive list of attributes to characterize any given innovation [6]. These include, among others, effectiveness, cost, return on investment, risk and uncertainty, compatibility with other aspects of the organization, complexity, perceived relative advantage, and communicability. It is important to distinguish between primary and secondary attributes of the innovation [7].

Primary attributes are those characteristics of the innovation which exist without reference to the specific adopting organization. Thus, for example, a financially well-endowed hospital and an organization with no endowment might describe a particular QA activity in the same way. Secondary attributes are those characteristics of the innovation that are highly interrelated with particular characteristics of the implementing organization. Thus, for example, a financially well-endowed hospital might classify a particular QA program as relatively inexpensive, while an organization with no endowment may classify the same innovation as prohibitively costly.

Perhaps the most critical attribute relative to QA activities is the effectiveness and cost of the activities. Does the program have an impact on the quality of care provided? At what cost? As stated by the Institute of Medicine (1976) report:

> Despite the potential future accumulation of evaluation data about MCEs (Medical Care Evaluations), today there are no reliable data on the number, topics, and associated cost of currently performing MCEs; the identified deficiencies of patient care; the remedial action proposed and taken; and the extent and duration of improvements in patient care. MCEs may have improved quality but reliable before and after assessments are not available. Any endorsement of the continued performance of MCE must be based on the recognition that in isolated instances performance has improved; the assumption that the questioning and

information exchange during conduct of audits may increase attention to quality issues, thereby informally leading to improvements; and the hope that future evaluations will provide more conclusive evidence [8].

Since 1977, there has been progress in the ability to detect problems in the quality and utilization of services [9]. Various assessment methods have been developed and in part evaluated in both inpatient and ambulatory health care settings [9-13]. Yet many questions remain [12]. Which problems respond best to which corrective measures? What problems respond just to exposure? Under what conditions is it more effective to rely on peer review, education, preadmission review, administrative changes, concurrent review or restriction of privileges? All these questions have significant policy implications.

For example, in the area of ambulatory care review the uncertainty that QA activities will have programmatic impact is seen as a primary factor inhibiting the development of such activity among HMOs [5]. Moreover with a few exceptions [15-19], little is known about the ability of QA activities to actually improve the care patients receive [20, 21].

Types of Innovations

The diffusion perspective emphasizes the need for greater attention to conceptual distinctions among innovations. For example, Downs and Mohr [7] suggest that a major reason for the inconsistency of research results is that the conditions associated with innovation vary with the type of innovation being considered.

A review of innovation literature in the health services field reveals a distinction frequently made between technological and programmatic innovations. However, the diversity of QA activities as a managerial innovation requires a more refined classification scheme. One such scheme is presented in Figure 12-1 in which the type of innovation is a function of the extent to which work activities are modified or the ends or goals of such work are altered. *Technological change* occurs when there is a change in means but not a change in ends. For example, the introduction

---

Figure 12-1 Types of Organizational Change

Types	Means	Goals
Technical	Changed	Unchanged
Adjustment	Unchanged	Changed
Adaptation	Changed	Changed

Source: Adapted from Kaluzny and Veney [22].

of a new technology and/or procedure is considered a technological change. *Adjustment change* occurs when the technological means for accomplishing some end remains the same but the goals are changed, e.g., the introduction of non-therapeutic abortion services or a primary care unit in a hospital setting. *Adaptation* occurs when there is a modification in not only the means the organization uses to reach its goals but also in the goals themselves. A classic but rarely observed example of such a change is where a community hospital provides preventive services for the entire community. This typology represents a continuum of risk in which adaptive change is the most extreme—requiring both a modification in structure and values—as opposed to a technical change in which there is little modification of structure or values.

Applying this distinction to QA activities would suggest the following type of classification. Technological change would include many of the innovative methods developed to enhance quality assessment. For example, criteria-setting methodologies such as the Delphi method [23], or the nominal group for problem identification [24], and computer feedback approaches [25] are all examples of more technical QA innovations. Adjustment innovation is illustrated by the use of fairly standard quality assessment methodologies that attempt to achieve new goals within and for the organization. There are few illustrations; however, one example is the QA program being developed by the American College of Radiology [26]. Under this program, systematic attempts have been made to measure the patterns of care provided by radiation therapists in both hospital and non-hospital settings, and to relate these patterns to specific outcome measures of morbidity, mortality, and quality of life. The inclusion of outcome represents a significant expansion of goals traditionally focused on assuring that the technology was correctly applied—independently of whether it made a difference in health status. In a sense, the quality assurance program represents an opportunity to incorporate technology assessment and use the organization as a laboratory for this activity.

Finally, adaptation includes activities which attempt to affect both the means and goals of the organization. As indicated, these types of innovations are rare; however, the health accounting approach developed by John Williamson [24] illustrates an adjustment change. Under this approach there is not only a change in the means, e.g., use of a nominal group to identify a problem area, but also an attempt to measure the outcomes of care, i.e., broadening the basic goal of the organization.

The above is presented only to illustrate the use of a classification scheme applied to QA activities. It is likely that each type of QA activity will follow a different diffusion pattern and reflect different adoption rates within the organization. While each of these requires examination, specific emphasis needs to be given the diffusion of adjustment and adaptive QA innovations. The study of QA activities provides a significant area in which to analyze the diffusion of these three types of innovations.

Patterns of Innovation

Research on innovation is often characterized by the normal diffusion curve [27]. That is, innovations are accepted slowly at first and then accelerated over time. Yet research from the health services field indicates that the rate at which innovations are implemented among health service organizations differs by type of innovation as well as adopting unit [28, 29]. Building on some classification of QA interventions, it is important to monitor the rate at which various types of QA activities are diffused among different types of adopting units. This information provides an opportunity to contrast diffusion curves with those already available for various programmatic and technological innovations, and to provide useful information to national organizations concerned with the extent to which QA activities are in fact underway throughout the country.

An equally important pattern is the order or sequence in which QA activities are implemented relative to other new programs, products and technologies. Sequence is an extremely important factor. That is, certain types of innovations must be implemented prior to the successful implementation of other types of innovations [30]. The introduction of QA activities may be contingent upon the availability of certain prerequisite resources or more specifically on the successful introduction of significant technological innovations. For example, a QA program at the Harvard Community Health Plan is based on a highly sophisticated computerized medical record system. Thus the implementation of the plan may be contingent on the diffusion of the computerized medical record system and the subsequent acceptance or adoption of that system as a technological innovation within the organization. Similarly, attention needs to be given to alterations in basic organizational structure that may be a prerequisite to the successful introduction of QA activities or a substitute for such activities. Palmer and Reilly [31] suggest that changing the process of care is not the only or even the best way to improve the institution's quality of care. Changing the process of care may be most cost-effective in the short run; but in the long run, changing the structure of care may prove far more effective.

ADOPTION PERSPECTIVE

The adoption perspective focuses on the process of bringing a new program, product, or technique into actual use or operation by an organization or individual. Three important questions for the study of QA are generated from this perspective.

— What are the distinguishing characteristics of organizations/individuals successfully implementing quality assurance programs?

— To what extent do individuals within organizations accept quality assurance activities; to what extent does data/information generated by such activities have an effect on decision-making processes within the organization?
— What are the most effective strategies for implementing quality assurance programs, and under what conditions?

Below is a detailed examination of each of these questions as potential areas for quality assurance research.

Distinguishing Characteristics of Individuals/Organizations Implementing Quality Assurance Activities

A great deal of time and energy has been devoted to the identification of factors associated with the implementation of various types of innovations.* Empirical research has focused on the effects of various environmental factors [36], structural factors [37, 38], and influence factors, i.e., the effects of values and selected characteristics of elite members of the organization, on the ultimate implementation of innovative activities [39, 40]. Similar research needs to be done on the implementation of QA activities. This analysis will provide an opportunity to test the generalizability of factors already identified as important to implementation and to identify those factors important to the implementation of QA activities.

In addition, it is important to consider innovation as a process involving a series of distinct stages. While there are various models [6] characterizing various stages of the process, for all practical purposes these stages center on the following: recognition of a problem, identification of a solution, implementation and final institutionalization or acceptance by critical actors within the organization. Using this perspective, the objective is to identify the organizational characteristics and attributes of the innovation and their interaction at various stages of the innovation process. Several points require special attention as we attempt to relate this perspective to quality assurance activities.

Performance Gap

A critical factor in the implementation process is the perceived discrepancy between how the organization is performing vis-a-vis how certain actors think the organization should be performing. This discrepancy creates a performance gap which when made visible to appropriate individuals within the organization provides a stimulus to initiate corrective action [41]. In other words, the performance gap is the driving force for organizational innovation: it provides the initiative

---

*For a detailed review of empirical studies involving programmatic and technological innovations in health services, see Kaluzny [28], Greer [32, 33], Gordon and Fisher [34], and NAS [35].

for a search process to identify corrective action and the rationale for ultimate acceptance by organization personnel. Attention needs to be given to identifying factors associated with the development of the performance gap, and to the relationship of the performance gap to subsequent stages of the innovation process.

Acceptance of the Innovation

Implementation of an innovation within an organization is not tantamount to acceptance by individuals within that organization. There are many cases where innovations are implemented within the organization and fail to be accepted via attitude or behavior by critical actors within the organization. Acceptance involves various degrees of attitudinal and behavioral change. Degree of acceptance may vary along a continuum ranging from compliance, identification, and internalization [42].

Compliance refers to the least amount of acceptance and focuses on behavior change which occurs because the individuals seek rewards or avoid punishment. Identification takes place when the individual imitates another behavior in order to gain approval of someone with whom he wishes to identify. In a sense, this behavior indicates a stronger level of acceptance, and is contingent upon relationship between the individual and a particular role model. Internalization reflects the highest degree of acceptance. It occurs when an individual perceives an action as relevant and credible so that he or she incorporates the action within his or her own value system and reorganizes perceptions in keeping with the new value behavior. In the case of quality assurance the ultimate occurs when the professional internalizes the activities of the QA program and when data generated by the program are used to affect policy decisions within the organization. This level of acceptance is difficult to achieve [43].

Despite the conceptualization of innovation as a process, research has tended to focus primarily on the implementation stage. With a few exceptions [44, 45], little attention has been given to the analysis of factors affecting the early stages of the innovation process; i.e., recognition of a problem and the identification of a solution to resolve that problem. This area of research is particularly critical to our understanding of QA activities since the implementation of many of the activities is voluntary. Even when mandatory, e.g., JCAH, acceptance by physicians and other health providers within the implementing organization is contingent on the extent to which providers recognize the problems and see the proposed assurance activities as solutions to them. Moreover, attention needs to be given to the relationship between attitudinal and behavioral acceptance and the way in which this affects the use of information generated by the QA program.

Since little research is available, two basic questions should guide research in the areas: (a) Do the same factors that were identified as important determinants of implementation have a similar effect on recognition and identification? (b) If these same factors are identified as important, is the direction of the relationships the same as that recorded for implementation?

A second area of research focuses on the generalizability of factors associated with different types of innovation. Research efforts in both the health services and other areas has tended to support the need for this approach. For example, Nathanson and Morlock [46] distinguish between social and technological innovations and find that hospital conditions favorable to social innovations differ from those conducive to more technological innovations. Similarly, Daft and Becker [47, 48] report that organizational and environmental factors associated with innovation activity in one area of the organization may not be associated with activity in other areas. Specifically, their research on schools reports that there are two distinct processes ongoing within the organization, contingent on whether the innovation is associated with administrative activities or with the more technical aspects of organizational performance.

Similar research needs to be conducted in the quality assurance area. As indicated in our discussion of the diffusion perspective, it is likely that different types of assessment and assurance activities are associated with varying degrees of risk. Research in other areas suggests that there are different factors within the environment and the organization associated with various types of innovations. Adopting more risky innovations needs to be considered. As Greer [32] suggests in her review of innovation as a field of study—there is little information available on the conditions that are conducive to the adoption of "disruptive, publicly visible or otherwise risky innovations." Moreover, research in the area of quality assurance needs to account for the secondary attributes of the innovation [7]; that is, those attributes of the innovation interacting with the characteristics of the adopting unit.

Utilization of Information

A critical problem facing quality assurance programs is whether the information generated by the program is actually used to influence policy and/or change physician behavior. While the utilization of information is a chronic problem in many organizations, the use of quality assurance information in health service organizations is difficult for two reasons. First, managerial activities in many health service organizations are embryonic or non-existent [49]. Thus while quality assurance mechanisms are mandated and viewed as managerial innovations there is no well-developed subsystem within the organization to track or coordinate this particular innovation.

Even where the managerial activities are well-developed, they are generally "loosely coupled" relative to other functions/activities of the organization [50]. That is, the various activities are tenuously related and while each is somehow "attached," each retains some identity and separateness in that the attachment may be circumscribed, infrequent, weak in mutual effects, unimportant and/or slow in response. Thus while the primary function of the QA mechanism is to control the various activities within the organization, the loose coupling nature of the managerial activities vis-à-vis other activities within the organization limits the ability of quality assurance to affect the ongoing operations of the organization in any systematic way.

Available innovation theory from either the diffusion or adoption perspective has limited utility in addressing these special problems. Emphasis from either perspective is mainly on implementation among or within organizations, and theory often assumes that utilization is a logical consequence of implementation.

To understand this process better we need to focus on other, related theoretical models. Perhaps the most relevant complement to the innovation concept is the growing body of theory and research focusing on the utilization of scientific information [51, 52]. The approach focuses on understanding how people send and receive information, how they make decisions and solve problems, and how they change and influence each other to change. These questions are generic to clinical decision making [53] and the operations of the QA program.

Moreover, focusing on the utilization of information provides an opportunity to gather important information about the quality assurance process. This can enhance our understanding of the utilization of information in an organizational setting, and direct attention to specific intervention strategies that may assure that information generated by a QA program has a significant impact on the ongoing processes of the organization. Perhaps at the simplest level it is appropriate to conduct a series of case studies to trace how information is in fact used in organizations and to identify barriers to use. This approach will provide the data to develop guidelines to improve existing QA activities.

Implementation Strategies

Within the adoption perspective, a final area of research is determining the most effective strategies for implementing QA activities. This investigation builds on our understanding of both the determinants of innovation and the identification of factors that facilitate or impede the utilization of information generated by QA activities.

Four basic strategies can be identified: re-education, persuasion, facilitation, and power [54]. Figure 12-2 provides the respective definitions and illustrative techniques associated with each strategy.

It is beyond our purpose to discuss specific strategies; however, it is important to emphasize that quality assurance provides a useful opportunity to evaluate the efficacy of various approaches. It allows us to determine the effectiveness of various strategies and the conditions under which each is most effective.

Figure 12-2 Implementation Strategies

Types	Definitions	Illustration
Re-education	The unbiased presentation of fact	Continuing education, survey feedback
Persuasion	The selling of an idea based on substantive fact or totally false information and/or manipulation of individuals	Successive approximations; avoidance reactance analogy social pressure
Facilitative	Activities which make the implementation of a specific change easier	Process consultation, team building, funds
Coercion	The use of sanctions and coercion to obtain implementation and subsequent compliance	Joint Commission on Accreditation of Hospitals/Quality Standards

Source: Based on Zaltman and Duncan [54].

To deal systematically with both requires a change in the way health service managers and providers approach problems. Managers and providers need to shift from advocacy of a specific approach to advocacy of the essential seriousness of the problem [55]. Their political position should be somewhat like the following: "This is a serious problem. We do not know which of these solutions is most effective—but we should initiate action on an experimental basis." By adopting an experimental stance, managers and providers can honestly evaluate results. By recognizing that more than one solution to a problem exists, they may substitute an alternative approach without compromising their position. Their job is to find a solution to a serious problem, to keep trying alternatives until the goal is attained.

This approach perhaps more than any other requires collaboration between program personnel and personnel trained in research/evaluation methodologies. The collaboration will require substantive change in the way both researchers and managers function. For managers, collaboration requires a recognition that they do not know whether a particular program or method of introduction will be effective and/or whether it is even relevant to the many problems faced by their organization. Thus, instead of advocating a particular solution or approach, the manager needs to present solutions as a series of options and develop ways to assess these options as they affect the organization. Similarly, researchers must translate theoretical concerns into practical policy and administrative issues [56, 57].

Attention also needs to be given to the basic design of QA activities and their compatibility with the characteristics of implementing organizations. Shultz and Slevin [58] refer to this compatibility as *organizational validity* or the "fit" between the innovation and the organization. Organizational validity is a multi-dimensional concept and consists of assessing the congruence of a number of factors such as attitudes of users, group dynamics, information flow within organizations, authority structure, previous background and a host of structural design characteristics bearing on the ultimate use of the particular program. The emphasis here is on designing these characteristics to enhance the ultimate acceptability and effectiveness of the program for the adopting organization. This approach has been used to facilitate the implementation of various operations research/management science approaches in industrial organizations, and appears equally appropriate to the design of QA activities in health service organizations. The extent to which modifications of design enhance adaptability and eventual utilization is an important area of investigation.

CONCLUSIONS

The purpose of this reading is to examine concepts from innovation theory and the research literature that may better guide research to understand the implementation of quality assurance activities. The available theory and research on innovation provides a good framework for some of the important research issues facing QA programs. Research on quality assurance activities developing from an innovation framework falls into two basic categories: diffusion and adoption perspectives. Each perspective provides a focus for identifying specific research issues. For example, the diffusion perspective highlights the innovation itself and focuses on the pattern of implementation among organizations. The adoption perspective focuses on the organization or the individuals within the organization as the adoption unit and considers factors that facilitate or impede the ultimate implementation, acceptance, and impact of the innovation. Each perspective has a useful role and a rich literature but it is important to keep clear the perspective in use.

Future research needs to focus on designing specific experimental studies to evaluate the effectiveness of QA activities, the conditions under which various types of QA activities have an impact, and the most effective strategies for implementing QA activities in various types of organizations. This type of evaluation needs to be an integral part of ongoing quality assurance programs in order to provide information relevant to the operations of QA programs and to contribute to the ultimate assessment of QA activities.

NOTES

1. Institute of Medicine. *Assessing Quality of Health Care: An Evaluation.* Washington, DC: National Academy of Science, 1976.
2. Kimberly, J.R. Hospital adoption of innovation: the role of integration into external informational environments. *Journal of Health and Social Behavior* 19:361, 1978.
3. Rubin, L. *Comprehensive Quality Assurance Systems.* Alexandria, VA: American Group Practice Association, 1975.
4. Miller Communication, Inc. Patient Care Evaluation Service. Norwalk, CT (no date).
5. Shapiro, E. et al. *Study of Quality Assurance and Utilization Review Mechanisms in Prepaid Group Practice Plans and Medical Care Foundations.* Baltimore, MD: The Health Services Research and Development Center, The Johns Hopkins University Press, 1976.
6. Zaltman, G., R. Duncan and J. Holbeck. *Innovations in Organizations.* New York: John Wiley and Sons, 1972.
7. Downs, G. and L. Mohr. Conceptual issues in the study of innovation. *Administrative Science Quarterly* 21:700, 1976.
8. Institute of Medicine. *Assessing Quality in Health Care: An Evaluation.* Washington, D.C.: National Academy of Sciences, November 1976.
9. HFCA. *Health Care Financing Research Report: Professional Standards Review Organization 1979 Program Evaluation,* 1980.
10. Mushlin, A. and F. Appel. *Developing a Quality Assurance Strategy for Primary Care, Final Report.* Baltimore, MD: The Health Services Research and Development Center, The Johns Hopkins University Press, 1978.
11. McAuliffe, W.E. Studies of process-outcome correlation in medical care evaluation: a critique. *Medical Care* 16:907, 1978.
12. Donabedian, A. Methods for deriving criteria for assessing the quality of medical care. *Medical Care Review* 37:653, 1980.
13. Donabedian, A. *The Criteria and Standards of Quality,* Vol. II. Ann Arbor, MI: Health Administration Press, 1982.
14. Goran, M.J. The evolution of the PSRO hospital review system. *Medical Care* 17 (supplemental issue): 1979.
15. Wennberg, J.E. et al. Changes in tonsillectomy rates associated with feedback and review. *Pediatrics* 59:821, 1977.
16. Dyck, F.J. et al. Effect of surveillance on the number of hysterectomies in the province of Saskatchewan. *New England Journal of Medicine* 296:1326, 1977.
17. Deuschle, J.M. Physician performance in a prepaid health plan: results of the peer review program of the Health Insurance Plan of Greater New York. *Medical Care* 20(2):127-142, February 1982.
18. Cohen, D.I. et al. Does cost information availability reduce physician test usage? *Medical Care* 20(3)286-292, March 1982.
19. Brown, C.R. and D.S. Fleisher. The bicycle concept—relating continuing education directly to patient care. *New England Journal of Medicine* 290:88, 1971.
20. Jessee, W.F. Quality assurance systems: why aren't there any? *Quality Assurance Bulletin* 3:16, 1977.
21. Jessee, W.F. Physician competence and compulsory continuing education: are they compatible? *Journal of Community Health* 2:291, 1977.

22. Kaluzny, A. and J. Veney. Types of change and hospital planning strategies. *American Journal of Health Planning* 1:13, 1977.
23. Romm, F.J. and B. Hulka. Developing criteria for quality of care assessment; effects of the Delphi technique. *Health Services Research* 14:309, 1979.
24. Williamson, J.W. *Assessing and Improving Health Care Outcomes: The Health Accounting Approach to Quality Assurance*. Cambridge, MA: Ballinger, 1978.
25. McDonald, C.J. et al. Physician response to computer reminders. *Journal of the American Medical Association* 244:1579, 1980.
26. Kramer, S. The study of the patterns of cancer care in radiation therapy. *Cancer* 39:1977.
27. Rogers, E. and F. Shoemaker. *Communication of Innovation: A Cross-Cultural Approach*. New York: Free Press, 1971.
28. Kaluzny, A. Innovations in health services: theoretical framework and review of research. *Health Services Research* 9:101, 1974.
29. Warner, K. A "desperation-reaction" model of medical diffusion. *Health Services Research* 10:369, 1975.
30. Kaluzny, A. et al. Scalability of health services: an empirical test. *Health Services Research* 6:214, 1971.
31. Palmer, R.H. and M.C. Reilly. Individual and institutional variables which may serve as indicators of quality of medical care. *Medical Care* 17:693, 1979.
32. Greer, A.L. Advances in the study of diffusion of innovation in health care organizations. *Milbank Memorial Fund Quarterly/Health and Society* 55:505, 1977.
33. Greer, A.L. Technology, assessment, diffusion and implementation. *Journal of Medical Systems* 5(1), 1981.
34. Gordon, G. and G. Fisher (eds.). *The Diffusion of Medical Technology: Policy and Research Planning Perspective*. Cambridge, MA: Ballinger, 1975.
35. National Academy of Sciences. *Medical Technology and the Health Care System*. A Report by the Committee on Technology and Health Care, Assembly of Engineering, National Research Council and Institute of Medicine, Washington, DC, 1979.
36. Russell, L. *Technology in Hospitals*. Washington, DC: The Brookings Institute, 1979.
37. Hage, J. and M. Aiken. Program change and organizational properties. *American Journal of Sociology* 72:503, 1967.
38. Moch, M.K. and E.V. Morse. Size, centralization and organizational adoption of innovations. *American Sociological Review* 42:716, 1977.
39. Hage, J. and R. Dewar. The prediction of organizational performance: the case of program innovation. *Administrative Science Quarterly* 18:279, 1973.
40. Kimberly, J.R. The Diffusion, Adoption and Effectiveness of Managerial Innovation. In P.C. Nystrom and W.H. Starbuck (eds.), *Handbook of Organizational Design*. Vol. 1. New York: Oxford University Press, 1980.
41. Downs, A. *Inside Bureaucracy*. Boston, MA: Little Brown, 1967.
42. Kelman, H. Compliance, identification and internalization—three processes of attitude change. *Journal of Conflict Resolution* 2:51, 1958.
43. Osborne, C.E. Relationship between medical audit results and the planning of continuing education programs. *Medical Care* 18:994, 1980.
44. Aiken, M., S. Bacharach, and J. French. Organizational structure, work process and proposal making in administrative bureaucracies. *Academy of Management Journal* 23:631, 1980.

45. Hernandez, R. and A. Kaluzny. Determinants of Program Initiation: The First Stage of the Innovation Process. Paper presented at the American Sociological Association Meeting, New York, August 1980.

46. Nathanson, C. and L. Morlock. Control structure, values and innovation: a comparative study of hospitals. *Journal of Health and Social Behavior* 21:315, 1980.

47. Daft, R.L. A dual-core model of organizational innovation. *Academy of Management Journal* 21:193, 1978.

48. Daft, R. and S. Becker. *The Innovative Organization.* New York: Elsevier, 1975.

49. Katz, D. and R. Kahn. *The Social Psychology of Organizations,* 2nd Ed. New York: John Wiley and Sons, 1978.

50. Weick, K.E. Educational organizations as loosely coupled systems. *Administrative Science Quarterly* 21:1, 1976.

51. Havelock, R.G. Research on the Utilization of Knowledge. In M. Kochen (ed.), *Information for Action: Reorganizing Knowledge for Wisdom.* New York: Academic Press, 1975.

52. Havelock, R.G. What do we know from research about the process of research utilization? *CRUSK* 1974.

53. Koran, L. The reliability of clinical methods, data and judgments. *New England Journal of Medicine* 293:642, 695, 1975.

54. Zaltman, G. and R. Duncan. *Strategies for Planned Change.* New York: Wiley-Interscience, 1977.

55. Campbell, D.T. Reforms as experiments. *American Psychologist* 24:409, 1969.

56. Shortell, S. Organizational theory and health services delivery. In S. Shortell and M. Brown (eds.), *Organizational Research in Hospitals.* Chicago: Blue Cross Association, 1976.

57. Mintzberg, H. The manager's job: folklore and fact. *Harvard Business Review* 49, July/August 1975.

58. Schultz, R.L. and D.P. Slevin. A Program of Research on Implementation. In R.L. Schultz and D. Slevin (eds.), *Implementing Operations Research/Management Science.* New York: American Elsevier Publishing, Inc., 1975.

13. Assertive Behavior in Nurses and Collegial Staff Relations: Implications for Patient Care Practices

SHARON J. REEDER and SHARON STEVENS

INTRODUCTION

It is generally conceded that the character of role relationships between the two key hospital care providers—physicians and nurses—may in part determine the quality of patient care. A body of expert opinion and research stresses the point that collaborative team effort leads to high quality care. The team effort should be characterized by a high degree of information exchange, mutual respect of health care providers for each other, and clarity of communications by nurses in apprising physicians of their patients' conditions and needs.[1-7]

Assertiveness by nurses in dealing with physicians and with their peers also is seen to contribute to the quality of patient care. In today's hospital in which a number of different medical specialists, residents, and technicians may intervene in the care of each patient, the staff nurses are the link between the patient and the cadre of care providers. Their sustained presence, if accompanied by articulate communication and forceful efforts aimed at assuring conformity to appropriate practices, may protect patients from incompetent actions and unintended consequences of hospitalization.[3,8]

In this reading, we will examine, specifically, nurses' perceptions of their assertiveness with physicians and co-workers and their perceptions of the degree of collegial relations with physicians in the hospitals in which they work. We are particularly concerned with how these perceptions may influence the rigor of patient care practices related to preventing infections. In addition, we also will discuss the effects of selected hospital characteristics and various background characteristics of nurses on patient care.

We will examine the hypothesis that nurses who report that they work in a collegial hospital milieu are more likely to engage in appropriate patient care practices. We also hypothesize that nurses who report a willingness to assert themselves to influence other staff members to conform to appropriate practices

199

are most likely to engage in appropriate practices themselves. Evidence for appropriate practice will be measured in this reading by the rate of nosocomial, or hospital-acquired, infections.

PERSPECTIVES ON COLLEGIALITY AND ASSERTIVENESS

The literature on professional collegial relations is characterized by variations in interpretation and definition of the term, although it appears that there has been an evolution of its meaning. In the 1950s and early 1960s increasing attention was paid to the dilemma of professionals and scientists working in formal organizations.[2,9-13]

The discussion revolved primarily around the issue of control and indirectly around the problem of accountability. Conventional bureaucratic methods became suspect as either appropriate or practical for controlling the work of professionals. For physicians at least, and perhaps all health care providers, it was believed that a kind of autonomy is required that is antithetical to Weber's model of rational-legal bureaucracy.[14] Indeed, it was felt by organizational catalysts in the 1960s that the value of the work of health care providers is substantially reduced when done "by the book" or otherwise subjected to the detailed and tedious directives of an administrative hierarchy. The way for such individuals to work is as members of a self-regulating "company of equals."[2,15]

However, physicians in the company of equals, for reasons of intrinsic prestige and monetary status, as well as supposedly superior training and knowledge, apparently are the most equal of the company of equals. Moreover, the predominance of males in the profession increases their standing.

The long history of nurses and physicians working together includes documented instances of outstanding collaborative effort. However, it is also marred by interprofessional and interpersonal conflict, a situation believed most common in these times of technological and specialty emphases in medicine.[16] A century ago, physicians had little of the technological and pharmacological supports that they now enjoy. The medical science knowledge base was primitive by today's standards. Hence, except for surgery, which advanced relatively early, physicians could do little more than nurse their patients. Disparity in knowledge and skills and economic compensation between the professions were not the issues they are today. Colleagueship was inhibited, however, by occupational sex aggregation, since nursing, like other women's fields, suffered in status and standing.[7,17-25]

Factors within the nursing field in the past also mitigated against collegiality. Up until the past two decades, nursing education occurred in a rigid, regimented, and often theoretically sterile environment, which emphasized obedience and passivity and negatively sanctioned any self-assertion by students.[24,26] Socialization messages were often mixed and contradictory: Be independent in knowledge and practice and an equal member of the health team, but do not question issues, assert your knowledge and competence, make policy, or compete with physicians. Although the context in which you work encourages you to practice with sound scientific knowledge, be "professional," ignore conflict, keep the environment tension free, remain affectively neutral, and do not expect reimbursement commensurate with educational background and work responsibility. Try to do what is best for the common good; if conflict occurs, do not let people know what you want by speaking out clearly. If all else fails, be silent and noncommittal.[18,26,27]

Assertive behavior may be conceived, on the one hand, as part of a generalized pattern of collegial activities and, on the other, as an independent dimension orthogonal to collegiality. The former view—that assertive behavior is a general pattern of collegiality—is plausible on the grounds that equalitarian interactions and sharing of ideas often require pressing a point and acting in a strong, aggressive manner.

The latter view—the orthogonal view—would hold that assertive behavior stems from one's "social personality makeup," that is, assertive behavior is superordinate to occupational role or any other role or role set.[28] Thus, individuals differ in the extent to which they will act in ways to encourage conformity with what they believe either affectively and cognitively to be right and proper depending on their overall socialization experiences. The issue of orthogonality between assertiveness and collegiality needs to be assessed empirically since peer relations among health care providers are considered to be the cornerstone of quality patient care. Thus, the analyses presented here include the examination of the interaction between self-perceptions of assertiveness and collegiality as well as an assessment of the relations of both assertiveness and collegiality to patient-care practices related to the prevention of nosocomial infections.

DATA AND METHODS

Nosocomial, or hospital-acquired, infections represent a major medical care problem in the United States from the standpoint of patient discomfort and mortality. It is estimated that as many as two million of the patients admitted to U.S. hospitals yearly acquire such infections and that 15,000 die. In addition to this excessive morbidity and mortality, financial costs of hospital care are markedly raised by prolonged hospitalization and extra services rendered to treat the infections.[29] Authorities in the nosocomial infection field differ in their opinions as to the efficacy of many eradication and prevention practices. However, there is rather general agreement that the way work in the hospital is organized influences the quality of patient care and, consequently, the incidence of nosocomial infections.[30-33]

The Study on the Efficacy of Nosocomial Infection Control (SENIC Project), sponsored by the Centers for Disease Control (CDC), is a national evaluation of programs and activities to prevent hospital-acquired infections.[34] It has provided an unusual opportunity to examine the complex relationships among health care providers, particularly those of physicians and nurses, as they relate to the provision of quality patient care.

The background and development of the SENIC Project have been described elsewhere.[34] Briefly, a random sample was selected from 433 hospitals, representative of all general medical and surgical hospitals that are short-term care, not federal or state owned, have at least 50 beds, and are located in the contiguous 48 states. Each sampled hospital participated in the Hospital Interview Survey (HIS) phase of data collection; 338 of them also participated in the second phase, the Medical Records Survey (MRS).

The objective of HIS was to measure the characteristics of each hospital's infection control activities as practiced in the calendar year 1976. This was accomplished through a structured set of personal interviews with the hospital staff, who play important roles in hospital infection control, including the chairman of the Infection Control Committee, hospital epidemiologist, infection control nurse, hospital administrators, and others. Since nursing care is a central factor in controlling nosocomial infections, a random sample of 7,188 staff nurses, both male and female, filled out a self-administered questionnaire. For this paper our analysis is restricted to 6,970 female nurses only, since the small number of male nurses made the analysis unrealistic.

The SENIC sample involves both individual- and group-level processes (that is, 433 groups or hospitals and 6,970 individual nurses). Since multiple regression techniques were employed as part of our analysis, there was the problem of dealing with individual- and group-level variables. Therefore, each nurse variable was aggregated to the hospital mean score, for the regression analysis. This type of analysis permits discussing *average* nurse behavior rather than *individual* nurse behavior.* To this hospital-level file we merged variables describing hospital structural characteristics obtained from the American Hospital Association (AHA) Annual Survey of Hospitals, 1976.

The aggregation technique allows us to merge hospital-level variables together with nurse variables in one model, reducing the number of nurses to 433, comparable to the number of hospitals. While we describe our nurse measures for individual nurses, below, we then aggregate them for our correlational and regression analyses.

Measures

The measurement of the nurse level and hospital-level variables will be discussed prior to a discussion of our results.

---

*This means also that average patient care practices will differ across hospitals.

Nurse Level

The dependent variable was the type of care nurses gave their patients. A proportional index was developed, which we termed the Patient Care Practice Index. This is a summed index of 11 items describing appropriate patient care relating to control of nosocomial infections. "Correct" practices were defined from current published recommendations.[35] We do not consider it a scale since the items are not homogeneous. The questions included in the index dealt with procedures relating to urinary catheter care, proper handling of breathing units or respirators, replacement of intravenous cannulas and administration sets, and whether or not patients had been given proper instruction regarding breathing techniques before undergoing surgery. A higher score indicates better patient-care practices.

The independent variables from the nursing staff questionnaire were divided into two groups: (1) sociodemographic measures and (2) perceptual measures. The sociodemographic measures consisted of the nurses' age (scored in number of years), the length of time the nurse had been employed in the hospital in which she is currently working (ranging from six months to ten years); and the proportion of registered nurses (scored 1 if the nurse is an RN and 0 if she is an LVN/LPN). We would expect each of these variables to be positively related to patient care. Although it could be argued otherwise, we assumed that older nurses are likely to have been in the profession longer and registered nurses were educated better than licensed practical nurses. Another variable included in this first category was whether any ongoing inservice training was presented in the hospital where the nurse worked. The measure for inservice training consisted of a proportional index of eight items pertaining to different training procedures and ranging in value from 0 (no relevant techniques presented) to 1.0 (all relevant techniques presented).* We expected this variable to be positively related to patient care practices, since more training implies an increase in nurses' knowledge.

The perceptual measures consisted of an assertiveness scale and a collegiality scale. These two sets of items measured how assertive the nurse says she or he is in speaking up directly to violators of patient care policies, and how collegial the nurse perceives the hospital milieu to be.

We defined assertive behavior as behavior that an individual considers appropriate or correct in the face of social pressure to do otherwise. It includes both a readiness to speak up to others, attempting to influence them when they are engaged in behavior that is inappropriate, and a readiness to voice objections or

---

*The items that went into the inservice index consisted of questions relating to techniques about handling urine specimens, intravenous fluid administration tubing, plastic cannulas for changing intravenous fluids, hospital's isolation techniques, aseptic management of subclavian catheters and central venous pressure lines, and handwashing techniques. The higher the score, the more inservice training had been presented to the nurse in the hospital where this individual worked.

refusal to be influenced when such compliance would result in behavior that is improper or inappropriate in a given circumstance. Nine items comprised the assertiveness scale, which was factor analyzed, resulting in one factor explaining 33 percent of the variance of the items; the average inter-item correlations are about .3, and Cronbach's (1951) alpha is .80, with a mean of 13.7, a standard deviation of 1.59, and a range of 1 to 19.*

Collegial relations were defined as relationships among individuals of equal and particularly of unequal status within an organization, which allow for readiness to be mutually helpful as well as to communicate constructively in order to accomplish the goals of the group or organization. It involves collaborative effort on both sides. Seven items were included in the collegiality scale, which was factor analyzed, resulting in one factor explaining 24 percent of the variance; the average inter-item correlation was about .2, and Cronbach's alpha is .67, with a mean of 8.9, a standard deviation of .96, and a range of 0 to 14.

The actual questions of the individual items comprising each scale together with their component mean scores is presented in Table 13-1 of the results section, where they are discussed in more detail.

Hospital Variables

Several hospital variables were included in our analysis as control variables; one is a continuous variable, the others are nominal variables. The continuous variable measures the ratio of the allocation of nurses or staffing adequacy. It is calculated as the ratio of full-time equivalent nurses divided by total number of hospital beds. A higher number indicates better (qualitatively) staffing of nurses. The other hospital variables, which were categorical, were: region (1 = Northwest, 2 = North Central, 3 = South, 4 = West); type of hospital ownership (1 = proprietary, 2 = nonprofit, 3 = local government); and organizational complexity in hospitals (1 = high, 2 = medium, 3 = low).** The last variable dealt with the hospital environment, which was scored 1 for medical-school–affiliated hospitals with a bed size greater than or equal to 200 and located in urban areas and 2 for

---

*The assertiveness scale dealt with the nurses' perceived willingness to speak up to violators of infection control practices—physicians as well as nurse peers and subordinate ancillary personnel. In order to see if this total scale was comparable to the collegiality scale, physician-only assertive items were correlated with the patient care index. The correlation was .31 (p = .001), which indicated the total scale was not significantly different from the partial scale. All results were rerun on the assertiveness scale without the urinary catheter care items, since urinary catheter care is so fundamental to patient care. Assertiveness was significant for both index constructions, hence, it was felt the large correlation was not merely artifactual.

**This variable is a count of the number of each organization's units, such as facilities and services. The index was collapsed into three categories based on an equal frequency trichotomization of high, medium, and low.

large hospitals in urban areas that are non-medical-school–affiliated organizations. Since only two of the hospitals with fewer than 200 beds were medical-school–affiliated, all with fewer than 200 beds were scored as 3 if they were located in urban areas or as 4 if they were in rural areas.*

FINDINGS

Female nurse perceptions toward various statements concerning speaking up directly to violators of proper patient care procedures and relations between professional colleagues are illustrated in Table 13-1. These statements are paraphrases of actual questions given the nurses in the nurse questionnaire. We see from Table 13-1 that the nurses are more inclined to speak up to violators who are nurses and orderlies than to physicians (items 2, 4, 6). This corresponds with the previous finding of Hofling et al, who reported that nurses were inclined to comply with an improper medical order (such as giving an obvious overdose of medicine to patients) when a physician gave the order.[36]

Nurses also have greater tendency to perceive they are on collegial terms with physicians when consultations and communications about a patient's progress are involved (items 12, 15, 16). Note that Duff and Hollingshead's in-depth study of a community hospital concluded that a lack of effective communication between physicians and nurses (for example, the "health team") was a significant factor in explaining the poor patient care they found.[37]

It is important to note that the *assertiveness* questions were hypothetical situations and not actual ones. A major finding in the Hofling study was that nurses reacted differently to an actual situation in compliance with erroneous medical orders than to a hypothetical one where the "correct" answers were idealized.[36] However, as Berrelson and Steiner have pointed out, there is a positive correlation between attitudes and behavior.[38] Others have noted that both attitudes and behavior are affected by the social frame of reference in which they occur.[39] A study by Acock and DeFleur of the relationship between attitudes may provide a baseline for decision making about action toward the relevant issue. Against this baseline, the individual raises other considerations such as the views held by his reference group and possible sanctions for acting one way or the other.[40]

Testing the Model

This part of our analysis focused on results derived from multiple regression procedures. As explained above, we not only want to know how nurses' perceptions of their behavior affect health care to patients but also want to examine the

---

*Six medical-school–affiliated hospitals were excluded from all analyses, since they were located in rural areas.

Table 13-1 Perceptions of Female Nurses Toward Various Statements Regarding Assertive Behavior and Collegial Relations

Statement	Mean Score*
Assertiveness Components+	
1. Would you speak up if you saw a nurse disconnecting the urinary catheter system to collect a specimen?	2.41
2. Would you speak up if you saw a surgeon with a boil on the arm making ward rounds?	1.79
3. Would you speak up if you saw a nurse's aide handle a dressing from an infected wound without washing his or her hands first?	2.93
4. Would you speak up if you saw a doctor disconnecting the urinary catheter system to collect a specimen?	1.84
5. Would you speak up if you saw a housekeeper with a boil on the arm performing duties in a patient's room?	2.41
6. Would you speak up if you saw a doctor remove sutures from an infected wound and proceed to examine another patient without washing hands?	2.20
7. Would you speak up if you saw a nurse with a boil on the arm giving patient care?	2.56
8. Would you speak up if you saw an orderly disconnecting the urinary catheter system to collect a specimen?	2.58
9. Would you speak up if you saw a nurse handle a dressing from an infected wound and proceed to examine another patient without washing hands?	2.83
Collegial Components‡	
10. Nurses here know that the doctor is pleased if they are informed of errors in written orders.	2.08
11. Doctors do not criticize nurses for informing them of progress of special needs of their patients.	2.31
12. Doctors consult regularly with the nurses regarding their patients' progress.	2.60
13. Doctors like a nurse calling attention to their "breaking technique."	2.14
14. Doctors actively seek the nurses' opinions when devising treatment plans for their patients.	2.05
15. Nurses feel free to inform the doctor whenever he has made an error in his written orders.	2.56
16. There is much communication between doctors and nurses regarding their patients' care.	2.46

*N is approximately 6,800, since it varies due to missing cases on each question.
+1 = would not say something; 2 = maybe, 3 = would say something.
‡1 = never characteristic, 2 = sometimes, 3 = usually characteristic.

influence of the hospital setting and various nurses' sociodemographic characteristics on patient care practices. As stated previously, this has been accomplished
by an aggregated or "contextual effects" model. From this point on, we can only
discuss our results for the average nurses in different hospitals, in order to make
between-hospital comparisons, rather than comparisons among individuals.

Correlation

The correlations of the continuous variables are presented in Table 13-2.

Assertiveness and collegiality are significantly correlated at $p < .01$, but the
relationship is small with a correlation of .17. Both of these measures are
positively related to patient care and they are significant at $p < .01$. However, the
correlation between patient care and assertiveness is .45, nearly three times as
large as that between patient care and collegiality.* Of the hospital and nurse
background characteristics, only inservice training, nursing staff ratio, and the
proportion of registered nurses are significantly related to patient care; age and
experience are not. However, age is significantly related to assertiveness, $p < .01$,

---

*For lack of space, we did not present the full correlation matrix including categorical variables,
which have been appropriately dummied for each categorical level. These results are available upon
request from the authors.

Table 13-2   Correlations, Means, and Standard Deviations for
Continuous Variables Only

Variables	1	2	3	4	5	6	7	8
1. Nurse staffing ratio		−.04	− .19*	−.32*	.10	−.11	.02	.13*
2. Proportion of registered nurses			− .07	−.11	−.07	.19*	.12*	.12*
3. Experience				.60*	.13*	.03	.01	.02
4. Age					.06	.22*	.01	.06
5. Inservice training programs						.26*	.15*	.45*
6. Assertiveness							17*	.46*
7. Collegiality								.16*
8. Patient care practice index								
9. Means	.68	.69	4.17	30.94	.64	13.69	8.87	5.55
10. Standard deviation	.21	.18	1.41	6.18	.13	1.59	.96	.95

N = 427 due to a listwise deletion of missing cases. All nurse variables have been aggregated to mean
hospital scores.

*Significant at $p \leqslant .01$.

and not to collegiality. Experience is not significantly related to either assertiveness or collegiality, while an inservice training program is significantly related to both behavioral measures at $p < .01$, although somewhat higher with assertiveness for a correlation of .26 compared to .15 between collegiality and training. Subsequently we test for possible interactions between the behavioral measures and various background variables of the nurses. We next examined the influence of these background variables and behavioral measures in predicting patient care for nurses between hospitals.

Regression

The regression results for the prediction of patient care are presented in Table 13-3. The first two columns of coefficients do not include the effects of assertiveness or collegiality; the second two columns do. The four categorical variables (hospital environment, region, hospital ownership, and organization complexity) have been appropriately dummy coded, and their coefficients will be discussed in relation to the omitted group for each respective category of variables. A stepwise regression analysis was performed with the hospital characteristic variables entered first, followed by the nurse sociodemographic variables, then the collegiality scale followed by the assertiveness scale, all regressed on the patient care practice index.

Before assertiveness and collegiality are entered in the model, it should be noted that hospital environment, organizational complexity, geographic region, and hospital ownership do not significantly contribute to how well a nurse says she or he performs in giving care to patients. The nurse staffing ratio (line 5, columns 1 and 2) is the most important hospital characteristic, suggesting that patient care will be better when the nurse per bed ratio is high. Two dummy-coded hospital variables such as geographic region and hospital ownership offer some interesting distinctions. In interpreting dummy-coded variables, each category is compared with the omitted group. In the case of the regional variable, the western sector of the United States has hospitals with nurses who on the average practice the best patient care, since the other geographic localities all have a negative coefficient. The northeastern sector of the United States appears to have nurses on the average with the worst level of patient care practice when compared with the other three regions. Nurses working in proprietary hospitals will, on the average, have higher levels of patient care practice than nurses in nonprofit or government-owned hospitals. Both sets of categorical variables (region and hospital ownership) are significantly related to our dependent measure only after controlling for the behavioral measures. This suggests that hospital structural effects are related to nurse behavior to some degree.

Of the nurse-aggregated variables in the first two columns of lines 6 through 9, only licensure and inservice training in the hospital significantly contribute to

Table 13-3 Predicting Average Nurse Patient Care Practices in United States Hospitals from Hospital- and Nurse-Background Characteristics and Nurse Behavioral Characteristics

| Independent Variables* | Unstandardized (b) and Standardized (B) Partial Coefficients | | | |
| | Coefficients Before Assertiveness and Collegiality are Included in the Regression | | Coefficients With Assertiveness and Collegiality Included in the Regression | |
	b	B	b	B
Hospital environment				
Large hospitals (beds ≥200)				
Medical schools	−.03	−.01	−.02	−.01
Nonmedical schools	−.23	−.11	.11	−.05
Small hospitals (beds <200)				
Urban areas	−.03	−.01	−.04	−.02
Rural areas (the omitted category)	.00	.00	.00	.00
Region				
Northeast	−.28	−.13	−.29†	−.13
Northcentral	−.10	−.05	.02†	.01
South	−.17	−.08	−.13†	−.06
West (the omitted category)	.00	.00	.00†	.00
Hospital ownership				
Proprietary	.29	.09	.35†	.11
Nonproprietary	.09	.05	.21†	.10
Local government (the omitted category)	.00	.00	.00†	.00
Organizational Complexity				
High	−.03	−.01	−.04	−.02
Medium	−.04	−.02	.01	.00
Low (the omitted category)	.00	.00	.00	.00
Nurse staffing ratio	.57‡	.13	.65‡	.15
Proportion of registered nurses	.78‡	.15	.30	.06
Hospital experience	−.04	−.06	.01	.01
Age	.01	.10	−.00	−.01
Inservice training	3.33‡	.45	2.42‡	.33
Intercept	(2.35)			
Variance explained	(27%)			
Collegiality			.02	.02
Assertiveness			.23‡	.39
Intercept			(−.02)	
Variance explained			(38%)	

*N = 427 due to a listwise deletion of missing cases; all nurses scores have been set to the average number per hospital.

†Set of dummy variables for entire category significant at $p \leq .05$.

‡Coefficient significant at $p \leq .05$.

explaining patient care practices. A nurse's age and experience in working in a particular hospital for any length of time do not contribute anything. By far the most important contributor is inservice training, with a standardized coefficient of .45, excluding collegiality and assertiveness.

When the behavioral measures are included in the equation, the most important predictor of the quality of care that nurses give to their patients is assertiveness, with a standardized coefficient of .39. Collegiality's effect fails to contribute anything. This says that even when we control for hospital size, geographic region, and training programs the personality characteristics of a nurse will influence better patient care. Thus, if nurses, on the average, are assertive in their behavior and inform patient care violators of their inappropriate procedures, patient care will be enhanced. Assertive behavior by nurses appears to be a crucial factor in predicting patient care practices rather than interpersonal relations between physicians and nurses. This finding refutes the claim to the importance of a "company of equals" among members of unequal status in the medical profession.

It is also interesting to note that including assertiveness in the model reduces the effect, somewhat, of inservice training. Although this variable is still significant it is not quite as important as assertiveness. The influence of the licensure of a nurse becomes insignificant when the behavioral measures are included.

It is also important to note that the type of hospitals nurses work in, the staffing ratio, and the geographic region where the hospital is located are still significant contributors to patient care practices. In fact, the staffing ratio of nurses is slightly higher when assertiveness is included in the model. Thus, it is important to understand how nurses' perceptions of their own behavior indirectly influence hospital factors and other salient nurse attributes. Some become spurious, others decrease in value, while others even gain in predictive capabilities.

Earlier we addressed the issue of whether collegiality is more of an important contributor than assertive behavior or vice versa. The aggregate regression coefficients for the nurses' perceptions of such behavior clearly indicates that the ability to speak directly to violators overshadows collegial relations (lines 11 and 13, columns 3 and 4). While collegiality is insignificant, our results suggest that assertiveness is important. This finding disputes the collegiality hypothesis of the importance of a team effort based on collaboration and a "company of equals" and lends support to nurses "speaking up," stemming from the personality makeup of nurses.

Although O'Kelly cites ample evidence of nurses' unwillingness to speak up or "rock the boat;"[23] in health care institutions, our results are contrary to this claim. This result suggests that in the context of the hospital, nurses, on the average, are more assertive and willing to speak up to violators of inappropriate patient care. Finally, including these perceptual measures into the regression equation enhances the ability to explain the variance in patient care practices. The R^2 increased to 38 percent from 27 percent (compare line 11 with line 15), with assertiveness as the variable primarily responsible for adding to the increment; collegiality's overall contribution was negligible.

DISCUSSION

While studying the processes involved in predicting the quality of care that nurses give their patients, we also addressed another relevant issue that deals with interaction effects. We sought to find out whether or not interactions between assertiveness and collegiality, as well as interactions between all of our independent variables with these two behavioral measures increased the predictability of what is being done for patients by nurses. In proceeding to empirically test for significant interactions, contrary to our expectations, we did *not* find any. Thus, the model we have been dealing with in this study is a main effects one and not an interactive one.

However, we have been able to learn something about nurse behavior in hospitals through our empirical analysis. Earlier we said that assertive behavior may be conceived in two ways. One is as part of a generalized pattern of collegial activities; the other as an independent dimension of assertiveness is orthogonal to collegiality. The first view argues that equalitarian interactions and sharing of ideas often require arguing a point and acting in a strong and aggressive manner. The orthogonal view holds that assertive behavior stems from an individual's social personality characteristics. Thus, individuals differ in the extent to which they will act in ways to encourage conformity with what they believe either affectively and cognitively to be right and proper, depending on their personality development and overall socialization experiences. We then proceeded to examine whether or not equalitarian relationships between nurses and physicians or the independent dimension of the nurses' willingness to speak up and assert themselves informing violators of proper medical procedures is associated with the quality of care that nurses give their patients.

We found that nurses who speak up to violators of patient care policies and are assertive practice a higher quality of patient care. This relationship was significantly related to patient care practices in our correlational and regression analyses. Collegiality did not significantly contribute to the predictability of nurse patient care. We have learned empirically, from this study, that the nurses' personality characteristics are more highly associated with quality of care than are role relationships between members of unequal social status. Advocates of a "company of equals" perspective might find it useful to question this frame of reference and begin to focus their thinking on social-personality characteristics of nurses as contributors to better patient care. This position is advocated by Herman, who argues that unless nurses are encouraged to speak up on issues of practice standards and policy, they will continue to find silence a way of life, and hence will continue to abrogate their responsibility.[3] The Herman position is one that appears most tenable given our results. One would also expect the normative climate of the institution to affect the extent to which assertiveness is expressed. Our aggregated model supports this assumption; that is, nurses' assertiveness is related to other nurses' qualifications and some hospital characteristics.

A third alternative needs to be explored. We have developed our model from the general hypothesis that assertiveness and collegiality influence the caliber of patient care. It may be that high quality care does, in fact, influence the degree of assertive behavior displayed by nurses. Thus, nurses who are knowledgeable and deliver appropriate care may become more assertive because they are confident of their knowledge and capabilities. This confident manner together with obvious good results would tend to stimulate a collegial atmosphere since physicians would be more likely to treat confident, capable practitioners, regardless of profession, as colleagues.

CONCLUSION

We employed a contextual model that examined relationships at the hospital and not at the individual nurse level. From this type of model we conclude that the characteristics of hospitals in which nurses work help shape their behavior. It is important to know something about the structure of the organizational setting and behavioral processes when attempting to predict behavior. The fact that the extent of assertive behavior by nurses differs by hospital ownership and U.S. region suggests that certain hospitals have some type of selection process that occurs within it for hiring a particular type of nurse. Finally, our results have suggested that hospitals that hire assertive nurses may enhance the quality of patient care.

Perceptions of assertiveness then are not only important for patient care but they also affect the type of hospital a nurse chooses to work in, the locality of the hospital, and the training program in it. Implicit in this finding are policy suggestions for the future. For example, inservice training programs in hospitals could also include assertion sessions as part of their course material. Also, such courses could have the ultimate objective of reducing nosocomial infections, a threat to almost every individual who enters a hospital today.

Finally, we suggest looking at our model in a slightly different manner. Since our dependent variable is a "global" measure of patient care practices, an analysis entailing examining specific indices of patient care such as urinary catheter care, irrigation solution procedures, or intravenous care would be useful. This analysis is currently in progress. In other words, we envision a parsimonious model, one that includes only the statistically significant independent variables found in this study regressed against these specific patient care practice indices. In turn, we might be able to evaluate not only nurses' patient care but also, more importantly, how independent measures such as assertiveness and training programs are related to specific components of patient care practices. Further studies capable of establishing causal linkages among the variables could result in important policy recommendations.

REFERENCES

1. Coser RL: Authority and decision-making in a hospital: A comparative analysis. *Am Sociol Rev* 1958; 23:56-63.
2. Friedson E, Rhea B: Process in a company of equals. *Soc Probl* 1963; 2:119-131.
3. Herman SJ: *Becoming Assertive*. New York, D Van Nostrand Co, 1978.
4. Hoeckelman RA: Nurse-physician relationships: Problems and solutions, in Chaska N (ed): *The Nursing Profession: Views Through the Mist.* New York, McGraw-Hill Book Co, 1978, pp 330-335.
5. Kramer M: *Reality Shock: Why Nurses Leave Nursing*. St. Louis, CV Mosby Co, 1974.
6. Reeder S, Mauksch H: Nursing: Continuing change, in Freeman HE, Levin S, Reeder LG (eds): *The Handbook of Medical Sociology.* New York, Prentice-Hall Inc, 1979.
7. Smoyak SA: Problems in interprofessional relations. *Bull NY Acad Med* 1973; 53:51-59.
8. Herman SJ: Assertiveness: An answer to job dissatisfaction for nurses, in Alberti R (ed): *Assertiveness: Innovation, Applications, Issues.* San Luis Obispo, Calif, Impact Publishers, 1977.
9. Ben-David J: The professional role of the physician in bureaucratized medium. *Human Relations* 1958; 11:225-274.
10. Goss ME: Influence and authority among physicians in an outpatient clinic. *Am Sociol Rev* 1961; 26:39-50.
11. Kornhauser W: *Scientists in Industry: Conflict and Accommodation.* Berkeley, University of California Press, 1962.
12. Solomon D: Professional Persons in Bureaucratic Organizations. Symposium on Preventive and Social Psychiatry. Washington, DC, Walter Reed Army Institute of Research, 1957, pp 253-266.
13. Wardwell WI: Social integration, bureaucratization and profession. *Social Forces* 1955; 34:356-359.
14. Weber M: *The Theory of Social and Economic Organization.* New York, University Press, 1957.
15. Barber B: *Science and the Social Order.* New York, Collier Books, 1962, p 195.
16. Aiken L, Freeman HE: A sociological perspective on science and technology in medicine, in Durban PT (ed): *A Guide to Science, Technology and Medicine.* New York, Free Press, 1980.
17. Broverman ID, et al: Sex role stereotypes and clinical judgments of mental health. *J Consult Clin Psychol* 1970; 54:211-213.
18. Bullough B, Bullough V: Sex discrimination in health care. *Nurs Outlook* 1975; 23:40-45.
19. Ehrenreich B, Deirdre E: *Complaints and Disorders: The Sexual Politics of Sickness.* New York: Feminist Press, 1974.
20. Feather N, Simon J: Fear of success and causal attribution for outcome. *J Pers* 1973; 41:524-541. Feather N, Simon J: Reactions of male and female success and failure in sex-linked occupations: Impressions of personality, causal attribution, and perceived likelihood of different consequences. *J Pers Soc Psychol* 1975; 31:20-31.

21. Levinson R: Sexism in medicine. *Am J Nurs* 1976; 31(March):426-431.

22. Millet K: *Sexual Politics*. Garden City, NY, Doubleday & Co Inc, 1970.

23. O'Kelly L: Revolution in 1976: The assertive nurse. *Weather Vane* 1976; June:453-5.

24. Reeder S: The social context of nursing, in Chaska N (ed): *The Nursing Profession: Views Through the Mist*. New York, McGraw-Hill Book Co, 1978, pp 235-245.

25. Scully D, Bart P: A funny thing happened on the way to the orifice: Women in gynecological textbooks. *Am J Sociol* 1973; 78:1045-1050.

26. Stevens S, Reeder S, Yokopenic P, et al: Nurse Assertiveness and Patient Care Practices. Presented at the annual meeting of the American Psychological Association, New York, 1979.

27. Yokopenic P, Stevens S: Hospital Nurse Assertiveness: Individual- and Group-level Determinants. Presented at the annual meeting of the American Psychological Association, New York, 1979.

28. Borgotta EF, Cattrell LS Jr: Directions for research in group behavior. *Am J Sociol* 1957; July:62 42-48.

29. Haley RW, Schaberg DR, Von Allman SV, et al: Estimating the extra charges and prolongation of hospitalization due to nosocomial infections: A comparison of methods. *J Infect Dis* 1980; February:141:248-57.

30. Kass EH: Surveillance as a control system, in *Proceedings of the International Conference on Nosocomial Infections*. Center for Disease Control, Atlanta, August 3-6, 1970; pp 292-293.

31. Williams REO: Changing perspectives in hospital infections, in *Proceedings of the International Conference on Nosocomial Infection*. Center for Disease Control, Atlanta, August 3-6, 1970; pp 1-10.

32. Schaffner W: "Humans, the animate reservoir of nosocomial pathogens, in Cundy KR, Ball W (eds): *Infection Control in Health Care Facilities*. Baltimore, University Park Press, 1977; pp 57-70.

33. Raven BH, Haley RW: Social influence in a medical context, in Bickman L (ed): *Applied Social Psychology Annual 1*. Beverly Hills, Calif, Sage Publications, 1980, pp 255-278.

34. Haley RW, Bennett JV, Quade D, et al: Study on the efficacy of nosocomial infection control (SENIC project): Summary of study design. *Am J Epidemiol*, to be published.

35. Bennett JV, Brachman PS: *Hospital Infections*. Boston, Little Brown & Co, 1979.

36. Hofling CK, Brotzman E, Dalrymple S, et al: An experimental study in nurse-physician relationships. *J Nerv Ment Dis* 1966; 143:171-190.

37. Duff JA, Hollingshead AB: *Sickness and Society*. New York, Harper & Row Publishers Inc, 1968.

38. Berrelson B, Steiner GA: *Human Behavior: An Inventory of Scientific Findings*. New York, Harcourt, Brace & World, 1964.

39. Raab E, Lipset S: *Prejudice and Society*. New York, Anti-defamation League of B'Nai B'rith, 1959.

40. Acock A, DeFleur M: A configurational approach to contingent consistency in the attitude-behavior relationship. *Am Sociol Rev* 1972; 37:714-726.

Part III

Issues in Implementation

14. Integrating Quality Assurance Mechanisms

WILLIAM R. FIFER

INTRODUCTION

The 1980 edition of the *Accreditation Manual for Hospitals (AMH)* published by the Joint Commission on Accreditation of Hospitals (JCAH) contains, for the first time, a comprehensive quality assurance standard. This standard sets forth a major change in the requirement for patient care evaluation, stressing, in particular, integration of quality assurance activities. It proposes a problem-finding, problem-solving approach that shall be evaluated for accreditation purposes in terms of problems found and problems solved. We will discuss in this chapter the rationale for and content and process of the integrated quality assurance system.

The word *system* implies an orderly plan, procedure, or method, and what exists now in the quality assurance world is plainly nonsystematic, in every sense. First, there is no agreement at the conceptual level about what quality assurance means, as applied to the patient care function, or even about the meaning of *quality*. Second, there is no agreement about the scope of a *comprehensive* quality assurance program. That is, it is not clear whether it should include, for example, a review of tissues to determine necessity for surgery, analysis of incident reports generated by the hospital risk management program, patient satisfaction surveys, discharge planning, or concurrent utilization review to determine appropriateness of resource allocation. Indeed, Stearns and coworkers have listed 23 separate data inputs to the hospital-based, comprehensive quality assurance system.[1] Two major confluences, the cost/quality interface and the relationship between quality assurance and risk management (prevention of patient injury), typify the most "comprehensive" systems and serve to illustrate the need to define the scope of the activity. Third, it is unclear where the locus of control should be located within health care institutions (for example, in the administration, medical staff, or some joint committee).

Thus, disintegration is the order of the day, conceptually and organizationally, and the consequences of this disintegration are borne mostly by the individual health care facility, the principal object of regulation and accreditation. The hospital is an intriguing locus of accountability on several scores: it is a well-defined, licensed corporation with deep roots in its community, as represented by its governing authority. It is professionally managed and thus capable of considerable organizational rationality. It provides a unique peer forum for a variety of kinds of health care professionals, and, finally, it documents more carefully than almost any other health care organization the transactions of patient care. This reading will assume that the hospital is the organizational locus of accountability most capable of integrating all the facets and dimensions of quality assurance activities. In doing so, it recognizes the importance of nonhospital quality assurance activities such as statutory credentialing (licensure), mandatory continuing education, recredentialing, and accreditation requirements for ambulatory care facilities, mental health clinics, alcohol treatment programs, and Health Maintenance Organizations (HMOs). We conclude that effective integration must be viewed from an organizational perspective, and we choose the hospital as the most visible candidate organization.

THE RATIONALE FOR INTEGRATION

Why all the fuss about quality assurance? At the most fundamental level, concern about bad medical care arises from the comparatively recent evidence that medical care can be good. (There was no clamor for equity of access when medical care was little more than the provision of supportive nostrums.) Further, there is probably less "bad" medical care now than at any time in history. However, because technologically oriented, science-based medical care is so expensive and so capable of being profoundly effective, we are more aware than ever before of differences in cost, quality, and effectiveness. The "evidence" that there is a "quality crisis" is fragmentary: the much publicized marginal practices of providers catering to the poor led to the perjorative term *medicaid mills*. It is clear that public programs will be abused by some providers financially, ethically, and scientifically, but we do not know the true extent of such "marginal" practices.

Flagrant malpractice trials such as *Gonzalez* v. *Nork*[2] indicate that our present credentialing and facility accreditation systems with their dependence on "peer review" do not protect patients from detectable patterns of substandard practice. Evidence arising out of the malpractice insurance "crisis" of 1975 indicates that there is a significant undercurrent of patient mishaps that attends modern medical care. The California Medical Insurance Feasibility Study concluded that almost five percent of all hospitalized patients experienced "potentially compensable events."[3] Egeberg has estimated that there are 2,000,000 patient injuries annually in U.S. hospitals, of which 700,000 involve negligence.[4] Finally, the data concerning "unnecessary" surgery has led a committee of the United States House of Representatives to conclude that "unnecessary" surgery costs four billion dollars and 12,000 lives annually.[5]

In sum, this brief discussion indicates that there is a rationale for introducing quality assurance mechanisms in health institutions. We now discuss the rationale for integrating those mechanisms, at least at the level of the individual hospital. Although lesser reasons exist (e.g., to eliminate costly, time-consuming, and inefficiently overlapping activities), the principal reason for integration is to enhance the effectiveness of existing activities. To capitalize on the potential impact of integration, we must understand the flaws of existing mechanisms and the potential of integration to correct these flaws.

Professional Credentialing

Individual professional credentialing can be divided into two parts: (1) statutory credentialing (licensure) and (2) professional credentialing (e.g., certification, registry). It seems likely that a cornerstone of quality care would be to certify the competency of those professionals allowed to provide services to the seekers of care. States attempt this through licensure and are aided by a vast array of professional societies that establish standards and award certificates and such to those qualified to meet the standards. Yet these activities are patently ineffective and are thus currently undergoing reform. Licenses have been criticized for being too broad, infrequently revoked (and for the wrong reasons), and, until recently, nonexpiring.[6] The latter concern has prompted a wave of reform emphasizing periodic relicensure. While the initial licensure decision may be relevant, it became clear that a one-time assessment, no matter how valid, did not attest to much of anything 20 years later, given the dynamic nature of health-related knowledge. For this reason many states now require relicensure. However, in the absence of any performance evaluation data, they usually require only proxy evidence of competence, such as participation in continuing professional education.

Professional credentialing, although undergoing reform similar to licensure to require periodic recertification, suffers from the same flaws of licensure, plus a possibly fatal one from the point of view of the public—it is voluntary. The principal problem with professional credentialing as a quality control mechanism is that it lacks a performance evaluation data base. In the absence of any professional performance data, an occasional license or certificate may be lifted for some flagrant (and usually irrelevant) legal or ethical breach. What is needed, however, is a dynamic and valid data system that tracks professional competence throughout a lifetime and sensitively adjusts permission to practice in accord with changing professional competencies.

Mandatory Continuing Education

The health professions are among the scholarly professions characterized by lifelong dedication to learning. It is, therefore, not surprising that continued participation in professional education would be proposed in the name of quality assurance. Mandatory continuing education is required by many states for relicensure of a variety of health professionals,[7] for continued membership in professional associations, and for recertification. Hospitals have become an important locus of continuing professional education, devoting space, equipment, and education expertise; keeping records for their professional staffs; and struggling to achieve and maintain accreditation status as educational providers. Yet despite the time and effort, there is little if any evidence of a relationship between continuing medical education (CME) and the quality of patient care.[8] The likely reason for this is that, despite the sentinel contribution of Clem Brown in 1971 stressing the importance of a "bicycle" relationship between professional care and professional learning,[9] most CME still lacks relevance in terms of being a response to demonstrated defects in the quality of patient care caused by cognitive deficiency. Most CME programs (including hospital-based ones) do not proceed from the results of needs-assessment efforts that begin with a rigorous analysis of the quality of patient care. Conversely, patient care evaluations usually lack the rigor to separate the "cognitive-lack" component from the general area of improvable professional performance or patient benefit so that they clearly isolate who needs to know what to improve the quality of care. Although refreshing exceptions are beginning to appear in medical literature,[10] there is a general lack of integration between quality maintenance and lifelong learning to the detriment of both.

Peer Review

It is accepted as an article of faith in professionalism that there exists some almost magical quality in the concept of peer review. While lawyers or teachers would not know "good" surgical technique if they saw it, peer (L. *pare,* "equal") surgeons would and, further, would accept as a component of professionalism the duty of reviewing their peers' performance and submitting their own performance to their review. The ultimate expression of this magical belief is that health professionals can be exempted from the legal controls that pertain to ordinary mortals.[11] The myth is exposed by most current investigations of medical care quality, which indicate, as might be expected, that perhaps 10 percent of health care practitioners are so marginal in their performance as to be (to use Nader's catchy phrase) "unsafe at any speed." Indeed, many physicians decry the need to evaluate the quality of professional performance, saying "we all know that 10 percent of the doctors in this hospital (this society, this city, this state) could not take care of your cat and, further, we all know who they are!" The fact that nothing is done about it is the ultimate condemnation of peer review as a quality assurance mechanism.[12]

To understand the failure of traditional peer review, one must, as Judge Goldberg did in *Gonzalez* v. *Nork*,[2] ask how it works. Peers review a random sample of patient medical records in order to make a judgment about the quality of care provided by their colleagues. Picking up the records one by one, peers review initial evaluations, treatment plans, operative reports, consultants' notes, laboratory data, and medication sheets to decide if the care represented by the record is "good" care. Lacking objective criteria or even some consensus among various reviewers, the judgment of "goodness" hinges on "whether I would have done it that way." Of the two possible answers, the affirmative is tainted by such subjectivity that the result is determined by the reviewer. The negative, which should provide the springboard for all remedial action in the peer review system, occurs only under the most flagrant or bizarre circumstances because (1) "it's only one case," (2) "I'm sure the record is an incomplete documentation of all the circumstances and contexts which existed at the time," and (3) "under certain circumstances I might have handled the situation that way myself, so who am I to judge my colleague?"

Medical Audit

Until recently, both the JCAH and PSROs have required that hospitals use medical audit as a central tool in the conduct of quality assurance activities. Despite fairly lengthy literature and extensive application and experimentation, the medical audit has not proved to be, by itself, an effective instrument of quality assurance.[12] One must therefore ask: "What caused the collapse of medical audit?" The list of suspects is long: physician resistance; professional defensiveness; fear of data being subpoenaed by unfriendly lawyers; fear of lawsuits by colleagues subjected to sanctions; and, perhaps most importantly, the failure to implement effective change strategies to assure that improvement in quality occurred once problems were identified. It is clear that many studies were completed by hospital medical staffs that tended to conclude that "all was well" and that no problems existed. Some of the initial ineffectiveness was likely due to choosing "safe" topics and the use of permissive, nondiscriminating, or at least irrelevant criteria in the screening step. When criteria were tightened up, a whitewash was sometimes evident at the subjective (peer review) step. Often the "front end" of audit was effectively tightened up, yet no action output occurred save for endless letters providing individual practitioners feedback as to the audit criteria and their own performance.

For some or all of these reasons, medical audit was considered ineffective in accomplishing its ultimate objective: documented evidence of improvement in the quality of patient care.[13] The JCAH concluded that hospitals responded with "paper compliance," filling in all the squares and spaces on the audit worksheets in keeping with the numerical requirements but not with substantive evidence of improvement in care quality.

Utilization Review

Both the JCAH and PSROs require a hospital-based, concurrent review of newly admitted and extended-stay patients for the purpose of minimizing unnecessary or inappropriate hospital admissions, stays, and ancillary tests and procedures. While a discussion of the effectiveness of concurrent review to accomplish its major objective (cost containment) is beyond the scope of this reading, utilization review was dissociated from audit and other "quality assurance" activities in the hospital setting. The cost containment job was seen as distinct from the quality maintenance job, even though what is "necessary" and "appropriate" clearly relates to the quality of patient management. It is likely that the utilization review coordinators saw numerous patterns of variant practitioner performance of patient outcomes, but there was no linkage (data or otherwise) to connect concurrent review to retrospective review, even as applied to the same patient! It is likely that the extended-stay case represented a prime candidate for review to detect complications, unimproved cases, or preventable morbidity, but it was used only as a focus for (ineffectual) administrative efforts to contain expenditures.

Continuous Monitors

The JCAH requires ongoing review of certain categories of patients and practices, presumably because there is room for improvement. Thus, the standard specifies tissue (surgical case) review; review of antibiotic use; review of transfusion practices, pharmacy, and therapeutics (drug use review); participation in a hospital-wide infection control and patient safety function; and medical records review. This diverse group of review activities has usually been handled by a separate committee for each, with a complete lack of integration.

As a group, these review activities were intended to provide the content for the ineffective and subjective "peer review" discussed above. Each committee met separately on a monthly or quarterly basis and tried to decide subjectively about the quality of an aspect of care out of the context of the many other aspects that relate to and influence each other in a given case. There is prima facie evidence of the ineffectiveness of most of their activities in causing practitioner behavior change or enhancement of the quality of care. As recently as a year ago, the claim that "unnecessary surgery" cost four billion dollars and 12,000 lives annually was unrefuted by alternate data, although the data used were criticized.[14] If, in fact, tissue (surgical case) reviews (which had been in place as a peer review mechanism in hospitals for decades) were effective, hospitals would have been able to show that the unnecessary hysterectomy issue had been dealt with long ago by effective medical staff action. Although there is no expert consensus even on such doctrinaire procedures as tonsillectomy,[15] criteria are beginning to become available for an objective review procedure.[16] It is certainly not conceptually farfetched to envision a criterion-based, on-line procedure that monitors surgical practice to prevent "unnecessary" surgery from being done, but such does not exist to our knowledge.

Evidence is beginning to appear that significant behavioral change in regard to blood use can be accomplished,[17] but most hospitals are still spending too much physician time reviewing single unit transfusions and similar unproductive efforts.

The publications of Simmons and Stolley,[18] Kunin and associates,[19] Achong and co-workers,[20] and others document clearly the extent of irrational overutilization of antibiotics, singly and in combinations, usually as prophylaxis for surgical procedures. Criteria are now available to permit objective review focused on areas shown to contain great potential for improvement. The time is here to coordinate antibiotic use review with the whole issue of nosocomial infection control, thus integrating the microbiology laboratory and clinical pharmacy with the expertise of the nurse epidemiologist and infectious disease clinician.

Medical records review is usually handled by a committee that approves new forms for laboratory slips and wastes physician time on quantitative review of the record for timeliness and completeness. Despite the long-standing existence of the standard, most medical staffs have not dared to intrude on the autonomy of their individual members by specifying the data base or type of documentation that attests to a clinician's thoroughness, analytic sense, or efficiency. The result is that medical records are still too often illegible, incomplete or uncompleted, and unauditable, to say nothing of living up to Weed's standards of instruments that "guide and teach."[21]

Finally, the patient safety function provides the bridge between quality assurance and risk management. There is likely a correlation between meticulous patient care and the prevention of patient injury, yet the traditional hospital risk management function is essentially administrative and has failed to involve the practitioner whose negligence may lead to the injured or dead patient and the million dollar lawsuit. The unnecessary hysterectomy probably carries with it the same potential for morbidity and mortality as the necessary one. The injudicious use of an antibiotic is attended by the same incidence of nephrotoxicity as when one that is indicated is used. It is time for the "incident report" to be expanded to include the medically related incident and to be pattern-analyzed to detect slippage in practitioner performance before patient harm occurs.

Credentialing and Continuing Education

Credentialing and continuing education, required by the JCAH, are essentially response steps to problems identified by a comprehensive surveillance activity.

Their genesis is logical enough—problems with the quality of patient care are either due to the fact that practitioners do not know (Rx: CME) or do not do (Rx: credentialing). In fact, both response steps (the assurance in quality assurance) are cut off from the surveillance (quality assessment) activities because there is no organizational or information link between them.

We have already made the point that CME as a problem-solving activity is generally disintegrated from patient care problems; credentialing in the hospital remains to be discussed.

Hospital-based credentialing possesses the potential to overcome many of the flaws of individual credentialing, discussed previously. It is not as broad as the license—clinical privileges are usually much more limited and are practitioner specific; it does expire—periodic reappraisal is required; and it has the potential to be data based—the JCAH standard, for example, says that the periodic reappraisal process should consider the practitioner's "patterns of care as demonstrated by reviews conducted by committees such as utilization review, infection control, tissue, medical record, pharmacy/therapeutics, and patient care evaluation."[22]

In point of fact, however, credentialing is as "blind" as CME, lacking an information system to give it direction in fine-tuning practitioners' credentials to match demonstrated competencies. At issue in both *Gonzalez* v. *Nork*[2] and *Purcell and Tucson General Hospital* v. *Zimbelman*[23] was the effectiveness of credentialing, the courts holding that hospitals and their professional staff committees "could have known or should have known" that these practitioners displayed a pattern of incompetence in the relevant clinical areas long before the harm occurred to these patients. The courts said, in effect, why didn't you (hospital) know of and interdict the interaction between these practitioners and these patients? In most hospitals today, "initial" credentialing is reasonably data-based in that the applicant provides verifiable evidence of his education, training and previous experience. Periodic recredentialing, however, still generally lacks data based on objective evaluation of practitioner performance to support most credentialing recommendations.

We have described many of the quality assurance activities required of hospitals to illustrate the present condition of disintegration of the components. To enumerate other activities is to further amplify the disintegration. For example, *nursing audit* has a long and distinguished history of its own.[24] Yet it grew up apart from medical audit and generally remains so, as though medical care and nursing care were unrelated aspects of patient management. Social workers evaluate the social work function using wholly separate topics, criteria, and data systems. Respiratory therapists evaluate respiratory therapy and rehabilitationists evaluate rehabilitation therapy. Except in settings where team care is a reality, "multidisciplinary audit" has been more form than substance.

THE CONTENT OF INTEGRATION

It seems clear that integration means more than simply making an exhaustive inventory of all the quality-related activities in the hospital and channeling all of their reports through a single committee. Functional integration means creating a clear relationship between the problem-finding and problem-solving components of quality assurance.

The first task of integration is to decide how to identify productive areas for evaluation, a step which might be called *problem identification.* John Williamson calls this a quest for ''ABNA—Achievable benefit not achieved'' and recommends a nominal group process (NGP) technique to identify candidate problems.[25] We prefer to think of it as construction of an *exception review system,* which begins with the assumption that most medical care proceeds nominally and that the key is to identify the patient care exception to find the potential for improvement. Examples of data capture points for exception review would be deaths, unimproved cases (overstays), complicated cases (nosocomial infections), and transfers to special care units or other acute care facilities. A beginning implementation of an exception review system is exemplified by the Medical Management Analysis (MMA) system of Craddick,[26] which uses generic criteria modified from the California Medical Insurance Feasibility Study.[3] The new JCAH quality assurance standard suggests the following data sources as being potentially useful in identifying problems (or exceptional cases): medical records, death review, continuous monitors, safety/infection control data, review of drug use, PSRO profiles, specific medical care evaluation studies, incident reports, laboratory/radiology reports, claims/settlements, utilization review findings, surveys of patients and staff, and fiscal data. However accomplished, the integrated model begins with a front-end activity whose objective is to identify problems with patient care and whose dimensions are appropriate to the clinical mission of the health care facility and program.

The next step in the integrated model is to employ objective problem assessment methods to validate the existence of the suspect problem turned up by the initial problem identification activity and to delineate its scope and cause. This central step is as important as the input (problem finding) or the output (problem solving) phases of the integrated model because it provides the objective evidence of the nature of the problem necessary to take appropriate action. It resolves the major cause of peer review ineffectiveness by providing objective evidence of the problem and usually its attribution to provide the psychological support necessary to take meaningful action. If one suspects unnecessary antibiotic use in the hospital, the subject may be discussed in committees or become the content of a seminar. If one knows that unacceptable (by valid, published criteria) and irrational antibiotic use occurs 62 percent of the time as prophylaxis for gynecologic surgery, the problem demands action, and its solution can be assigned to appropriate responsible people.

There is a misconception that the new JCAH quality assurance standard means the end of the "audit" requirement for accreditation. On the contrary, patient care evaluation studies that derive their content from the problem identification activity and use objective evaluation methodology are a keystone of the problem assessment (middle) phase of integrated quality assurance. The new standard attempts to leave behind lock-step, inflexible "medical audits" that were limited to collecting data from the patient medical record retrospectively about the technical processes of professional performance. It does not do away with the need to assess problems objectively. It suggests, however, flexibility in regard to the time frame, data to be used for analysis, and objectives (input, process, outcome, or some combination) of the study. Objective evaluation methodologies have been developed in addition to "audit." The mental health or alcohol treatment unit may prefer to use the "goal attainment scale" (GAS) methodology of Kiresuk and Sherman to evaluate its performance.[27] A support service such as dietary may plug candidate problems into an already well-developed management by objectives (MBO) system. Utilization review may use claims form data to identify exceptional resource use adjusted for case mix. The emergency department may collect data concurrently to support or refute a suspicion that its triage is not timely or maximally effective. Audit lives!—not as a paper shuffling activity to provide window dressing for some inspection agency, but as a flexible and innovative tool of objective assessment that validates the existence of a suspected problem.

The final step in the integrated quality assurance system is problem solving, thus completing the integrated model (Figure 14-1).

The ineffectiveness of hospital-based quality assurance mechanisms up to now is principally due to their lack of action output. Granted, when no problems were found (due to ineffective first and second steps) no action output was possible. However, some early evaluation efforts unwittingly turned up significant and often major defects in care quality only to have no action taken. Why? It was principally because there was no forced integration, functionally or organizationally, between the problem-finding and problem-solving activities. Problems withered on the vine because committee personnel changed annually like a game of musical chairs so that "institutional memory" was nonexistent. (From beginning to end a patient care evaluation study may require two or more years.) Problems died because the committee that discovered them possessed only fact-finding and recommending authority, as opposed to the capability of taking action; and, the organizational wires were cut between staff work (problem finding) and line authority (problem solving). Knowing that "something should be done" to address incontrovertible problems, "education" was often handed the baton and did its thing even though the people in the seats may have been fully cognizant. Believing that feedback alone would be sufficient to cause behavior change,

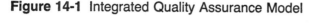

Figure 14-1 Integrated Quality Assurance Model

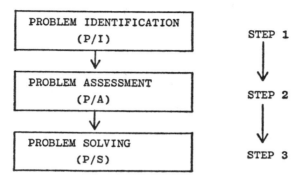

mimeographed letters and completed audit worksheets were stuffed into already-full physician mailboxes, never to be read.

Only by having guidance from the problem assessment step as to the scope, cause, and attribution of the problem can problem solving be relevant, and relevance is the key to effectiveness. If the problem is cognitive, who needs to know what to resolve it? If the problem is performance, what behavior change must be accomplished by counseling, by monitoring, by adjustment in clinical privileges, or by sanctions? If the problem is organizational, what policy or procedure must be changed or what task must be reengineered or reassigned?

Two examples of the quality assurance system will serve to illustrate the content of functional integration:

Example 1

Problem identification:
    The literature stresses the nephrotoxicity of injectable aminoglycoside antibiotics and recommends close monitoring of renal function.

Problem assessment:
    Pharmacy records are searched and the last 50 administrations of parenteral aminoglycoside are reviewed. Only 12 percent were adequately monitored relative to renal function. All services and practitioners were involved.

Problem solving:
    Policy and procedure change was effected such that pharmacy released the drug only when renal function was within limits set by policy. All physician overrides were individually and pattern-analyzed by the service chief.

Example 2

Problem identification:
   PSRO areawide length of stay data disclose that the hospital has a 30 percent longer stay for stroke patients than the area mean.

Problem assessment:
   Consecutive case study of the last 50 stroke patients is completed by multidisciplinary team. Case mix is okay. Nursing care is okay. The problem is lack of effective discharge planning process.

Problem solving:
   Discharge planning was reorganized after consultation to involve both nursing service and social work service. Protocol was reworked to include a screening step. Duties were assigned and training was accomplished. The length of stay was to be monitored by the director of nurses and reported quarterly to the chief executive officer.

THE PROCESS OF INTEGRATION

   The process of integration of quality assurance mechanisms in the individual health care facility should be flexible and uniquely suited to the clinical mission of the facility. The new JCAH quality assurance standard requires a written plan as the first step, allowing the individual hospital to determine the dimensions of its quality assurance program or system, but requiring that it think through what will be done and who will do it before beginning.
   There are two basic dimensions of this process of integration: (1) organization and (2) information flow. Organization implies that the form is created to follow the function, and that aspects of authority and responsibility are clearly defined. It presumes timeliness, job descriptions, reporting relationships, and clear charges to committees and task forces.
   Resistance to implementing a truly comprehensive quality assurance system that articulates with cost containment and risk management programs is often due to reluctance to add a new administrative superstructure to the already excessive number of committees and staff aides created by prior accountability requirements. Also, the assumption that the fundamental raison d'etre for the hospital's organizational structure is to provide *quality* medical care, making a separate system for quality assurance an organizational redundancy.
   My own predilections are that most hospital committee structures are overblown and that a hospital should take advantage of a new requirement such as the JCAH quality assurance standard to simplify and collapse the structure. More importantly, I believe that the disintegration that has characterized previous quality assurance efforts is at least partly due to separation of the staff (problem

finding) from the line (problem solving) function. My instinct is to decentralize the quality assurance function organizationally to make each department or service director responsible for the quality of performance of the personnel and functions of his or her own department: Within each department would reside the responsibility and authority to implement and document all three steps of the integrated process: problem identification, problem assessment, and problem solution. I see the need to aggregate the generic components of quality assurance (credentialing, continuing education) conceptually but not operationally. Thus, I believe each department head should be required to use the same generic data base for the credential function (health status and patterns of care data) but adapt it to the specific departmental or professional function to assure relevance. Two examples are provided below:

- The chief of surgery will maintain a current professional performance profile on each active surgeon that systematically tracks unjustified procedures, complication rates, inappropriate use of blood or antibiotics, deaths and significant morbidity (overstays), status of physical and mental health (including age), and other relevant performance parameters.
- The directors of medical/nursing/other education will provide staff work to assist department heads to identify and remediate knowledge lack at the departmental or other appropriate level.

Information flow presents the same general overkill problem that organization does. It is clear that the lifelines of integration are the information exchanges that support the relationships between the problem identification, problem assessment, and problem solving components of the system. While continuing to favor a decentralized information system that fits the decentralized organization of the integrated quality assurance system, it is of value to be exposed to the dimensions of a single comprehensive system for the individual hospital. The reader is referred to *Solutions* as the best attempt to date to construct a comprehensive "QIS" (quality information system) for the modern hospital.[1]

REFERENCES

1. Stearns G, Imbiorski W, Fox L: *Solutions*. Chicago, Care Communications Inc, 1979.
2. Hedgepeth JH: Court decision would extend liability . . . but the publicity is premature. *Trustee* 1974; 27(2):19-27.
3. California Medical Association: *Report on the Medical Insurance Feasibility Study*. San Francisco, Sutter Publications, 1977.
4. Egeberg R, cited by Schwartz WB, Komesar NK: Doctors, damages and deterrance—An economic view of medical malpractice. *N Engl J Med* 1978; 298:1282-1289.

5. House Committee on Interstate and Foreign Commerce, Subcommittee on Oversight and Investigation: Cost and quality of health care: Unnecessary surgery, publication no. 052-070-03295-2. Government Printing Office, 1976.

6. Cohen HS, Miike LH: Toward a more responsive system of professional licensure. *Int J Health Serv* 1974; 4:266.

7. *New York Times,* September 9, 1979, p Educ 3.

8. Berg AO: Does continuing medical education improve the quality of medical care? A look at the evidence. *J Fam Pract* 1979; 8:1171-1174.

9. Brown CR, Fleisher DS: The bicycle concept—relating continuing education directly to patient care, in Stearns NS, Getchell ME, Gold PA (eds): *Continuing Medical Education in Community Hospitals.* Boston, Massachusetts Medical Society, 1971.

10. Achong MR, Wood J, Theal HK, et al: Changes in hospital antibiotic therapy after a quality-of-use study. *Lancet* 1977; 2:1118-1122.

11. Freidson E: *Profession of Medicine.* New York, Dodd, Mead & Co, 1973, p 47.

12. Anderson OW, Shields MS: Quality measurement and control in physician decision-making: State of the art, *Health Services Research,* 1982, 17:125-156.

13. *Report of a Study: Assessing Quality in Health Care: An Evaluation.* Washington, DC, National Academy of Sciences, 1976.

14. Jacobs CM, Christoffel TH, Dixon N: *Measuring the Quality of Patient Care.* Cambridge, Mass, Ballinger Publishing Co, 1976.

15. Carden TS Jr: Tonsillectomy—trials and tribulations: A report on the NIH consensus conference on indications for T and A. *JAMA* 1978; 240:1961-1962.

16. Breo DL: AMA-HEW project: Study will report "unjustified" surgery is less than 1%. *Am Med News* 1979; (November 9):8.

17. Henry JB, Mintz P, Webb W: Optimal blood ordering for elective surgery. *JAMA* 1977; 237:451.

18. Simmons H, Stolley P: This is medical progress? Trends and consequences of antibiotic use in the U.S. *JAMA* 1974; 227:1023-1028.

19. Kunin CM, Tapaci T, Craig WA: Use of antibiotics: A brief exposition of the problem and some tentative solutions. *Ann Intern Med* 1973; 79:555-560.

20. Achong MR, Hauser BA, Krusky JL: Rational and irrational use of antibiotics in a Canadian teaching hospital. *Can Med Assoc J* 1977; 116:256-259.

21. Weed LW: *Medical Records, Medical Education and Patient Care–The Problem-Oriented Record as a Basic Tool.* Cleveland, The Press of Case Western Reserve University, 1969.

22. *Accreditation Manual for Hospitals, 1980.* Chicago, Joint Commission on Accreditation of Hospitals, 1980, p 99.

23. *Purcell and Tucson General Hospital v Zimbelman,* 119312, CAC IV 130 (Superior Court of Pima County 1972).

24. McGinnis S: History of nursing audit, in *Nursing Audit. Quality Review Bulletin* (special edition). Chicago, Joint Commission on Accreditation of Hospitals, 1978.

25. Williamson JW: Formulating priorities for quality assurance activity: Description of a method and its application. *JAMA* 1978; 239:631-637.

26. Craddick J: An alternative approach: Medical management analysis (MMA). *Audit Action Letter* 1978; 4 (June).

27. Kiresuk TJ, Sherman RE: Goal attainment scaling—a general method for evaluating comprehensive community health programs. *Community Ment Health J* 1968; 4:443-453.

15. Medical Peer Review and Information Management: The Dead-End Phenomenon

HARRY M. ROSEN and WILLIAM FEIGIN

Reprinted with permission from Health Care Management Review 7(3). Copyright © 1982, Aspen Systems Corporation, 59-66.

The output of hospital peer review activities can be characterized in two ways: either as code compliance or as medical management information. The result of this characterization has important implications for the way the output is used, and for its ultimate impact. Code compliance carries the connotation of "getting by with the minimum," while management information carries the connotation of supporting, rather than avoiding, decisions. This issue has become a matter of greater concern since the approval of the new Quality Assurance Standard of the Joint Commission on Accreditation of Hospitals (JCAH) in April 1979.

The standard states: "There shall be evidence of a well-defined, organized program designed to enhance patient care through the ongoing objective assessment of important aspects of patient care and the correction of identified problems." It further states that "Quality Assurance activities should be integrated/coordinated . . . (should) assimilate information gathered . . . (and) enhance communication."[1]

A body of theory that can be brought to bear on the notions of "integration" and "assimilation" can be drawn from the literature of management information systems. This of course assumes that the results of a hospital's mandated medical peer review activities should be viewed as medical management information. It also assumes that hospital management has an important role to play by providing the environment in which important decisions about the quality of care can be made. These assumptions have been used to review several basic concepts of management information systems (MIS), and to compare them with the results of an informal survey of peer review activities at several hospitals. With this as background, deficiencies in the management of medical peer review information come to light—deficiencies that can be remedied by simple mechanisms suggested by basic MIS concepts. The result would be more effective use of available information and more efficient use of the time invested by medical and administrative staffs.

BASIC MIS CONCEPTS

There are three basic concepts of MIS theory that are germane to the problem of managing medical peer review information. They are the distinction between data files and a data base, the concept of an access structure and the concept of record linkage.

Most data are assembled into files as they are collected. Files may be the ordinary kind with metal drawers and manila folders, or the computer-sensible kind which reside on punch cards, magnetic tapes or magnetic discs. In either case, a file is a collection of records that contain similar data and are arranged in some particular order.

For purposes of this discussion, the minutes of medical staff committees such as pharmacy and therapeutics, medical audit or credentials would form independent files as they accumulate over time. They would most probably be filed in chronological order, a procedure that would be logical and useful from the point of view of each committee. As long as a problem or decision requires the data of a single file, the above arrangement is perfectly adequate, if not optimal. The users, in this case committee members and staff, can be close to their own data and make use of them as they see fit. But if a decision must be made which could benefit from information from other sources, a "data base," rather than an individual file, is required.[2]

A data base is a set of files that are linked by some mechanism so that a potential user can gain access to bits of information from more than one file for a given problem. As the capabilities of computer hardware have improved, and the need by researchers and managers for more complex arrays of information has expanded, a whole new field of "data base management" has emerged. Some of the data base management systems that are currently available are remarkably powerful, and can even draw together pieces of relevant information which are stored in several independent, but communicating, computer installations.[3]

However, while these systems are complex in their implementation, they are simple in their basic concept. They are indexing or cross-referencing systems that can identify appropriate information in the data base in a manner that is analogous to a subject index in the back of a book. The index of a history text, for example, might guide a reader interested in constitutional reform to material on the Magna Carta, the Mayflower Compact and the U.S. Bill of Rights. Returning to the medical peer review example, files of the various medical staff committee minutes could be linked by a simple system of index cards.

This leads to the notion of an "access structure," which is essentially a map that guides either a user or a computer system to the location of pertinent information.[4] For example, the vice-president for personnel of a multinational corporation might need information on rates of increase in executive salaries to set a corporation-wide policy on executive compensation. If the data access structure were hierarchical, a request (computer-based or manual) might have to go to each national office, then into each office's personnel files to identify people at the appropriate executive level, and finally to the payroll files to compute rates of increase. This particular access structure might be less technically efficient than one that could go to payroll files directly, but it might add some measure of confidentiality. In terms of the above discussion, the access structure defines the bounds of data base management capability.

Finally, linkage involves the identification of particular bits of information that will "link" records in the same file or other related files. For example, the hypothetical multinational corporation might have an employee numbering code so that the first digit identifies the corporate division, while the second identifies the level within the corporate hierarchy so that all employees with the same second digit would have similar levels of responsibility in any corporate division. This would enable the kind of search described above to be carried out. In another setting, such as medical peer review, the link might be the subject of a committee's deliberation rather than a code number.[5]

In all aspects of the above discussion, it is important to emphasize three things. First, the information contained in a system need not be quantitative. Second, information management is not necessarily achieved with the aid of a computer. (In fact computerization may be utterly useless in many situations.) And finally, benefits of any attempt at information management are achieved by first assessing the needs of users and then applying basic concepts.[6,7] Complexity and elegance are only dictated by the nature of information and its uses.

THE PROBLEM OF PEER REVIEW

Peer review activities of 11 hospitals in the greater New York metropolitan area were examined with a particular emphasis on the sharing of determinations made by standing committees of each medical staff with other committees or units of the hospital. Since medical staff organizations may establish committees that are irrelevant to another hospital, observations were limited to those committees most similar to eight suggested by JCAH in its quality assurance guide.[8] They were: credentialing, tissue/surgical case review, morbidity/mortality, pharmacy and therapeutics, medical audit, infection control, utilization review, and risk control. All 11 hospitals had standing committees charged with responsibility to review all of the above aspects of patient care.

Study hospitals ranged in size from 1,212 to 235 beds. All were acute general care hospitals with, at a minimum, organized clinical departments of medicine, surgery, pediatrics, obstetrics/gynecology and psychiatry. The prevalence of subspecialty divisions varied widely. Three hospitals were under municipal auspices, four were major teaching affiliates of schools of medicine and three were community hospitals with no teaching affiliation. Hospitals were selected to reflect the above ranges of size and clinical complexity. (See Table 15-1.)

Research assistants were instructed to identify the person or persons responsible for coordinating quality assurance activities, chairing the above medical staff committees or providing administrative support for them. These individuals were interviewed and committee minutes were examined to determine what use was made of findings by committees. Only those examples of committee determinations that had a direct bearing on patient care were selected. Committee activities that centered on administrative problems, such as form completion, were not observed.

Results indicated that only 2 of the 11 hospitals had any system in place that guaranteed that information generated by one of the above committees would be used by another. In both cases, a link was established between the risk control and medical audit committees. Medicolegal hazards identified by the former committees from their review of claim settlements or pending legal actions were referred to the latter for a hospital-wide analysis of the hazard's prevalence.

There was no other example of peer review information moving beyond the confines of its original file. Inquiries, reports and warnings were sent to physicians or their clinical chiefs for follow-up, but simple follow-up fails to take full advantage of the information generated by these different committees. With the exception of the two linkages discussed above, all of this information reaches a dead end within its own committee. Furthermore, there was no evidence of physicians serving on more than one of the eight committees studied who might have provided informal information linkage. Two case studies will illustrate this problem, and suggest new relationships.

Table 15-1 Basic Characteristics of Survey Hospitals

| | Beds | | Auspices | |
Number	Frequency		Type	Frequency
0-399	2		Municipal	3
400-599	3		Voluntary	8
600-899	3			11
900+	3			
	11			

Range: 235-1212

| | Affiliations | |
Type		Frequency
Primary medical school		4
Major teaching affiliate		4
Unaffiliated		3
		11

Case I: Monitoring Aminoglycoside Prescriptions

In one of the community hospitals in the study, the pharmacy and therapeutics committee reviewed the cases of three physicians who, in the opinion of the hospital's chief pharmacist, had not adequately monitored the renal function of patients for whom antibiotics in the aminoglycoside group were prescribed. This was considered to be a serious clinical problem because if this series of drugs is prescribed over an extended period of time, kidney impairment or hearing loss may result.

Ten patients were reviewed and none of them documented adequate monitoring of renal function. In fact, one patient developed renal failure, while another was discharged with an observable loss of hearing. The committee recorded these findings in their minutes and notified the appropriate department chairmen of the problem.

One might raise several questions regarding the above committee action, not the least of which is whether the three physicians changed this clearly unsafe clinical practice. But another dimension exists. If other medical staff committees at this hospital had the above information available to them, several additional actions are likely. The risk control committee might have wished to open a file on each of these cases (particularly the kidney failure and hearing loss) to begin preparation for possible malpractice suits. This would represent a different use of the same information.

The medical audit committee might have wished to develop a hospital-wide study to determine how frequent this dangerous practice was throughout the entire medical staff. And perhaps the credentials committee could use this, and other information, in their decision to reappoint members of the attending staff. While moving peer review information outside of its original file does not guarantee the above actions and decisions, it is clear that without a linkage and access structure, the full potential of the original observations to improve patient care would not be realized.

Case II: Managing Cardiac Arrhythmias

The mortality committee of a large academic medical center considered the records of three deaths that occurred in the emergency room over a 48-hour period. All three were associated with cardiac arrhythmias which, in the opinion of the committee, were not managed properly by the junior house officers in charge. The matter was referred to the chief of cardiology for action.

The committee file indicates that, as a result of this information, the on-call schedules of cardiology fellows were revised to provide more supervision in the emergency room, and junior residents were informed that this improved back-up service was available. This was evidence of a definitive response by the hospital to improve quality of care for cardiac patients in the emergency room setting.

The point here is not to question this particular chain of events; they are perfectly acceptable in their own right. In fact, the evidence of follow-up is laudable and an important part of JCAH's Quality Assurance Standard. However, improvement management of this information might have led to even greater benefit and better coordination of peer review activities.

For one thing, unnecessary deaths clearly represent a medicolegal vulnerability that requires some preparation. An access structure which made the above mortality committee determination available to the risk control committee would have ensured that at least some assessment of the potential for a malpractice suit would be made. Without an established linkage, medicolegal consideration might only have occurred by chance.

Furthermore, one could postulate that the three cases came to the mortality committee's attention simply because they occurred in the same unit over a short time span. The problem may, in fact, pervade the entire hospital, but could only be known after a broader study conducted by the medical audit committee. Unless this committee was aware of the information currently available only in the mortality committee's file, they might not consider it to be a priority for hospital-wide investigation.

The above two examples were, admittedly, chosen to prove a point. But anyone familiar with the workings of peer review-oriented medical staff committees would concede that they are reasonably representative. And furthermore, the brief survey reported above indicated that regardless of bed size, complexity or auspices, hospitals simply do not coordinate information generated by medical staff committees.

Figure 15-1 shows the traditional peer review information flow represented by the two case studies. Four committees mentioned in the cases are used as examples. Reviews are conducted by each committee acting independently. They maintain their own files, make notifications and recommendations as necessary, and report to the medical board. There are no established linkages between files or between the committee review processes. Reports and recommendations for medical policy changes will flow to the medical board, but a more dynamic and cooperative use of available information is obviated; hence the notion of a dead end.

When recommending improvements, consultants and computer hardware firms often tend to leap to a complex, computer-based MIS. But managers prefer to follow a basic tenet of information theory that holds that the nature of an information system ought to be dictated by the needs of the people who must use it.[9] In this case, there are several constraints that must be understood.

First, the information is very sensitive. Judgment by physicians of the care rendered by their peers is a time-honored method of professional assessment, but

Figure 15-1 Traditional Peer Review Information Flow

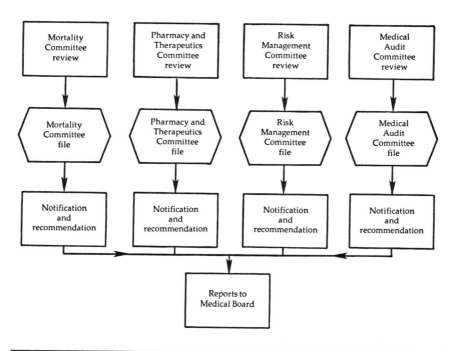

has always been performed in an atmosphere of strict confidentiality.[10] In fact, the dead-end phenomenon in peer review information can be viewed as the logical result of a need by the physician community to keep peer judgments limited to specific issues. Therefore, if physician confidence is to be retained, the access structure must stress moderation rather than easy penetration of the data base.

It has been argued that all information concerning the quality of patient care in a health care institution can be conceptualized as a common data base that is provided by many activities of the organization, including such things as strategic planning, medical audit and operational control, and can be used in many other activities such as new program development, medicolegal affairs and compliance with regulatory codes.[11] This notion is esthetically pleasing to someone concerned with optimal utilization of information, and suggests a broader definition of quality assurance activities. Efforts to improve the quality of patient care must move in this direction. However, initial efforts to improve the management of medical peer review information must proceed with caution by sharing valuable information that is already available, and by maintaining a sensitivity to the professional concerns of a medical staff and to legal questions of discoverability.

WHAT IS TO BE DONE?

The JCAH's initiative in quality assurance, as well as the evidence of linkages in medical peer review information uncovered by our survey, represent important steps toward improved information management. Some further steps are indicated, which require minimal effort and no hardware. These steps can also be accomplished within the bounds of professional and legal propriety.

Establishing a Central File

A committee or office with responsibility delegated by the medical staff for coordination of institutional quality assurance could maintain a file which is, in essence, an access structure for the hospital's peer review data base. The linkages would be the subjects of reviews and assessments performed by the various peer review committees. This index file would be confidential and only available to the chairpersons of a specific set of committees. It would have the same legal status as other committee files which, at the moment, have only limited discoverability for courtroom proceedings.

It is important to note that only those matters that might represent a hospital-wide tendency or would be of some interest to other committees would be referenced in this central index file. Procedural matters or warnings to individual physicians are not an important part of this proposed peer review data base and would be retained in the committees' own files. (An even more ambitious proposal for a peer review data base might include a central file which records specific incidents of physician performance that surface through analysis done by the several peer review committees.)

Once a determination is made that a favorable or unfavorable situation has broader consequences, a brief abstract would be placed in the central file. A title, such as the headings for the two case studies, would then be assigned. Abstracts would be filed by their respective titles. The committee that performed the initial study would also be indicated. A major teaching hospital estimated that each of its 11 committees charged with peer review responsibility might generate an average of six matters to enter in the proposed reference file.

Later, as committee chairpersons prepare their respective agendas, they could scan this file for potential review topics. Further information on a particular determination would be available in the file of the committee that performed the review through its chairperson. The chairperson would then be free to decide whether or not to further investigate a given matter, to use the same information in a different context or to avoid duplication of effort by moving on to other matters. This central file would also prove useful in establishing priorities for the improvement of patient care throughout the institution. This mechanism would comply with both the letter and spirit of the JCAH standard, which calls for an institution-wide plan that sets priorities and provides for appropriate action.

Of course there would be no compulsion for committee chairpersons to use the central access file, and no way to force committees to share their privileged deliberations. Implementation of the system would not be a simple matter requiring both commitment from the hospital's medical board and a skilled person to manage the process. The medical board would want some assurance that the access structure is functioning appropriately, and committee chairmen might have to be coaxed into participation.

Figure 15-2 depicts the structure of the proposed interactive information system using only the four committees from Figure 15-1. Note that the central file facilitates management of information generated by review activities of peer

Figure 15-2 Revised, Interactive Peer Review Information Flow

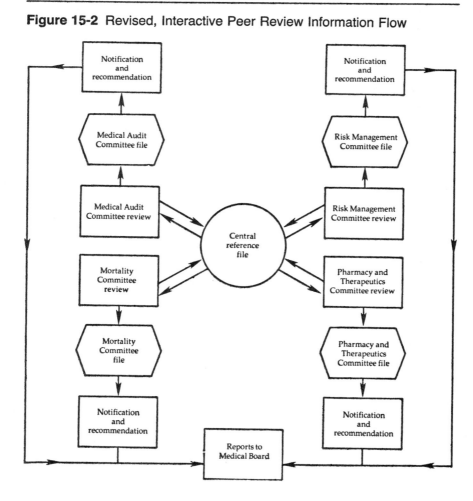

review committees. Their own files, which must be maintained for a variety of purposes, can remain independent. Also, the structure does not interfere with direct lines of committee reporting to the Medical Board from which they receive their mandates. Committees such as pharmacy and therapeutics, and mortality would be expected to be most familiar with patterns and practices in their respective areas of concern and are free to make their recommendations accordingly. In fact, pressure on these issue-specific committees to design hospital-wide studies may be alleviated by this system if committees such as audit and risk control can use the other committees' entries in the reference file as an important source of topics for their investigations.

Improved management of peer review information will not guarantee that better coordination or ultimate quality improvement will take place. However, another tenet of information theory asserts that if professionally meaningful information, which demonstrates a gap between actual and desired performance, is made available, organizational change is more likely.[12] The system proposed above may help to provide the appropriate information that will facilitate action by responsible professionals.

Ensuring Confidentiality

Finally, it should be noted that physicians and administrators in several of the institutions studied indicated a desire to share peer review information, but felt hampered by concerns over confidentiality and the long-standing tradition of committee independence. These sentiments were echoed in statements made by members of the education and training staff of JCAH who are responsible for working with hospitals as they strive to implement procedures that are consistent with the new Quality Assurance Standard. The conceptual model provided here should facilitate this effort. Again, quality assurance is an issue for management intervention, not simply medical staff organization.

REFERENCES

1. Joint Commission on Accreditation of Hospitals. *Accreditation Manual for Hospitals* (Chicago: JCAH 1981) p. 150.
2. Atre, S. *Data Base: Structured Techniques for Design, Performance, and Management* (New York: John Wiley and Sons 1980).
3. Ibid.
4. Thompson, G. and Handelman, I. *Health Data and Information Management* (Woburn, Mass.: Butterworth 1978).
5. Ibid.
6. Lucas, H.C., Jr. *Information Systems Concepts for Management* (New York: McGraw-Hill 1978).

7. Keen, P.G.W. and Morton, M.S.S. *Decision Support Systems: An Organizational Perspective* (Reading, Mass.: Addison-Wesley Publishing Co. 1978).

8. Joint Commission on Accreditation of Hospitals. *The Q/A Guide: A Resource for Hospital Quality Assurance* (Chicago: JCAH 1980).

9. Lucas. *Information Systems Concepts for Management*.

10. Friedson, E. *Profession of Medicine* (New York: Dodd, Mead and Co. 1970).

11. Rosen, H.M. "Quality Assurance, Technology, Assessment, and Health Care Management: Proteus Reborn." *Journal of Health and Human Resources Administration* (forthcoming).

12. Anthony, R.N. and Dearden, J. *Management Control Systems* (Homewood, Ill.: R.D. Irwin 1980).

16. Patient Classification: Implications for Quality Assessment

PHYLLIS B.J. GIOVANNETTI

It is an interesting time for nursing because a great number of generally disconnected events and practices are beginning to come together. Specifically, the contiguous relationship between planning, delivering, and evaluating care, although perhaps always recognized, is becoming more than a theoretical notion. This is reflected not only in emerging patterns of nursing practice and administration but also by mandate in the new JCAH nursing standards.[1]

As an example of the merging of traditionally discontiguous activities in nursing, this reading will discuss the relationship between patient classification and quality assessment. It should be emphasized that both patient classification and quality assessment play an interactive and important role in the overall task of planning for the delivery of nursing care. Patient classification systems serve, in part, to define nurse staffing resources, while quality assessments serve to provide feedback regarding the appropriateness and completeness of the staffing resources. Aydelotte's framework for defining the four major elements of a nurse staffing program serve to illustrate the point.[2] The four major elements are defined as:

1. a precise statement of the purpose of the institution and the services a patient can expect from it, including the standard and characteristics of the care
2. the application of a specific method to determine the number and kinds of staff required to provide the care
3. the development of assignment patterns for staff from the application of personnel guidelines, policy statements, and procedures
4. an evaluation of the product provided and judgment reflecting the impact of the staff on quality.

The classification of patients according to an assessment of their requirements for nursing care relates directly to the second of the elements of staffing; the application of a specific method to determine the number and kinds of staff required to provide the care. Quality assessments relate to the fourth element of staffing: an evaluation of the product provided and judgment reflecting the impact of the staff on quality. In this manner, patient classification and quality assessment are interrelated and contributory. A direct relationship between the two exists to the extent that resource allocation affects program performance. An indirect relationship also exists, although it is largely dependent on the specific application and extensive uses to which the patient classification system is put. For example, patient care categories may serve to define or select specific process or outcome criteria. Or, the rate of progression from one category to another may for specific groups of patients serve as criteria for process and outcome measures.

Before examining the nature of the relationship between patient classification and quality assessment, it is perhaps useful to elaborate on the concept and design of patient classification systems, the methods used for their quantification, and their uses.

CONCEPT AND DESIGN OF PATIENT CLASSIFICATION

Patient classification in nursing generally entails the categorization or grouping of patients according to an assessment of their nursing care requirements over a specified period of time. The assessment may provide either a general indication of requirements or a precise measure of the nursing care time involved. Similarly, the assessment may be directed toward certain aspects of patients' requirements for care, such as physical care, or related to the entire gamut of requirements, including psychosocial care and teaching in addition to physical care. It is generally agreed in nursing that if patient classification is to provide us with a data base on which to respond effectively to patients' requirements for nursing care, then it should encompass all aspects of the nursing care process, that is, physical, psychosocial, and teaching.

The primary purpose of patient classification systems in nursing is to respond to the variable demand for nursing care. The time frame to which a particular patient classification refers depends on the constancy of a patient's requirement for care and the application of the system. In most acute care settings, classification assessments refer to the patients' requirements over an 8- to 24-hour period. This time period seems adequate to respond to the question of patient variability while providing a practical basis for the determination and allocation of nursing personnel time.

Most patient classification systems in use today can be recognized as belonging to one of two types: (1) prototype evaluations or (2) factor evaluations.[3] The difference between the types is generally one of design. Prototype patient classifications are characterized by broad descriptions of the typical patients in each category. A patient is then classified into that category of care that most closely matches the prototype description. The factor evaluation type involves the delineation of specific elements of care for which the patient is rated independently. Ratings on the individual elements are then combined to provide an overall rating, which, when compared to a set of decision rules, identifies the appropriate category of care. Both types attempt to provide mutually exclusive and exhaustive categories graded in terms of an ordinal scale.

Although there are advantages and disadvantages of each, the factor evaluation type handles more discriminately the case of patients who may require, for example, minimal nursing involvement in the carrying out of physical functions but extensive nursing involvement in other areas, such as therapies or teaching. Thus, when patients' care requirements are not uniform across all of the assessment indicators, the factor evaluation method permits greater discrimination.

The number of categories that may be identified depends to a large extent on the degree of precision required and the potential diversity of the care requirements. Again, in the acute care settings, most patient classification systems include between three and five categories, ranging from minimal care to extensive care. Although additional categories may be useful in specifying more precisely the nursing care requirements, the increased precision is of limited practical value for the usual practice of determining and assigning nursing care hours on a per shift basis.

In spite of the fact that there are a large number of different patient classification systems implemented throughout the country, the critical indicators or patient care descriptions which form the basis of each system are fairly universal. They generally include factors relating to the patient's dependency in the areas of eating, bathing, and mobility; the need for special treatments, procedures, and observation; and requirement for psychosocial support and teaching.[4]

QUANTIFICATION OF PATIENT CLASSIFICATION

The quantification or measurement of a patient classification instrument refers to the estimate of the nursing care time or workload associated with each category of care. Quantification is central to the primary purpose of patient classification—the determination and allocation of nursing personnel time and skills. A variety of approaches for determining the time requirements of patients has been used. These include continuous observation or sampling of the care provided, established standard care times for selected nursing activities, and nurses' judgment or assessment of appropriate care times. A number of sources discuss these approaches in detail.[4-8] The quantification may involve an estimate of all patient-related activities or, more commonly, relate only to direct nursing care. To date, there has been little effort directed toward the effects of using different quantification methods, and the choice of methods has rested largely with the preferences of either the institution involved in self-implementation or the proprietary establishment involved in developing the system. What may perhaps be more important than the particular approach to quantification is the sophistication of the data collection effort. Institutions are becoming more discriminating in their selection and approval of appropriate techniques. The benefits of this have been twofold: greater credibility within the nursing profession and greater acceptance by administration.

While the method of choice for quantification may remain a debated issue, there is widespread agreement that the figures developed for one nursing unit may not be applicable to another nursing unit within the same institution. Similarly, the transfer of figures from one institution to another without adjustment has met with little success. The provision of care is indeed a complex process and appears to be a function of a wide variety of factors, including therapeutic modalities, unit structure and design, philosophy of care, and assignment patterns.[9]

The quantification of patient categories also provides the basis for validation of the classification instrument. The validation obtained at the initial measurement period, however, cannot be assumed indefinitely. Care modalities do change and the factors that contribute to differences in the care times between nursing units may alter to invalidate the system over time. Validation, then, must be considered an ongoing process, and periodic checks should be made to ensure that the instruments continue to perform in the manner intended.

Reliability of patient classification instruments relates to the magnitude of agreement among nurses in the selection of the category of care for each patient. Such agreement is important not only among nurses within a particular patient unit, but between nurses from all patient units. As with validity determination, reliability represents a continuous process, and periodic reliability checks should be conducted to assure that nursing personnel are categorizing in the same manner.

PATIENT CLASSIFICATION USES

The development of patient classification systems in nursing has been in response to the variable nature of the demand for nursing care. It is recognized that in many patient care settings there are wide swings in the demand for care, not only from day to day but from shift to shift. Moreover, these fluctuations are, in many instances, independent of the number of patients.[10] Thus, traditional methods of staffing based on standard ratios of hours of care per patient day have often been shown to be insensitive to the concerns of effective allocation and utilization of nursing resources.

From the introduction of patient classification systems for nursing in the 1960s to their widespread use today, their major focus has been to address the difficult and complex challenges of nurse staffing determination. Although their contribution has been worthy, it is important to realize, as illustrated by the aforementioned framework developed by Aydelotte, that they provide only a part of a comprehensive nursing staffing program. Moreover, it should be noted that, in general, they provide evidence for only one part of the personnel requirement question.

To be more specific, patient classification systems generally respond only to the question of *number of staff*. For the most part, they have not provided definitive answers to the question of *kinds of staff* or appropriate staffing patterns. By staffing patterns is meant the mix or combination of nursing personnel such as ratios of registered nurses, licensed practical nurses, and aides, orderlies, and attendants. While patient classification systems make use of patient care indicators that are suggestive of major nursing care time and effort, who is best qualified or who should exert the effort depends on many other factors. Staffing patterns vary widely across the country; they vary, for example, according to hospital size, ownership, complexity, geographic area, extent of service, occupancy rates, and manpower supply and availability.[9,11] It would be difficult if not unwise to expect the categorization of one set of variables to respond to a second set of variables whose complex interrelationship remains undefined. Moreover, the question of staffing patterns is closely related to the individual philosophy and standards of nursing care, which historically have been left within the confines of each care institution. Thus, once the categories of patients have been defined in terms of anticipated care hours, it rests with the institution to distribute those care hours using a staffing pattern consistent with their philosophy, their standards of care, and their nursing care delivery system.

Despite the limitations of patient classification systems with respect to the issue of staffing patterns, they do respond, as suggested, quite specifically to the question of number of staff. The process generally involves three stages. First, patient classification information is used to identify appropriate baseline staffing: the number of personnel who ought to be assigned to a particular unit and shift on a permanent basis. Second, patient classification information is used to prospectively estimate the number of staff required to meet fluctuations in the workload from day to day and from shift to shift. Third, professional nursing judgment is used to either support the findings of patient classification or provide justification for additional alterations.

All nursing units have a complement of permanent staff. Our concern for cohesive work groups, specialization, and continuity of care have dictated this. Once a patient classification system has been implemented, monitoring of the workload over a period of several months can aid in determining the number of permanent staff or baseline component for each unit and each shift. At the expense of oversimplifying, the baseline staff is identified as the number of staff that, if maintained on the unit over a period of time, would have resulted in the least number of shifts that were either overstaffed or understaffed. Occasionally, cyclical patterns of workload are identified such that more than one baseline per shift is identified. For example, the workload may be consistently higher or lower on a particular day of the week or during a certain time of the year. Surprisingly, the identification of appropriate baseline staff is often ignored in the process of developing a staffing program. Its importance, however, should not be underestimated as it has a direct bearing on the magnitude of the day to day allocations that will be necessary as a result of the variable nature of the demand for care.

The second stage in the determination of the numbers of staff makes use of the number of patients in each category from shift to shift. As previously noted, a prospective approach toward classification is generally used. The procedure is very simple. Patients are classified on one shift according to their anticipated care requirements for the next shift or 24-hour period. The results are totaled to provide an estimate of the workload and, thus, the number of staff that will be needed on the following shifts. This requirement is then matched to the number of scheduled staff. Any differences suggest the need to augment or delete the scheduled staff or alternatively to alter the demand for care by either transferring patients or controlling admissions. The advance knowledge of anticipated requirements permits nursing to plan more efficiently and more effectively.

The third stage exemplifies the fact that patient classification systems represent a minimum data set in relation to the process and delivery of care. The nature of the quantification methods coupled with the complexities involved in the delivery of care require that the decision-making process include professional nursing judgment. Very simply, this involves ratification by experienced nurses that the number of staff suggested by the system is in fact correct. Departures can and do arise for numerous reasons. First, the majority of patients in any one category may be at the extreme ends of the care continuum, suggesting that greater or lesser care may be required than that suggested by the classification system. Second, the nursing component available for care at any one time may consist largely of either experienced or new graduates. This may suggest that more or less workload can be adequately managed than that dictated by the classification system. Third, unanticipated transfers, admissions, and patient condition changes may significantly alter the projected level of workload. Any one of these situations can be significant enough to suggest that more or less staff than indicated by the system should be allocated to the unit. Thus, professional nursing judgment is needed to ratify or alter the dictates of the system.

Patient classification systems have also been useful in a wide variety of other care-related functions. Advance knowledge of the care requirements of individual patients can greatly facilitate the assignment of nurses. Calculations of equitable workloads per staff member can be determined. Nursing assignments based on patient mixes that do not demand either wide variations in skills or care requirements can be identified. The assignment of students or new graduates can also be facilitated and monitored by the knowledge of specific patient care requirements.

The processes of quantifying patient classification instruments have frequently provided detailed information on the practice of nursing. In many cases the systematic evaluation of the methods, procedures, and facilities for the delivery of care has been helpful in improving the manner in which scarce and costly nursing resources are managed. Specifically, the detailed activity analyses often used for quantification have resulted in changes in scheduled times for medications, treatments, staff coffee breaks, and mealtimes, in the interest of a more even distribution of the workload throughout a shift. These same studies have been useful in identifying improved organizational relationships and more clearly defined job descriptions.

A great deal of attention has been focused on the charging of patients according to their category of care.[4,12] The practice seems to result in a more equitable cost basis for the patient and offers to the nursing department the opportunity to be identified as a revenue-producing department. While this practice is relatively new, it demonstrates increased acceptability and understanding of patient classification systems beyond that of the nursing service departments. The movement will undoubtedly demand greater attention to the issues of reliability and validity of the systems themselves and, from nursing, greater justification and verification of the care time provided to individual patients. This is seen as a most positive force and may well provide the groundwork for that intractable question that asks what is the relationship between nursing care time and quality.

Patient classification systems have been used to aid in the placement of patients within a facility.[13] In addition to the usual considerations of sex, service, type of accommodation requested, and bed availability, knowledge of the level of care requirement can be useful. To the extent possible, patients can be assigned to units where workload and staff availability is more favorably matched. This type of action can lessen the occasion of nursing staff reallocation between units and the hiring of float or agency personnel, while improving the patient's chance that his or her requirements for nursing care can be met. Selective admissions, particularly with elective patients, on the basis of anticipated care requirement levels from day to day does provide yet another opportunity to control peak workloads when staffing complements cannot be augmented.

Finally, patient classification systems can be used for a wide variety of other purposes. They can provide information for improved distribution of equipment and supplies and for inventory control. The monitoring of a patient's category of care throughout the period of hospitalization has potential both as a quality indicator and as a basis for constructing recovery models. Although efforts in this area have been limited, the benefits are promising and are more likely now to be pursued with the renewed interest and commitment to patient classification and quality determination.

RELATIONSHIP BETWEEN PATIENT CLASSIFICATION AND QUALITY ASSESSMENT

As previously mentioned, the relationship between the classification of patients and the assessment of quality may be described as contributory. While a direct relationship between the two may be identified, the two concepts are also related indirectly. At the outset, it is important to recognize that the selected indicators of care that characterize patient classification systems are primarily time related; they represent only one plane of the complex and multidimensional system of care. Classification systems must be viewed therefore as minimum data sets. They do not necessarily delineate the critical indicators that are required for the assessment or measurement of quality. Thus, the use of patient classification instruments to define the components of quality assessment is limited.

The direct relationship between patient classification and quality assessment is most frequently described in the hypothesis relating the adequacy of staffing with the quality of care. While there is general agreement with this hypothesis, the nature of the relationship remains intractable. *The existence of a patient classification system does not guarantee adequate staffing.* A well-developed and implemented system, however, can be instrumental in developing a staffing program that attempts to match patients' requirements for care with nursing resources. It is assumed, therefore, that effective utilization and appropriate allocation of nursing resources do have a positive influence on the quality of care, specifically in relation to the measurement of structure. As suggested by Donabedian, the allocation of time and other resources affects the performance of individual practitioners as well as the performance of programs.[14] The difficulty is knowing at what point increased or decreased nursing care time ceases to have a positive influence on the quality of care.

Indirectly, patient classification and quality assessment are related in a variety of ways. First, patient classification systems have been useful in providing guidelines for the application of quality assessments. Haussmann and coworkers, in their development of process quality measures, identified specific quality indicators appropriate to each of the categories of care identified from a patient classification system.[15] They found that for each patient care category there were specific quality indicators that were more appropriate than others. Daubert, on the other hand, referring to community health nursing agencies, used a patient classification system as the basis for applying predetermined and objectively measured outcome criteria.[16]

Second, there is the notion of patient profiles. While little effort has been directed to the study of this concept, it is conceivable that the rate of progression from one patient category to another during an individual's hospital stay may serve as an appropriate process or outcome measure. Moreover, it is this kind of information that is needed to assist us in identifying the relationships between diagnostic-related groupings and patient requirements for nursing care.

Third, patient classification systems can provide the bases for the long-term planning of nursing personnel resources. It is often suggested that the lack of long-term planning is in part responsible for the extensive use of agency personnel that has characterized many institutions. While we have yet to identify the impact of the increased use of agency personnel, there are serious concerns about their effects on job satisfaction, costs, and quality of care.

Fourth, the use of patient classification systems as a means of equalizing the workload among nurses may also have implications for quality assessment. Equitable workloads will need to be defined both in terms of preestablished standards of performance among nurses, as well as of preestablished standards of care for patients. Subsequently that care will have to be evaluated.

Finally, the practice of charging patients by level of care may also lead to indirect measures of quality. The mechanisms that will no doubt be required to assure that assessed care requirements are indeed provided, thus justifying patient charges, may well lead to significant contributions in quality assessment. The contributions may not be limited to specific quality measures but may reflect as well specific levels of quality for which the recipient is willing to pay.

Systems of patient classification and quality assessments are increasingly being implemented in nursing. Although the present techniques are recognized as both general and imperfect, their increase in acceptance and usage suggests that nurses are seeking more objective methods to help them plan and evaluate their care. It is with the continued experience in the use of these systems, however imperfect they may be, that improvements can and will be made. As the measurement of quality becomes more precise, it is likely that our methods of patient classification and assessment will also become more precise and, in turn, more responsive to the true nature of patient needs. Both patient classification and quality assessment are dynamic; they must keep pace with changes in health care delivery in general and more specifically with changes in the professional delivery of nursing care. We must make use of them in a dynamic fashion, continuously evaluating and altering them so that they can serve us and our clients in the best possible way.

REFERENCES

1. *Nursing Standards*, Chicago, Joint Commission for Accreditation of Hospitals, 1979.

2. Aydelotte MK: Staffing for high quality care. *Hospitals* 1973; 47:58,60,65.

3. Abdellah FG, Levine E: *Better Patient Care Through Nursing Research*, New York, Macmillan Publishing Co Inc, 1965.

4. Giovannetti P: *Patient Classification Systems in Nursing: A Description and Analysis*, US Dept of Health, Education, and Welfare publication No. (HRA) 78-22, July 1978.

5. Aydelotte MK: *Nurse Staffing Methodology: A Review and Critique of Selected Literature,* US Dept of Health, Education, and Welfare publication No. (NIH) 73-434. Government Printing Office, March 1973.

6. Chagnon M, Audette L, Tilquin C: Patient classification by care required. *Dimens Health Serv* 1977; 54(9): 32-36.

7. Giovannetti P: Understanding patient classification systems. *J Nurs Adm* 1979; 9(2):4-9.

8. *Methods for Studying Nurse Staffing in a Patient Unit, A Manual to Aid Hospitals in Making Use of Personnel,* US Dept of Health, Education, and Welfare publication No. (HRA) 78-3, May 1978.

9. Young JS: Giovannetti P, Lewison D, et al: Factors affecting nurse staffing in acute care hospitals: A review and critique of the literature, US Dept of Health, Education, and Welfare contract No. (HRA) 232-78-01-50. Baltimore, The Johns Hopkins University, September 1980.

10. Giovannetti P: Measurement of patients' requirements for nursing services, in *Research on Nurse Staffing in Hospitals, Report of the Conference,* US Dept of Health, Education, and Welfare publication No. (NIH) 43-434. Government Printing Office, March 1973, pp 41-56.

11. Aydelotte MK: Trends in staffing of hospitals: Implications for nursing resource policy, in Millman ML (ed): *Nursing Personnel and the Changing Health Care System.* Cambridge, Mass, Ballinger Publishing Co, 1978.

12. LaViolette S: Classification systems remedy billing inequity. *Mod Health Care* 1979; 9(September):32.

13. Sjoberg K, Bicknell P: *Nursing Study Phase III–The Assessment of Unit Assignment in a Multi-Ward Setting.* Saskatoon, University of Saskatchewan, 1971.

14. Donabedian A: *The Definition of Quality and Approaches to its Assessment, Vol I, Explorations in Quality Assessment and Monitoring.* Ann Arbor, Mich, Health Administrative Press, 1980.

15. Haussmann RKD, Heggvary ST, Newman JT: *Monitoring Quality of Nursing Care, Part II, Assessment and Study of Correlates,* US Dept of Health, Education, and Welfare publication No. (HRA) 76-7, July 1976.

16. Daubert EA: Patient classification system and outcome criteria. *Nurs Outlook* 1979; (July): 450-457.

17. Quality Assurance in Nursing: The State of the Art

CATHERINE E. LOVERIDGE

In deciding how best to approach the study of quality assurance in nursing, it is helpful to remember the Indian legend of the blind men and the elephant. While each of the blind men who examined the elephant was partly right in his perception, the true nature of the elephant eluded their understanding. So, too, with quality assurance—many touch portions of the issue, but too often they appear to comprehend only their own particular area of exposure. This reading will attempt to examine the nursing quality assurance literature from a researcher's perspective of the phenomenon. The purpose of this reading is not to provide an exhaustive review of quality assurance research in nursing but rather to report selectively the major research and to identify areas requiring further development.

Nursing research in quality assurance has followed the familiar structure, process, and outcome framework suggested by Donabedian.[1] The simplicity of this triad belies the complex interaction found to underlie a dynamic health care system. Nevertheless, it is a useful perspective for examining the many influences that are believed to impact the quality of care provided in health care systems.

STRUCTURE

The dimension of structure includes consideration of factors such as the setting in which care is given including the physical facilities, the equipment and personnel, and the policies governing professional work. Pugh further defined this dimension by explicitly identifying six structural variables: (1) specialization and differentiation, (2) standardization, (3) formalization, (4) decision making, (5) traditionalism, and (6) configuration.[2]

As applied to nursing, *specialization* refers at the individual level to the depth of knowledge acquired through education and experience that prepares the nurse to make sound clinical judgments regarding a patient's nursing care needs. *Differentiation* is the form by which responsibilities are subdivided among the members of the nursing staff. This is often reflected in the mode of delivery, such as primary or team nursing that is used on a particular nursing unit.

The educational requirements for the generalist in nursing as well as for the nurse specialist have been determined by the American Nurses Association in cooperation with the National League for Nursing. Publication of these educational standards has contributed to the evaluation of quality in nursing care by providing parameters within which the preparation of the staff can be measured. The presence of well-prepared staff has not been shown to ensure high quality care, but its absence does preclude the hope of ever attaining such quality.

Research comparing the quality of care provided under different modes of delivery has concentrated on comparisons between team nursing and primary nursing. Team nursing developed in response to a critical shortage of professional nurses during and after World War II.[3] Auxiliary staff are assigned to less critically ill patients by a team leader who is the professional nurse responsible for the care provided to a group of patients on a particular nursing unit. Primary nursing assigns the responsibility for planning, providing, and evaluating the care of a particular patient to one nurse for the duration of the patient's hospital stay. In her research, Marram found that primary nursing units demonstrated more staff nurse satisfaction, lower turnover rates, and a higher patient perception of individualized care.[4] McCauley's findings were similar,[5] while Shukla found no difference in cost between the two modes of delivery but did identify increased staff and patient satisfaction, continuity of care, accountability, and physician-nurse communication.[6]

The variable *standardization* refers to the extent to which nursing care can be codified so that the variance in the quality of nursing care is limited. Basic research regarding the contribution of technology in organizations[7-9] has provided the foundation used by a number of nursing researchers to develop instruments to specify empirically the dimensions of technology found in various types of nursing units within hospitals.[10-12] Very little research has examined the relationship of technological differences to the quality of nursing care.

The extent of *formalization* in the nursing service organization is also related to the perception of the complexity of nursing care as well as to the nature of the environment in which care is provided. Lawrence and Lorsch reported several organizational studies that concurred in their findings relating the degree of formalization to the degree of routineness of the technology and the extent of environmental turmoil found in the industry.[13] Successful organizations operating in a stable environment with routine, standardized production activities were highly formal in their organizational structure. Less formal organizations were more often found in rapidly changing, nonroutine production arenas.

Acute care hospitals, which are the predominant settings in which nursing care is provided, can be described as complex, dynamic environments. Their organizational design has traditionally been bureaucratic regardless of the technology found in the institution.

Alternative structures, including the matrix form of organization[14] and the shared governance model,[15] are receiving attention in regard to hospital organization. Measurement of the relationship of formal structure to the quality of nursing care awaits the development of valid indicators sensitive to the differences found in the health care field.

The structure of *decision making* in acute care hospitals is reflective of the tensions existing within the health care industry and society itself. On an individual basis, decisions regarding patient care are made by the nurse responsible for the patient's care and the primary physician. The interdependence of these decisions is a function of the specialization and differentiation found in modern health care settings. However, the value of each contribution to the goal of patient progress is often a political function reflecting the physician/male dominance of the health care industry, which has been well described by Freidson.[16] Recognition of the fact that the nurse is accountable to the patient for the nursing care provided is essential to the formation of appropriate decision-making structures in the organization.

Assessment of the relationship of decision making to the quality of nursing care has been conducted by several researchers. Hinshaw's work relates the complexity of nurses' clinical decisions to the professional decision-making model.[17] Nurse administrators' decision-making approaches have been the focus of the work of others.[18,19] As organizational structures continue to be modified, effects on the decison-making processes must be examined.

Traditionalism has had a strong influence on the organizational structure of nursing services. Traditionally, the nurse has been viewed as an assistant to the physician instead of to the patient. Ironically, this position was fostered by Nightingale, who fought for recognition of her nurses' contributions to patient care by demanding an official request for nursing care from the physician before nurses were permitted by Nightingale to minister to the sick and injured.[20] This physician order concept has been institutionalized by requiring a physician's order for third-party reimbursement for nursing services.

Against this tangled web of relationships, nurses have been striving to reassert their special relationship to patients. The growth of visiting nurse services, the modernization of nurse practice acts, the emergence of independently practicing nurses, and the development of the nurse practitioner role are all evidence of the movement toward recognition of the accountability for nursing care that professional nurses have always maintained. The traditional values of nursing such as caring for, helping, and supporting patients and families during health and illness need to be retained while meaningless traditional practices are abandoned. Unfortunately, as important as this structural variable may be in nursing, no research was found that directly related traditionalism to the quality of nursing care.

The variable *configuration* has already been discussed to some extent in terms of modalities of nursing care delivery. The determination of preferable configurations of professional and paraprofessional nursing staff is currently under study.

In leaving the discussion of structure it is important to note that research in this area is needed because organizational structure can be manipulated by management to improve the capacity of the institution to produce quality outcomes. Despite the progress made to date, gaps exist in the measurement of technology in various nursing settings, in the precision of structural indicators related to quality of care, and in the comparison of different nursing care delivery systems. It is encouraging to note, however, that at a recent National Conference on Nursing Administration Research a full 20 percent of the papers presented focused on the structural dimensions of nursing practice.[21]

PROCESS

Evaluation of the process of nursing care as an indicator of quality has received more attention from nurse researchers than have the other dimensions identified by Donabedian. Implicit in its emphasis on process is the assumption that thoughtful application of the principles and findings of the art and science of nursing will produce high quality nursing care.[22] However valid this assumption, the major contribution of this research has been to establish measurement tools that permit comparison of the performance of nurses providing care to patients.

The Slater Nursing Competency Rating Scale is an important example of work done in this area. The scale was designed to measure the quality of performance of staff nurses by direct observation of nurse-patient interactions. An 84-item questionnaire using Likert-type scales was the principal tool for scoring performance. Items were selected through review of the literature and the experienced judgment of the developers. The six categories included (1) psychosocial-individual, (2) psychosocial-group, (3) physical, (4) general, (5) communication, and (6) professional implications. Inter-rater reliability was high ($r = .77$), and predictive validity was evidenced by correlations of the Slater Scale with instructor clinical experience grades, theory grades, National League for Nursing achievement tests, and Social Interaction Inventory Scores.[23] This instrument served as the basis for development of the Quality Patient Care Scale (QualPaCS), which measures the quality of the nursing care received by a patient while care is being provided.[24]

Another significant instrument, commonly referred to as the Rush-Medicus or Nursing Process Model, was developed by Hegyvary and Haussmann. They used the nursing process (that is, assessment, planning, intervention, and evaluation) as the conceptual frame of reference for determining criteria. In testing the instrument, several analyses were used to refine each dimension. An asset of this instrument is that it allows for selection of subsets of criteria according to the severity of illness of the patient so that measurement can remain sensitive across groups of patients with different nursing care needs.[25]

Yet another approach to evaluating the process of nursing care was developed by Phaneuf. In the Phaneuf Nursing Audit Instrument the construct of nursing was defined according to the legal definition of nursing common to most nurse practice acts of that time. Seven criteria describe the areas to be measured. These are (1) execution of physician orders, (2) observation of symptoms, (3) supervision of patients, (4) supervision of others participating in care, (5) execution of the nursing process, (6) teaching, and (7) reporting and recording.[26] Determination of whether or not criteria have been met is made by reviewing the patient record. It is, therefore, less costly to use than the Slater, QualPaCS, and Rush-Medicus instruments, which require direct observation of nurse-patient interactions. A drawback, however, is that it does rely heavily on the accuracy and completeness of the patient's record.

The above instruments represent major examples of the tools that have been developed to evaluate the quality of the nursing process. Many other instruments have been developed that conceptualize nursing care that is appropriate for specific health care problems or diagnoses. Over 350 of these instruments have been reviewed and compiled in a two-volume manual entitled *Instruments for Measuring Nursing Practice and Other Health Care Variables.*[27]

Although many gaps exist in the research focus or process, a comparison of the quality of performance between different structural configurations can be helpful. Felton, for example, found that the quality of nursing practice was higher on a primary care unit when compared with a team nursing care unit when a combined score from the Slater, QualPaCS, and Phaneuf instruments was used to measure nurse performance.[28] Although this study was too small to generalize to a larger population, it identifies the elements of a productive research design.

Other areas needing attention are the replication of findings in different populations in order to increase generalizability, the standardization of terminology used in the evaluation of nursing process, the continued refinement of valid and reliable criteria for measurement, and the linkage of quality nursing processes to quality patient outcomes.

OUTCOME

One of the most difficult aspects of nursing research has been to relate the process of nursing care to patient outcomes. Horn and Swain have tried to limit the effect of confounding variables by focusing their development of health status outcomes on the areas in which nursing has major responsibility and should be held accountable. Their framework for defining these areas was derived from

Orem who described nursing practice within the parameters of nine health status domains. These domains are (1) air, (2) water/fluid and food intake, (3) elimination of body wastes, (4) activity and rest, (5) solitude, (6) social interaction and productive work, (7) protection from hazards, (8) normality, and (9) necessities arising from health deviation.[29] While providing a sound theoretical foundation for the construct, the measures need continued testing in order to decrease measurement error.

A more specific delineation of nursing outcome research was conducted under the auspices of the Western Interstate Commission on Higher Education (WICHE). Lindeman, Krueger, and Hagen developed a program of targeted research in defining quality of nursing care.[30] Fourteen work groups of five to six nurses each were formed from representatives in the fields of nursing practice, education, administration, and research. Five groups worked on the development of valid and reliable measures of patient outcomes of nursing care, while the remaining nine groups focused their attention on identifying which nursing activities appeared to result in changes in patient outcomes. Areas of study included the relationship between operating room nursing activities and patient outcomes,[31] the relationship of nursing activities to acute confusional states of the elderly patient,[32] the relationship between nurse counseling and sexual adjustment after hysterectomy,[33] as well as several areas of instrument development.[34-37] Although this work represents a productive beginning, development of outcome measures of nursing care continues to be challenging.

An approach taken by Zimmer incorporates the findings of evaluation research and the demands of the clinical setting.[38] In her model of 11 steps in the process of quality assurance review, nurse peer groups are charged with the responsibility for conducting the evaluation. These steps include (1) identification of a specific patient population, (2) selection of a focus for evaluation, (3) determination of the critical time periods for measurement, (4) definition of variables, (5) selection or development of tools, (6) testing and ratifying the measure, (7) comparison of practice with the standards for measurement, (8) evaluation of variations from the standards, (9) reporting results, (10) implementation of corrective action plans, and (11) restudy of that patient population to determine the results of the actions taken to improve care. Those who are familiar with the requirements of utilization review and other oversight activities will recognize the parameters within which Zimmer developed this portion of her overall evaluation program.

CONCLUSIONS

The state of the art of quality assurance in nursing reflects the difficulties inherent in the analysis of a dynamic phenomenon. Like the story of the elephant and the blind men, each approach exposes only a portion of the areas under study.

When examined together, however, directions for the future become clearer. Although the findings reviewed above are encouraging, more work needs to be done in looking at the interaction of structure, process, and outcome and their separate and joint relationships to the quality of nursing care. This may be the most productive area for future nursing research focused on the quality of care. However, other areas need research attention.

The measurement tools already developed by nursing researchers need to be applied more widely in clinical settings so that their relevance and limitations can be assessed. In particular, it is suggested that as quality assurance takes on a greater organizational focus, priority in tool development should be given to the testing of the structural determinants of the quality of nursing care.

The development of nursing theory must continue so that constructs for the evaluation of nursing care will have sound theoretical bases. In other words, it will never be possible to develop valid measurements of quality if the elements of nursing practice are not properly conceptualized and made more explicit.

Finally, there must be encouragement of a healthy dialogue among nurses and between nurses and other practitioners of clinical or social sciences so that meaningful research can continue to underlie the practice of professional nursing.

REFERENCES

1. Donabedian A: Some basic issues in evaluating the quality of care, in *Issues in Evaluation Research*, publication No. G1242M, New York, American Nurses Association, 1976, p 7.
2. Pugh D: Context of organizational structures. *Adm Sci Q* 1969; 14(3):91.
3. Young J, Giovannetti P, Lewison D, et al: *Factors Affecting Nurse Staffing in Acute Care Hospitals: A Review and Critique of the Literature*, US Dept of Health, Education, and Welfare publication No. (HRA) 81-10, 1981, p 5.
4. Marram G: The comparative costs of operating a team and primary nursing unit. *J Nurs Adm* 1976; (May)6:21.
5. McCauley D, Schefelacqua M: Primary nursing: Its implementation and six-month outcome. *J Nurs Adm* 1978; (May)8:29.
6. Shukla R: Structure vs. people in primary nursing: An inquiry. *Nurs Res* 1981; (July/August) 30:236.
7. Woodward J: Management and technology, in *Classics of Organizational Theory*. Durham, NC, Moore Publishing Co, 1978, p 190.
8. Thompson J: *Organizations in Action*. New York, McGraw-Hill Book Co, 1967, p 51.
9. Perrow C: A framework for the comparative analysis of organizations. *Am Sociol Rev* 1967; (April)32:96.
10. Overton P, Schneck R, Hazlett C: An empirical study of the technology of nursing subunits. *Adm Sci Q* 1977; (June)22:203.
11. Leatt P, Schneck R: Nursing subunit technology: A replication. *Adm Sci Q* 1981; (June)26:234.
12. Schoonhoven C: Problems with contingency theory: Testing assumptions hidden within the language of contingency "theory." *Adm Sci Q* 1981; (September)26:353.

13. Lawrence P, Lorsch J: *Organization and Environment: Managing Differentiation and Integration.* Cambridge, Mass, Harvard University Press, 1967.

14. Hellriegel D, Slocum J: *Organizational Behavior.* San Francisco, West Publishing Co, 1976, p 129.

15. Cleland V: Shared Governance in a Professional Model of Collective Bargaining. *J Nurs Adm* 1978; (May)8:39.

16. Freidson E: *Profession of Medicine.* New York, Dodd Mead & Co, 1973, p 47.

17. Hinshaw AS: *Professional Decisions: A Technological Perspective,* unpublished dissertation, University of Arizona, 1975.

18. Daniel W, Terrell S: An introduction to decision analysis. *J Nurs Adm* 1978; (May)8:20.

19. Taylor A: Decision Making in Nursing: An Analytical Approach. *J Nurs Adm* 1978; (November) 8:22.

20. Davis F: *The Nursing Profession.* New York, John Wiley & Sons, 1966.

21. National Conference on Nursing Administration Research: *Abstracts.* University of Washington, April 20-21, 1981.

22. Scott WR: *Organizations: Rational, Natural and Open Systems.* Englewood Cliffs, NJ, Prentice-Hall Inc, 1981, p 329.

23. Wandelt M, Wandelt S, Slater D: *Slater Nursing Competency Scale.* New York, Appleton-Century-Crofts, 1975, p 68.

24. Hartman M: An historical perspective of quality assurance, in *Pathways to Quality Care,* National League of Nursing publication No. 20-1636. New York, 1976, p 3.

25. Hegyvary S, Gortner S, Haussman D: Development of criterion measures for quality of care: the Rush-Medicus model, in *Issues in Evaluation Research,* publication No. G1242M. New York, American Nurses Association, 1976, p 108.

26. Horn B: Establishing valid and reliable criteria. *Nurs Res* 1980; 29(March/April):88.

27. U.S. Health Resources Administration: *Instruments For Measuring Nursing Practice and Other Health Care Variables,* US Dept of Health, Education, and Welfare publication No. (HRA) 78-53, 1979.

28. Felton G: Increasing the quality of nursing care by introducing the concept of primary nursing: A model project. *Nurs Res* 1975; 24(January/February):27.

29. Horn B, Swain MA: An approach to development of criterion measures for quality patient care, in *Issues in Evaluation Research,* publication No. G1242M. New York, American Nurses Association, 1976, p 74.

30. Lindeman C, Krueger J, Hagen D: Targeted research: An empirical approach to defining quality of nursing care, in *Issues in Evaluation Research,* publication No. G1242M. New York, American Nurses Association, 1976, p 95.

31. Lindeman C, Holloway JR, Winn MC, et al: *The Relationship Between Nursing Activities and Patient Outcomes: An AORN-WICHE Report.* Denver, Association of Operating Room Nurses, 1978.

32. Willaims M, et al: The relationship of nursing activities to acute confusional states in elderly hip fractured patients. *Nurs Res* 1979; 28(January/February), pp 25-35.

33. Krueger J, Hassell J, Coggins DB, et al: The relationship between nurse counseling and sexual adjustment after hysterectomy. *Nurs Res* 1979; 28(May/June), pp 145-150.

34. Blair E, Hauf B, Loveridge C, et al: Instrument development: Measuring quality outcomes in ambulatory maternal child nursing. *Nurs Adm Q* 1978; 12(Summer), pp 91-83.

35. Lewis F, Firsich S, Purcell S: Clinical tool development for chemotherapy patients: Process and content. *Int J Cancer Nurs* 1979; (April)2:pp 99-108.

36. Adams M, Hanson R, Norkool D, et al: Psychological responses in critical care units. *Am J Nurs* 1978; 78(September), pp 1504-15012.

37. Lum J, Chase M, Cole SM, et al: Nursing care of oncology patients receiving chemotherapy. *Nurs Res* 1978; 27(November/December) pp 340-346.

38. Downs FS, Zimmer M: A nursing service administrator's perspective. *Nurs Res* 1980; 29 (March/April) pp 94-99.

18. Program Evaluation: Resource for Decision Making

MARIE E. MICHNICH, STEPHEN M. SHORTELL, and WILLIAM C. RICHARDSON

Reprinted with permission from *Health Care Management Review* 6(3). Copyright © 1981, Aspen Systems Corporation, 25-35.

EDITORS' NOTE: Quality assurance, perhaps because of its importance to the health care field, is too often treated as a unique and distinctive subject. As a consequence, related developments in other, closely related areas tend to be overlooked and not incorporated into the quality assurance literature. Inclusion of this reading in this book serves to draw attention to the interdependence and parallels between quality assurance and program evaluation concepts, methods, and applications.

Recent reports indicate a significant trend taking place in the health care sector. DeVries has predicted the demise of the independent, autonomous hospital.[1] Stull cites the inability of health services to be accommodated within traditional organizational boundaries.[2] Multi-institutional relationships of various forms are becoming common. The effect on the way health care organizations are managed is bound to be substantial. As described by Sheldon and Barrett:

> Legislators have shown a greater propensity to regulate health care costs; consumers' expectations are on the rise; community representatives demand to be heard; money is limited, and its use more and more restricted . . . Janus-like, the [health care administrator] must look in two directions at once—attending to the needs of his own organization and responding to the needs of other health institutions sharing the same environment . . . [he] cannot afford to run his institution as though it existed in isolation.[3]

It is inevitable that management decision making will be under keen scrutiny in this atmosphere. Accountability seems foremost in the eyes of the public as well as the health care governing boards. A sound, documented foundation for management actions will be required. That accountability may include justification of inaction, as well as evidence that the full range of options has been explored. It will be increasingly important for the manager to understand and take advantage of

263

264   Organization and Change in Health Care Quality Assurance

decision-making tools that can be of service in meeting this challenge. Formal program evaluation is a decision-making method that will be of growing importance to health care administrators.

Evaluation has always been an integral component of the management process. Evaluative logic is so ingrained in day-to-day organizational performance, it may be considered intuitive good judgment, even by the administrator credited with it. For some, it will be difficult to imagine an instance when a manager is *not* actively engaged in evaluation to some degree. This view is further supported by growing organizational dependence on sophisticated management information systems and the increasing number of administrative support staff formally trained in evaluative skills.

Health care administrators are constantly on the alert for new developments that could improve some aspect of their organization's design and performance. Their focus includes both areas of clinical interest, such as diagnostic treatment and services, as well as managerial concerns, such as staffing patterns, financing, and organization of services. As described by D'Costa and Sechrest, "Experimentation with a new system is . . . an important responsibility of the health administrator. Any time there is concern with an existing system and new ones are to be tried out, evaluation is the instrument of choice to justify the ultimate implementation of such change."[4]

Since evaluation is already well established in the health care field, why bother to go further? The answer is that the increasing complexity and magnitude of health care programs require a corresponding level of evaluative skills. There is a growing number of situations where traditional organizational evaluative capabilities can no longer meet the requirements of the job at hand. In these instances, the contribution of formal program evaluation is necessary.

Before discussing formal program evaluation, it is useful to define the terms involved. Here, a program is defined as "an organized response to eliminate or reduce one or more problems where the response includes one or more objectives, performance of one or more activities, and expenditures of resources."[5] Given this definition, it is easy to imagine the broad range of activities that fall within this realm. A health care organization may embody a single program, such as a free-standing suicide prevention center, or contain dozens of separate programs, as found in most major hospitals or medical centers. Similarly, programs may be large and national in scope, such as the Medicare or Medicaid programs, or small with a specific or narrow interest, such as a local effort to screen children for lead poisoning in a single neighborhood.

The word *evaluator* is also subject to broad definition. The term can describe anyone who exercises judgment in the determination of relative worth or quality. However, when we link "evaluator" with "program" and, further, add the "formal" requirement, we are identifying someone with specific expertise, having access to resources and command of methods not routinely available.

FORMAL PROGRAM EVALUATION

To develop a perspective on what is and what is not formal program evaluation, formal evaluation can be compared with other common evaluation activities. Examples of informal evaluations are easily identified in most health care settings. These activities include evaluating employee performance, periodic review of various departmental functions, most budget review processes, evaluation of the performance of a new billing system, and the typical "keeping-a-finger-on-the-pulse" activities characteristic of good management practice. In these evaluations, implicit standards and criteria for determination of acceptable performance originate from independent professional judgment and experience or commonly available guidelines from accrediting agencies, procedure manuals, consultants and professional associations.

Scientific Method

Formal program evaluation may be distinguished from informal or other types of evaluation activities by its application of the scientific method to augment professional judgment.[6] Through the use of research methods, it seeks to discover the congruence between performance, that is, what is taking or has taken place, and objectives, that is, what was supposed to occur. It further attempts to identify the reason or *cause* of a particular event or outcome, thus offering a more explicit basis for selecting among possible options for future action.

The distinction between formal program evaluation and what is considered research is not the methods employed but rather the way the results are used. The former is designed to supplement "real world" decision making; the latter, to add to disciplinary knowledge. For example, suppose an organization develops a cardiac rehabilitation unit. Formal program evaluation may be used to answer questions about the unit's cost effectiveness or its success in achieving a desired level of patient education or behavior change. Simultaneously, as is the case in many medical centers, this same unit may be engaging in research aimed at evaluating a patient's clinical response to a new antiarrhythmic drug or the effect of diet on the future incidence of heart attacks.

Unfortunately, this distinction between research and evaluation is not always clear. As in the case above, the program evaluation may identify with future incidence of heart attacks as an outcome measure of the cardiac rehabilitation unit's success. Consequently, the causal link will be of interest to researchers too. It is often difficult to explain how and why a program achieved its aim without some underlying theory that probably stimulated the development of the program in the first place. In fact, these overlaps are viewed as beneficial, though they make our comparison somewhat less effective.

It should also be pointed out that sound program evaluations need not be expensive. Simple and easily performed evaluations may provide the basis for informed judgment without elaborate investigative efforts. With some programs or program components, results may be attainable in relatively short periods of time, in the absence of excessive cost.

Timing

Within the domain of formal program evaluation, there are two basic types. The distinction originates in the timing of the evaluation as compared with the development status of the program. As portrayed, the above evaluation was used to determine the degree of success of the cardiac rehabilitation unit. This is called *summative* or *outcome* evaluation. Program evaluation may also be employed in the early stages of a program's development to assess whether the program is being implemented as it was originally intended. This is referred to as a *formative* or *implementation* evaluation.

Using the same cardiac rehabilitation unit example, if we back up a year or so in time, the questions that might have been asked in a formative evaluation would include whether the unit staff members were recruited in the numbers and categories as prescribed, whether the needed supplies and equipment (for example, ECG treadmill, patient education films, pamphlets) were in place and operational and whether the referral system was adequate.

Sometimes, an outcome or summative evaluation is initiated prematurely, before all phases of program implementation are completed. When, or after a program becomes operational, some new development or perceived need results in a shift in some aspect of the program's original purpose (for example, the patient population is different than anticipated or a key staff member leaves and is replaced by someone with a different idea about the way things should be done). If this occurs the program may be unfairly faulted for less than desirable outcomes simply because the evaluation was initiated too soon. This result may be unavoidable if evaluation timing is related to funding or budget cycles; nonetheless, the evaluator should be informed of any delays in program development and attempt to build this constraint into the evaluation design.

Internal Versus External Evaluation

It will also be useful to draw a distinction between internally initiated and externally imposed evaluation. Internally initiated evaluations serve the needs of the organization's decision makers. The evaluator is employed to answer their concerns. Thus the administrator will be instrumental in posing the key evaluation questions. Externally imposed evaluation is usually linked with federal or other outside funding sources. In these instances, the funding agency requires information about program performance to fulfill some very basic decision-making needs of its own. Consequently, the role of the evaluator is to provide them with information as well as to work with management and program staff.

Again, some very large health care organizations employ formally trained evaluators. While this has become more common in state health agencies, local health departments, prepaid health plans as well as major medical centers, most often formal program evaluators are based outside the organization, typically at universities and other research centers. Weiss describes the former as an *internal* evaluator; the latter, an *external* evaluator.[7] The position of the evaluator relative to the program being evaluated is an important factor in the evaluation's conduct and ultimate credibility. There are relative advantages and disadvantages of internal and external evaluators that should be considered when selecting an evaluator.

Internal evaluators have the advantage of intimate knowledge of the organization, the program, the data sources, the people and the needs of the decision makers. Because they are part of the organization, they may be perceived as "one of us" and thus move freely in and out of program activities without creating much notice. They may have the benefit of being called in early in the program planning stages and the ability to build in evaluation data bases before the program develops. However, they can be more susceptible to organizational politics, even if they are isolated from direct program pressures. Some organizational structures are set up so that the evaluation team is peripheral to the main hierarchy, reporting only to the chief executive officer or the governing board. However, there may be a potential to discount or give lighter weight to internally generated evaluation reports to make them fit in with other organizational plans.

The external evaluator is usually accompanied by the prestige factor associated with outside expert consultants. Often, this person is a well-known researcher, thus more likely to have an ego involvement in the validity and objectivity of the evaluation design. Efforts will be made to broaden the scope and the implications of the evaluation. Similarly, the external expert's reputation may increase the weight given to evaluation findings. However, the organization, particularly the program staff, may feel a need to "look their best." As a result, some information may be concealed and the program staff may dispute evaluation methods and findings as "irrelevant" because the outside person does not really "know how things are around here."

Objectivity Requirement

Formal program evaluation is intended to be as objective as possible. Management and funding agencies depend on the accuracy of the evaluation results for future decision making. Consequently, every effort should be made to ensure the highest level of scientific inquiry on the part of the evaluator. On the other hand, health care organizations are faced by pressures from both internal and external sources. These apparently conflicting demands may be best accommodated by selecting an evaluator who can remain insulated from the pressures and performance of the program and yet remain able to gain insight into program operations. A strong distinction should be apparent between those who are members of the program staff, and the evaluator of the evaluation team.

To fulfill the objectivity requirement, the evaluator cannot have a vested interest in the eventual outcomes of the program. While this may appear to be a reasonable and obvious prerequisite, it is sometimes difficult to put into practice. Programs are generally initiated with a great deal of enthusiasm, resource expenditure and overall organization commitment. The people charged with making the program work necessarily feel a strong identification with their responsibility. In fact, their jobs may depend on the program's success. Evaluators can be perceived as a potential threat. Nonetheless, for the evaluation to be effective, the evaluator needs access to data and frequently depends on the participation of the program staff in the evaluation design and data collection process.

Situations do arise where internal evaluators work in conjunction with external experts. The outside evaluator contributes to the design and, in essence, "audits" the evaluation process. The logic behind this arrangement is an attempt to maximize the benefits of both. Although more of this type of alliance may be seen in the future, its feasibility is limited. More often, outside evaluators are sought when formal program evaluation is indicated. Most organizations are unable to sustain the level of expertise and objectivity indicated within their structures.

Aside from resources and expertise, the importance of the issue, the amount of money involved and the time frame of the evaluation can be used as guides in choosing between an inside or outside evaluation. In general, the more important the program, the greater the amount of money tied up in the program, and the longer the period of time available for the evaluation, the more advisable it will be to select an external evaluator.

THE EVALUATION PROCESS

The integral relationship between the administrator, program development and the evaluation process is most easily portrayed through the use of the D'Costa and Sechrest model, shown in Figure 18-1. Above, the changing role of the health care administrator and the corresponding Janus-like viewpoint were discussed. The D'Costa and Sechrest model reinforces that expanded focus while describing the stages of formal program evaluation.

Figure 18-1 Stages in Program Evaluation

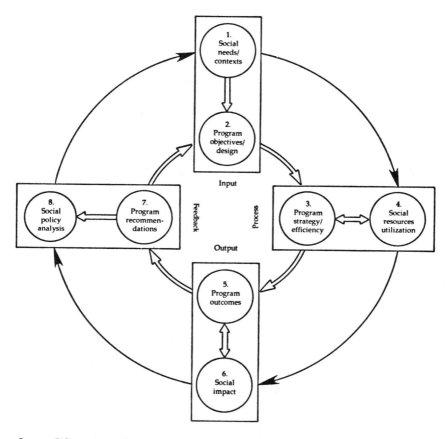

Source: D'Costa, A. and Sechrest, L. *Program Evaluation Concepts for Health Administrators* (Washington, D.C.: Association of University Programs in Health Administration 1976) p. 21.

The model shows that the evaluation process is cyclical, with each component having some dependence on other components. The core is the individual program's evaluation process and the perimeter is the environmental or social evaluation process. For each component or stage in program evaluation there is a corresponding social component in a fully integrated evaluation design. Stages 2, 3, 5 and 7 typify the traditional focus of administrative concerns about demand, efficiency, efficacy and continuation within the organizational structure. Stages 1, 4, 6 and 8, the societal viewpoint, are increasing in both organizational and evaluative significance.

The following questions, stimulated by the model, should be asked of any health care program by both administrators and evaluators.

- What is the setting in which the program is to be implemented?
- What are the problems for redress or what improvements should the program aim at?
- What are some good strategies to achieve these aims? What resources are available?
- How well have the resources available been used?
- What outcomes have been achieved? Not achieved? What unintended outcomes or side effects have been obtained?
- Are these outcomes worthwhile? What has been the impact on society?
- How could the program have been implemented better?
- What policy changes would society benefit from?

All steps in the model are considered important and may be discussed in detail. However, for purposes here, stage 2 is the keystone in the program, administrator, evaluator interface. Assuming that the function of formal program evaluation is to determine whether a program has achieved what it was designed to achieve, program objectives must meet the dual demands of defining the parameters of program performance and providing the foundation for the evaluation process. While programs are developed for many reasons, shift in focus over time and often represent multiple agendas, they are intended to fulfill a purpose and provide the means to accomplish that end. That purpose is often stated as a global, nonmeasurable concept, such as "to provide quality, family-oriented preventive care to children," or "to provide comprehensive cardiac rehabilitation services."

The *objectives* of a program ideally define *how, when, where*, with *whom* and to *what* degree program goals may be achieved. For example, an objective of a program to introduce new health practitioners in ambulatory care may be to increase patients' access to care. On the surface, "to increase access to patient care" appears to be a reasonably well-stated objective; however, to the program evaluator, a more clear, concise and measurable statement will be sought. The evaluator will want to know how you will know if it worked. Will it work if waiting times are decreased by 10 percent? 20 percent? 30 percent? Or is a decrease in the length of time between making an appointment and the actual visit also important?

Considerable effort should be expended on the development of program objectives to ensure that they fulfill their dual function. Preferably, this event occurs very early in the program planning stage conjointly with program developers and the evaluators. Both parties and the program itself can benefit from the exchange that is inevitable during objective setting.

To facilitate that process, the following description developed by Shortell and Richardson[8] can be used as a "preflight checklist" to ensure that all aspects of program performance are considered prior to program implementation.

- Is the nature or content of the objective clear?—Is the program intended to produce changes in information, opinions, attitudes or behavior? For example, some programs are primarily designed to change people's behavior (such as behavior modification programs for smokers) while others are designed to change attitudes (such as educational campaigns on the benefits of fluoridation).

- What is the order of the objectives?—In some instances, one objective depends on the completion of another objective. For example, in a program to decrease the incidence of hospital-related (nosocomial) infections, one objective may be to identify sources of contamination while another is to revise air flow systems. The success of the latter may depend upon the results of the former.

- Who is the target group?—For what specific population is the program intended? What are the geographic boundaries of the group? For example, is an ambulatory care clinic's outreach program designed to reach specific age, sex, ethnic categories? Is it aimed at a particular geographic area?

- When are the effects to be realized?—How quickly is the program intended to produce a change? For example, the development of a vaccine for polio can produce immediate effects, while the development of new personnel programs, such as the National Health Service Corps, or programs requiring new organizations (for example, Professional Standards Review) usually require at least several years before effects can be observed. In general, the more complex the program being initiated, the more diverse the target group to receive the program, and the more complex the environment in which the program must operate, the longer the time needed to observe program effects. It is with these programs that implementation assessments, or formative evaluations, become so important.

- What is the magnitude of the change?—How large an effect is expected? For example, is a smoking-cessation program intended to result in a 30 percent decrease in smoking, a 50 percent decrease or a 75 percent decrease? Or will *any* decrease, no matter how small, be accepted as a positive indicator of program success?

- How stable is the change?—How long are the effects produced by the program intended to last? For many programs, the effects are meant to be permanent, but for others, particularly continuing education programs and programs involving changes in one's behavior, it is recognized that additional retraining or reexposure to the program is necessary.

- How many objectives are there? Are they compatible?—Most programs have more than a single objective. These objectives may be conflicting. For example, an outreach program may increase access to care but may also increase program costs.

- Are the objectives interrelated?—The objectives may be highly related and similar to each other or unrelated and dissimilar. An example of similar and related objectives is a program designed to increase patients' knowledge of hypertension and increase adherence with medical regimen. An example of a program with less similar and less related objectives is an outreach program in a poverty community designed to increase use of health services while at the same time intervene in the "cycle of poverty" within the community.

- How important is each objective?—Objectives will differ in importance and individuals will often disagree about the importance of each objective. For example, in the case of university-based programs for the mentally retarded and developmentally disabled, faculty members are more likely to place greater importance on education and training, while direct care providers and community groups are more likely to emphasize service to clients.

- Will there be unintended and unanticipated consequences?—The program may produce effects not intended but anticipated, or even unanticipated, by its initiators. For example, an unintended effect of a methadone maintenance program may be the further addiction (to methadone) of those who were not true addicts previously. It is important for those involved in the evaluation to try to think through in advance the various possible "side effects" of the program under question.

Finally, and of great importance, early in the stages of program evaluation design, a distinction needs to be drawn between the services offered within a program and the program itself. Particularly in large programs, it will be important to isolate particular program components for the evaluation to offer useful information. For example, in a health promotion and disease prevention program, screening for colo-rectal cancer would not be included unless it could be ensured that efficacious methods for detection were available. Otherwise, the evaluation would be unable to determine if the results were consistent with existing evidence of efficacy.

APPLICATIONS OF FORMAL PROGRAM EVALUATION

Programs are classified according to their evolutionary status and purpose. Within that framework, six program types where formal program evaluation may be best applied are identifiable in health care settings.[9] These are (1) developmental programs, (2) modified ongoing programs, (3) ongoing programs, (4) natural experiments, (5) demonstration projects and (6) social experiments.

Developmental programs are often initiated by an organization to explore an innovative idea. They may be viewed as a pilot test. Here, a formative evaluation can be most helpful. Early involvement of the experienced evaluator can help in the conduct of both the planning and introduction of the exploratory effort. These types of programs require a great deal of latitude and a flexible environment. The evaluator's purpose is to keep track of the activities and offer formative appraisals of the evolutionary process. For example, a hospital may be interested in documenting the development of an early discharge planning program. This would involve clarifying the program's objectives, determining patient eligibility criteria, estimating the volume and resource requirements, working out the collaborative relationships with the relevant nursing units, financial office and admitting department, and related activities. The evaluator's documentation and assessment results would enable the administrator to make decisions about continuing or modifying the program.

Modified ongoing programs occur when an operational program is targeted for updating with new methods, equipment, or organizational schemes or when the services are offered to a broader range of consumers. The evaluator may be brought in before the modification takes place to collect baseline data and participate in the development of objectives for the modification. For example, a hospital may consider the implementation of primary care nursing in nursing services. This type of modification may be viewed by upper levels of nursing management as a "better way"—consequently, there may be pressure exerted on management to prove that this change will be an improvement. Program evaluation may be sought to provide justification for the change in addition to documenting the outcome of the program. Again, the evaluator will work very closely with management to ensure that decision-making needs are met.

Ongoing program justification may be necessary with budget cuts or accountability demands. Chances are that many existing programs have never received formal evaluation. In addition to documentation of relative program value, the evaluation may reveal areas that could benefit from modification, thus potentially strengthening or enhancing program performance in the future. For example, a marginally performing outpatient surgery center may be threatened with termination because of newly proposed budget restrictions. The evaluation may reveal widely varying utilization rates and inefficient staffing patterns. When the full picture is examined, the evidence may suggest that the program as conceived is worthy of retention but that patient scheduling, physician referrals and staffing improvements are needed to yield a more efficient and effective service.

Natural experiments occur when a situation arises that essentially creates a program without regard to evaluation or prior planning. It may be referred to as an experiment because the events take place in a manner that allows inferences and conclusions to be drawn with comparative data usually through retrospective analysis. Occasionally, concurrent or even prospective assessment of the change may be possible, depending on the nature of that event. Natural experiments frequently arise when funding for existing programs or services are unexpectedly terminated or reduced. One can then assess the impact of the fully funded program versus the partially funded in regard to issues of access and quality of care. In other cases, new programs unexpectedly develop which can serve as points of comparison for an ongoing program. For example, the relative success of foundation-sponsored initiatives to recruit and retain physicians in rural underserved areas might be compared with federal efforts in the same areas.

Demonstration projects are usually externally funded with the evaluation taking a more dominant role. Programs that fall within this category can be responsive to local needs, thus a formative evaluation may be employed. Federal agencies will often require a strong evaluation component to distinguish the demonstration from a direct source project which is ineligible for federal funding. The Emergency Medical Service (EMS) projects are examples of this program type. The evaluators must meet the needs of the funding agency to provide information about program success, taking into consideration the variations at the local level. Managers involved with these programs may be called upon to organize and supervise the program's compliance with reporting requirements or to serve as the liaison between the program staff and the evaluation team.

The social experiment is less common but included to fully describe program types. Its main purpose is the evaluation of the intervention. For example, the Rand Health Insurance Study is designed to test the effects of different organizational and financing characteristics on providers and consumers of health care services. Research design and hence the role of the evaluator is the prominent force in the program. In this situation, management will be asked to ensure that, to the highest degree possible, the needs of the research design are foremost in the program conduct.

The first three areas where program evaluation may be applied—developmental, modified and ongoing programs—portray the administrator as a central figure in virtually every aspect of the evaluation. In the natural experiment, administrative input and control will depend on the unique circumstances of the individual program. In the latter two areas, demonstration projects and social experiments, the major purpose is usually the evaluation itself. Here external funding agencies and the evaluator will usually assume more dominant roles.

In all program types, the evaluator, the administrator and the program staff can interact. The timeliness and quality of that interaction may exhibit a significant impact on the formal program evaluation process. Hence, the role of the administrator deserves special attention.

THE ADMINISTRATOR'S ROLE IN FORMAL PROGRAM EVALUATION

The degree to which management can contribute to the evaluation process can be important to eventual quality and utility of the evaluation results. Administrators who are aware of the needs of the organization, the program staff and the evaluators, and are able to anticipate and intervene in potential problem areas can optimize the benefits to be gained by engaging in a formal program evaluation. Four areas have been identified where management offers a major contribution in the evaluation process: (1) initiation of the evaluation itself, (2) facilitation of the process, (3) mediation of the relationship of the evaluator(s) and the program staff, and (4) implementation of the evaluation results.

Initiation

In addition to recognizing the type of programs where formal evaluation is appropriate, the administrator should answer the question concerning why the evaluation is being sought. Is this effort proposed to offer scientific input to the decision-making process and thus intended to be used, or is the evaluation being proposed for ulterior or covert purposes and likely to result in a token, cursory exercise? Similarly, is the organization willing to commit the resources required for a valid program evaluation or will the effort be poorly supported, with minimal probability of any major impact? Organizational motives and resources should be carefully examined before initiating formal program evaluation.

A second activity which may occur simultaneously with determining organizational motives and resources is selecting an evaluator. An experienced evaluator will be able to assist in deciding if formal program evaluation is indicated and what resources will be needed to carry out the evaluation. From the administrator's perspective, these discussions may be very important. Often, one evaluator may recommend another evaluator. This may be because of time constraints or the availability of another person whose skills and/or geographic locale may be more suitable for a particular type of program. For example, an administrator contemplating an evaluation of a hospital-based ambulatory care program may call an evaluator from a major university in another state who recommends another evaluator in the administrator's own state with extensive experience in health care program evaluation and who has recently been working with ambulatory care programs. These early contacts will also allow the proposed evaluator to schedule the time and resources needed to perform the evaluation.

The last consideration that falls within the area of initiation is timing. Timing has two components, one being related to organizational or program readiness to be evaluated and the other a factor of the type of evaluation being proposed. Some consensus on the former should take place before the evaluation team is contacted.

The latter has to do with whether a formative or summative evaluation is proposed. It is usually better to summon the evaluator very early, even if an outcome or summative evaluation is proposed. However, it is neither necessary nor wise to perform an outcome evaluation if a program is not yet fully operational or if it has been operational for a short period of time.

In brief, at the initiation stage the administrator is essentially involved in conducting an "evaluability assessment." As developed by Schmidt, Scanlon and Bell,[10] this consists of determining whether the following criteria have been met:

- Is the program well defined?
- Is the program description acceptable to those policy makers and managers interested in the evaluation results?
- Does the program description validly represent the activities to be carried out?
- Are the expected results plausible given the program activity?
- Is the evidence required to support the program reliable and economical?
- Are management's expected uses of evaluation information plausible?

Facilitation

Most often, the administrator is charged with the responsibility of ensuring that the evaluator receives whatever is necessary from the organization to get the job done. This may include people, ideas, data, space and authority to work within the organization. Introductions need to be made, meetings need to be held, data sources need to be available and interpreted. The administrator, in essence, "paves the way" for the evaluator.

Perhaps the most important area where the administrator may facilitate the evaluation is in the area of formulating program objectives. Through an understanding of the needs of the evaluation and the function of the program, it may be that the administrator is the best person to take a lead role in objective setting. Mechanic has noted that "even when the intent of a program is clearly specified at the highest administrative levels, the translation at the local units can be quite bizarre; and the operational units tend to have their own agendas and priorities and often quite different goals."[11] Through active involvement in this process, the administrator may be instrumental in both the organizational sense and the evaluative sense.

Mediation

The relationship between program staff and evaluators is sometimes less than mutually supportive. While some degree of anticipation and planning may minimize the need for mediation, conflicts can occur and may compromise the performance of both. In general, the greater the distance between the evaluators and the program staff, the higher the probability that each may view the other with increased suspicion.

The potential for program staff-evaluator conflict is due to very basic value differences. The program staff is service oriented and thus gears their performance to expanding program activities. They necessarily view their service as beneficial, contributing to some component of health care. The evaluator is research oriented, seeking to maintain the integrity of the research design. Suppose a health program is designed to introduce a new method of health education for individuals with epilepsy. The program staff will want to offer their services to as many people as possible while the evaluator may want a control group or another group of individuals who receive a different or partial intervention. The staff may find this practice unreasonable and, possibly, ethically offensive.

Also, program evaluation consumes resources that program staff may view as better spent on direct services. Evaluation can be expensive and time consuming. Program personnel may resent fulfilling data-recording requirements or attendance at meetings concerning the evaluation process. They may also resent anyone who attempts to pass judgment when that person is not bearing the day-to-day responsibility and drudgery involved in direct service. The evaluator may be seen as the recipient of special privileges, showing up at irregular intervals, meeting with the "higher-ups" and, in general, not subject to the basic constraints of line performance.

If the evaluation is being performed to serve as a part of the program development, such as formative evaluation, the role of the evaluator is more likely to be perceived as a supportive, contributory effort. If the evaluation is summative and funding decisons are depending on the evaluative results, a level of program staff anxiety and defensiveness is to be anticipated.

Similarly, if the evaluation is a "built-in" component that was initiated early in the program planning stages, there will probably be less conflict than if the evaluator is called in to make a "one-shot" assessment. In the former instance, the development of program objectives, the evaluation data collection requirements, and the role of the evaluator will become an integral part of program operations; in the latter, it is more likely to be viewed as an intrusion by the program staff.

Evaluations that are linked to external funding requirements can be seen by the program personnel as a necessary nuisance, not really central to their mission; however, when someone higher up in the organizational chain of command initiates the effort, the immediacy of that act and its implications may create greater attributions of significance to the evaluation. This effect is not necessarily either positive or negative but usually results in greater interest on the part of the program staff.

Experienced evaluators are familiar with most of the conflicts that can arise with the evaluation of health care problems. They will welcome, if not rely on, the participation and cooperation of management. It is management that can best assume the mediator function. Often, it is the manager who introduces the evaluation team to the program staff. The way that team is presented may be critical to the eventual program receptivity to the evaluation effort. Managers can minimize conflicts by (1) ensuring that time be allocated for discussions and the development of mutual understanding, and (2) if conflicts do arise, engaging in conflict resolution as swiftly and equitably as possible.

Implementation

Health care organizations and funding agencies expend considerable resources to produce formal program evaluations to augment their decision-making abilities. (Evaluation results are intended to be used; however, the full impact of the effort is often diluted.)

As portrayed in the D'Costa and Sechrest model, evaluation results have significance for the individual program and policy formulation as well. (Yet, in many instances, evaluation reports are skimmed by one or two individuals and filed away on a shelf.) O₁, the report is distributed to the funding agency and the individual program receives a summary or the format is such that the results have little relevance to their own decision-making needs. Even more frustrating, evaluation results may be reported through such a confusing myriad of statistics and qualifications or technical language that they offer minimal direction for the decision makers.

An administrator who works closely with the evaluator can shape the form of the evaluation to be sure the key questions are answered and reported in a manner that makes sense to the intended audience. For example, certain test statistics may be very important for data analysis, but the results may be more clearly portrayed through the use of percentages, graphs or charts with the more technical display contained in one of the appendices. Evaluation reports that are difficult to wade through will not be read. Many evaluators have recognized these problems and will provide executive summaries to allow for broader review of the findings.

IMPORTANT RESOURCE FOR DECISION MAKING

Formal program evaluation is an important resource for decision making in the health care field. Through its application of the scientific method, this form of evaluation offers a more valid and justifiable foundation for resource allocation and planning. At the program level, this method can be employed by the administrator to provide detailed information to monitor and guide the development and determine the effects of a program. On a broader level, the results of program evaluations may be aggregated to form a basis for health care policy decisions.

REFERENCES

1. DeVries, R.A. "Strength in Numbers." *Hospitals, JAHA* 52:6 (March 1978) p. 81-84.
2. Stull, R.J. "Many Concepts Mold Multi-Institutional Systems." *Hospitals, JAHA* 51:5 (March 1977) p. 43-45.
3. Sheldon, A. and Barrett, D. "The Janus Principle." *Health Care Management Review* 2:2 (Spring 1977) p. 77-87.
4. D'Costa, A. and Sechrest, L. *Program Evaluation Concepts for Health Administrators* (Washington, D.C.: Association of University Programs in Health Administration 1976).
5. Kane, R.L., Hanson, R. and Deniston, O.L. "Program Evaluation: Is It Worth It?" in Kane, R.L., ed. *The Challenge of Community Medicine* (New York: Springer Publishing Co. 1974) p. 213-233.
6. Shortell, S.M. and Richardson, W.C. *Health Program Evaluation* (St. Louis: C.V. Mosby Co. 1978) p. 7.
7. Weiss, C.H. *Evaluation Research: Methods for Assessing Program Effectiveness* (Englewood Cliffs, N.J.: Prentice-Hall 1972).
8. Shortell and Richardson. *Health Program Evaluation* p. 18, 19.
9. Ibid. p. 99-101.
10. Schmidt, R.E., Scanlon, J.W. and Bell, J.B. *Evaluability Assessment: Making Public Programs Work Better* (Washington, D.C.: The Urban Institute, October 1978).
11. Mechanic, D. *The Growth of Bureaucratic Medicine* (New York: John Wiley & Sons 1976) p. 187.

19. A Multi-Institutional Approach to the Assurance of Quality

VERLA COLLINS

In this era of resource constraint, the corporate organization of a group of hospitals is emerging as one of a variety of multi-institutional arrangements that are likely to succeed in supporting a survival course for hospitals.[1-6] Multihospital systems offer not only the possibility of achieving economies in the general management and organization of health services, but also the potential for introducing cost and quality control mechanisms that may be more effective than if implemented independently by individual hospitals.

We suggest that one reason cost and quality control activities of hospitals have, in the past, not been particularly effective is that they are being implemented in relatively small organizations that, as a consequence, lack essential resources and capabilities to carry out such activities. This is particularly true of the small rural hospital; but it may also be true of many large free-standing hospitals, since these often do not have properly trained staff and adequate information systems to assure control over the cost and quality of care.

The purpose of this reading is to illustrate the advantages and disadvantages of multihospital approaches to control. We do this by using the quality assurance program of Intermountain Health Care, Inc. (IHC) as our example.[7] IHC is a nonprofit system of community hospitals located in Utah, Idaho, Wyoming, and Nevada. It owns, leases, or manages 22 hospitals with approximately 3,000 beds and currently has shared-service arrangements with 32 additional hospitals with about 2,500 beds. In all, IHC provides about 60 percent of all hospital care in Utah and 30 percent in Idaho. IHC is thus one of about 30 major hospital chains in this country, which together represent approximately 400 hospitals and over 84,000 hospital beds. IHC is an especially appropriate system to examine for possible advantages and disadvantages of quality assurance mechanisms because it includes within it the full spectrum of small and large, and urban and rural hospitals; it is a regional system, thus offering the potential for making "system" changes, as needed; and it is a nonprofit system, thus paralleling the ownership structure of most voluntary hospitals in this country.

While there are many advantages and disadvantages in the multihospital approach to quality assurance, the following are the ones that have appeared most prominently in the IHC system:

Advantages:

- strengthens accountability control
- enhances analytic capability
- facilitates more economic use of limited resources
- increases capability of achieving reliability in measurement
- legitimizes standards, analyses, and recommendations for change
- facilitates the integration of related managerial functions
- provides the capability for making needed "systems" changes.

Disadvantages:

- disparities among hospitals in perceptions of the relative advantages of shared programs
- conflicts between local and central boards
- conflicts with regulatory bodies focused on single institutions or on hospitals in only one state (when the multihospital system spans several states)
- incongruities among hospitals in both needs and capabilities.

ADVANTAGES

A multi-institutional organization has the potential for developing superior quality assurance programs primarily because of the relatively greater resource base. The interaction and resource exchanges that occur among large and small, urban and rural, and specialized and general hospitals in a consortium provide opportunities for the delivery of care whose overall quality may be better than the sum of the constituent institutions. In effect, the larger resource base has the potential for generating a kind of synergism, resulting in a number of advantages for quality assurance.

Strengthens Accountability Control

The responsibility and authority for the development and management of the quality assurance program lies with the chief executive officer and executive board of an institution. In the case of the multi-institutional organization, accountability for compliance with, for example, the JCAH standards, is placed at the corporate level. This ensures that system resources will be deployed effectively, increasing the likelihood that each institution within the system will meet accreditation requirements.

The corporate board of IHC, for example, has clearly demonstrated its interest in the quality of patient care. The board carries out its responsibilities through the work of an oversight committee established by the board. The committee is comprised of members of the board and of top corporate management. This committee supports the board by expecting each hospital and health care program to set appropriate quality standards that correspond to the goals of the corporation; monitoring reports on the compliance of the hospitals and their health service programs with the established quality standards; providing resources to those hospitals and their health service programs that request assistance in complying with the standards; and establishing policies that govern the action of the corporation on questions of quality.

The overall quality assurance objectives for the IHC hospitals are developed by the corporate director and staff for quality assurance. The director and the staff also provide consultation services, educational services, and review of performance to local hospitals, as needed. On the other hand, primary responsibility for setting specific standards for evaluation and for implementing quality assurance programs rests at the local level.

The hospital administrator is the pivot person at the local level. This individual coordinates the work of the medical professionals, the hospital department heads, the local board members, and the corporate board; a role that expands the administrator's accountability to a marked degree. In summary, the administrator of each IHC hospital is the officer accountable to the board and is responsible for organizing the quality assurance programs and the risk control functions through a staff assistant to the chief executive officer, thus ensuring direct reports to the administrator. Provision is made for adequate and appropriate funding for clerical assistance in data retrieval and reporting.

Specific responsibilities of the hospital administrator include:

- establishing an organizational structure for quality assurance with a delegated staff of adequate size
- coordinating the quality assurance program throughout the hospital
- providing a direct route for local hospital staff to report to the hospital administrator
- integrating the hospital's quality control and risk management functions
- designating a member, or members, of the medical staff to be responsible for quality control and assuring that they receive special preparation for this role
- developing and implementing a method for collecting, analyzing, and reporting the data generated and used in the program and
- establishing a system for ongoing evaluation of program costs and results.

In the IHC system, all individuals with professional responsibilities and who have direct contact with the patient are included in the quality assurance program. For example, physicians are involved in the development of criteria and standards. People in management and on the local boards of trustees also support the quality assurance programs and are made aware that quality assurance is an essential component for the successful provision of hospital services. We believe that this degree of involvement in quality assurance is greatly enhanced by the multi-institutional structure of the IHC system. The corporate structure layers on an important additional source of organizational authority, thus giving impetus and support to quality assurance activities through the use of formal accountability mechanisms.

Enhances Analytic Capability

The multi-hospital approach offers the capability of collecting and examining sufficient data to allow comparisons between and among a variety of hospitals. This has been well demonstrated, for example, in the quality assurance programs of the Kaiser Health Plan. An example of this advantage in the IHC system is represented in the applications currently being made of a nursing quality assurance tool.

The IHC nursing personnel developed and tested a quality assessment tool that enables them to examine the similarities and differences that exist in six complex tertiary centers, eight community hospitals, and eight rural hospitals.

A panel of 31 registered nurses, selected from within IHC, developed the Intermountain Health Care Quality Assurance Tool. These nurses reviewed a list of 455 items identified from the literature and other sources as standards for nursing care. The panel categorized each item according to level of "best care," "average care," or "minimal care." For the trial instrument, items having 75 percent agreement of the panel were considered to reflect the "best care."

Four expert clinicians then reviewed the trial instrument and reduced the items to 30, reflecting topic clusters. These 30 items were later reduced to 18, making the tool easier to administer and to score. A number of statistical analyses were conducted to determine the reliability and validity of the tool.

The tool evaluates the nursing care received by the adult care patient population in terms of the nursing process:

- the acquisition of patient baseline data, a nursing or patient history or both
- the development of an initial or continuing patient care plan or both
- the implementation of the plan of care, including written descriptions of care (for example, problem-oriented records and nurses' notes) and demonstration of the knowledge base of the nurse assigned to provide the patient's direct

care (to be obtained by an interview). (Direct care is defined as the services performed by the person giving the majority of bedside care.)

- evaluation based on the interpretation of audit scores for each hospital unit.

Audits based on the tool are now obtained from each unit of a hospital on a random basis and are based on 30 percent of the admissions per unit per month. Each month, these are submitted to the corporate office for computer analysis and data are reported back to the hospital units for review and as a basis for recommending changes and reevaluating the care provided.

Deficiencies found in a particular unit of any hospital are located, causal agents are identified, and corrective actions are instituted. Our experience is that deficiencies usually fall into educational, structural, or management categories.

In general, we have found that participation in tool development and data collection increases the nursing staff's belief in the credibility of the data and their acceptance of corrective action. Further, we have found that the involvement of nurses from other hospitals as well as the impact of the interhospital comparisons reinforces the overall acceptance of and commitment to the quality assurance program.

Facilitates More Economic Use of Limited Resources

Much has already been said about the advantage of sharing resources among the hospitals in a multihospital system. In this section, we give a few additional specific examples.

The identification and analysis of problems is simplified and made less costly when data from quality assessment are fed into a central review process for comparative analysis against predetermined standards. *Example:* The scores indicated on form A and form B (Exhibit 19-1) provide an example in which performance in the areas of nursing/patient history, care plan, and nurses' notes were found to be relatively low. These scores represent a composite of contributions from a number of nurses who work at one specific hospital. Once deficiencies are identified, they are then addressed through corrective actions directed toward the entire staff of the particular unit. The point is, such analyses would not always be feasible if each hospital had to develop its own information systems to support the quality assurance effort.

Central office staff who are familiar with standards and their interpretation can assist each department in each hospital to conduct quality care evaluations in a systematic, organized, and consistent manner. *Example:* Assistance from central quality assurance staff has resulted in a noticeable improvement in care as measured by outcome audits. Specifically, nursing care audits based on predetermined criteria have resulted in a significant increase in the quality of nursing care patients have received.

Exhibit 19-1 Monthly Report Form Prepared From Data Submitted by Hospital Units

INTERMOUNTAIN HEALTH CARE, INC.
NURSING QUALITY ASSURANCE

Hospital:
Unit:
Number of Audits: 19

Form A

1. Nursing History	— No History	0.0%	
	— First Item Recorded	10.5%	
	— Second Item Recorded	0.0%	
	— Third Item Recorded	89.4%	
2. Nursing Care Plan	— No Care Plan	15.7%	
	— First Item Defined	15.7%	
	Plan of Action		15.7%
	— Second Item Defined	21.0%	
	Plan of Action		21.0%
	— Third Item Defined	47.3%	
	Plan of Action		47.3%
3. Charting	— No Acceptable Charting	0.0%	
	— First Item Defined	0.0%	
	Nursing Action		0.0%
	— Second Item Defined	0.0%	
	Nursing Action		0.0%
	— Third Item Defined	100.0%	
	Nursing Action		100.0%
	Form A Subtotal — Mean	87.7%	
	Std. Dev.	13.8	
Staff Classification	— Aide		0.0%
	— LPN		42.1%
	— 2 Yr RN		5.2%
	— 3 Yr RN		31.5%
	— 4 Yr RN		10.5%
	— Masters		0.0%
Employment Status	— Outside Med Pool		0.0%
	— Parttime 1-2 Days		0.0%
	— Parttime 3-4 Days		0.0%
	— Fulltime		89.4%

Exhibit 19-1 continued

Form B

	Month: Mar 79
4. Patient Diagnosis	89.4%
5. Read Nursing Care Plan	52.6%
6. Observations Regarding Pt Condition	
A. None	0.0%
B. First Observation	0.0%
C. Second Observation	0.0%
D. Third Observation	100.0%
7. Patient Problems/Therapy	
A. Discomfort/Concern Identified	100.0%
B. Therapeutic Measure Identified	100.0%
C. Effects Identified	100.0%
8. Plan for Teaching — None	10.5%
— Plan 1	21.0%
— Plan 2	68.4%
9. Current Teaching — None	10.5%
— Plan 1	31.5%
— Plan 2	57.8%
10. Teaching Recorded	36.8%
11. Discussion: Plan of Care	
A. No One	0.0%
B. Health Professional	5.2%
C. Patient/S.O.	89.4%
Form B Subtotal — Mean	88.0%
Std. Dev.	8.1
Unit Total — Mean	87.8%
Std. Dev.	9.0
IHC Goal — Mean	85%
Std. Dev.	9

Increases Capability of Achieving Reliability in Measurement

The collection of sufficient data in a consistent manner in a variety of hospitals assures that a high level of reliability in measurement can be achieved. The capacity for pooling comparable data is a decided advantage for small institutions with limited data bases.

Legitimizes Standards, Analyses, and Recommendations for Change

We believe that the multihospital system with its central coordination capabilities and central resources makes it easier to establish a communications network that facilitates meaningful feedback at all levels within the system. Not only does this promote a more efficient means of studying the quality of a large number of hospitals, but it also serves to legitimize and validate the results in the eyes of those who must act on the implications of findings.

Facilitates the Integration of Related Managerial Functions

Quality assurance programs in the IHC system are a means not only of assuring that the care given to patients is of a high quality but also of controlling the costs of care, improving educational programs, and revising management procedures (e.g., patient billing). We think that a multihospital system provides a unique environment within which a broad program of management control can be developed, some of the advantages of which are illustrated in what follows.

Productivity

The centralization of computer services makes it possible to combine analyses of productivity and quality. *Example:* Data retrieved from hospitals are submitted to the central office for analysis and development of monthly summary reports. In addition, all data from the IHC hospitals (e.g., admissions, length of stay), are plotted and charted on a combined productivity report that uses a patient classification system and the quality scores. Such an analysis is illustrated in Exhibit 19-2. This allows nursing administration staff the opportunity to analyze the relationship of the staffing component to the quality scores.

Staffing

Staff can be distributed throughout the system on a shared basis. *Example:* A patient classification system that is used in quality assurance is also used to determine staffing requirements based on patient acuity levels. This system allows administrators to deploy personnel from units/systems with lesser needs to those with greater needs.

Self-insurance and Risk Management

One of the strengths of a multihospital system is its ability to develop a self-insurance program to respond to litigation. An important outcome of such a program is the change in attitude among hospital staff toward preventing incidents that could harm the patient. A multihospital system's self-insurance program also requires a concomitant risk management program that encourages incident detection, evaluation, and prevention in each of its constituents. *Example:* The attitude in IHC that "This is our Insurance Company" has converted staff to the opinion that "These are our dollars—let's do everything we can to avert problems." Each hospital in the IHC has created an in-house risk manager who works closely with those in charge of patient care activities and reports directly to the hospital administrator. Risk managers immediately follow-up on untoward incidents. Their initial efforts are to anticipate potential problems and to resolve them immediately by initiating appropriate changes that will either avert or prevent similar accidents from happening in the future. The program, thus far, has been very successful, particularly in the area of improved and more immediate adjudication of patient grievances and claims. More important, it shows great promise for effecting a major reduction in patient injuries in the future. The interdependence between this program and quality assurance is, obviously, very substantial. Although the two programs are separated in the IHC system, they share information on possible problems within the system on a regular basis.

Utilization Review

Savings realized from central billing and uniform record systems are obvious means of controlling costs and assuring quality. *Example:* Examination of radiographic charges to determine whether charges are appropriate or whether radiography is overused or underused is relatively simple with a centralized system. This also allows the comparison of individual patient bills with a number of bills for patients with like illnesses, thus enabling the discovery of incorrect charges. In addition, this type of review has led to the savings of thousands of dollars after a change of procedure was determined to be needed and, consequently, instituted. Such reviews also promote awareness among the professional staff of less expensive procedures or medicines that may be available and the interdependence between cost and quality control.

Provides Capability of Making Needed Patient Care Delivery System Changes

The multihospital system permits the corporation to make changes in the delivery system, based on an assessment of community needs and resources. Services that are duplicative or fragmented may be phased out and provided by another institution in geographic proximity.

The maintenance of underutilized beds in sparsely populated areas, for example, has both cost and quality implications. The ability to refer patients freely from one hospital to another within the same system has both financial and public relations implications. Many of the benefits of a multihospital system seem to

Exhibit 19-2 Adjusted Workload per Patient Acuity*

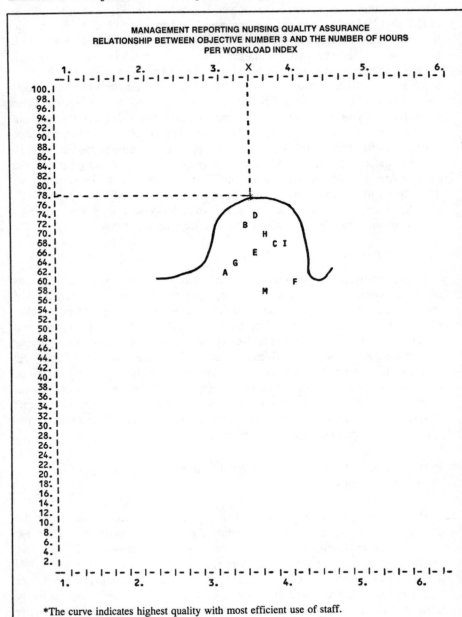

MANAGEMENT REPORTING NURSING QUALITY ASSURANCE
RELATIONSHIP BETWEEN OBJECTIVE NUMBER 3 AND THE NUMBER OF HOURS
PER WORKLOAD INDEX

*The curve indicates highest quality with most efficient use of staff.

```
- |- |- |-  7.|-|-|-|-|8.|-|-|- |- |-|-|-|-|-|-|10.|-|-|-|-
                 L|                 9.              |
```

LEGEND
A=3RD—ORTHO
B=YOUTH
C=PEDIATRICS
D=4TH—SURGICAL
E=5TH—SURGICAL
F=GYNECOLOGY
G=6TH—MEDICAL
H=7TH—MEDICAL
I=I.C.U
K=C.C.U.
L=I.A.C.U.
M=POST PARTUM
O=WELL BABY NS
P=INTENSIVE CA
Q=INTERMED CAR
R=BORDER BABY

```
|- |- |- |- |- |- |- |- |- |- |- |- |- |- |- |- |- |- |- |- |- |- |-
     7.            8.            9.            10.
```

accrue to the smaller community or rural hospitals. However, if rural patients requiring specialty care are referred to the large, complex metropolitan hospitals, this tends to increase bed utilization and the flow of care dollars. Exchange of information at the provider levels also contributes to the development of colleague/peer relationships.

DISADVANTAGES

While we tend to see more advantages accruing to the multi-institutional approach to quality assurance, our experience has certainly taught us of a number of disadvantages that limit the effectiveness of this approach.

Disparities Among Hospitals in Perceptions of the Relative Advantages of Shared Programs

Large, complex metropolitan hospitals often have difficulty conforming to the requirements of a central office. They often have available to them many of the necessary resources and thus do not perceive the full advantages of shared programs (e.g., quality assurance) as do smaller hospitals.

Conflicts Between Local and Central Boards

The local boards often feel constrained by the authority of the central office and are not always supportive of the mandates from the central office administration. *Example:* The restraints placed on specialty services (such as newborn and intensive care units) in small hospitals are sometimes resented, particularly when referral systems are suggested as alternatives. These restraints are often resented, even when they may be justified in both quality and cost terms. The same holds true for the implementation of the quality assurance program.

Conflicts with Regulatory Bodies Focused on Single Institutions or on Hospitals in Only One State (When the Multihospital System Spans Several States)

The single-institutional focus of the JCAH, for example, may pose problems for the accreditation of a multihospital system. The centralization of some functions and resources at the corporate level challenges site team members to adjust their evaluative strategies to fit a multi-institutional perspective. Also, multihospital systems operating in several states threaten the effectiveness of the individual state regulatory agencies, since the latter implement standards and rate setting under unique state regulations.

Incongruities Among Hospitals in Both Needs and Capabilities

Quality assurance programs of multi-institutional systems must be careful to allow for the differences in needs and capabilities of the member hospitals. To fail to do so may create resentment at the local level and, therefore, resistance to program objectives. The small rural hospitals, for example, often have very different quality problems than do large urban hospitals. Even if the problems may be the same, the feasibility of alternative solutions may differ substantially between the two types of hospitals.

CONCLUSION

In summary, during the past decade the multihospital system has emerged as an organizational structure of potential mutual benefit to all of its components. The IHC example illustrates that in this system the advantages potentially outweigh the disadvantages in the management of an integrated, interorganizational quality assurance program. The trend toward interorganizational alliances seems certain to accelerate in the face of increased demands for cost containment, cost effectiveness analysis, utilization review, certification of need, and competition, for example. Accepting this as a given, we make the following recommendations for changes in the area of quality assurance:

- *That the JCAH continue to develop an accreditation strategy that recognizes the multihospital structure.* Currently, each hospital is accredited as a freestanding unit. With the joint programs that are implemented among the hospitals in a given network, serious consideration needs to be given to the feasibility of accrediting the multi-institutional cluster. The multihospital quality assurance program established within the IHC system represents only one example of why this is needed.

- *That the feasibility of developing voluntary consortia to conduct quality assurance and cost containment programs in small hospitals be explored.* Centralization of the management of the quality assurance function appears to be cost saving. For example, system-wide data collection and analysis by central office personnel with special expertise means that one person can do the job for several hospitals, thus decreasing the cost of this service. The potential for pooling data for purposes of conducting cost and quality studies also argues for a consortia approach to cost and quality control.

- *That standardized tools be developed to permit intraorganizational and interorganizational comparisons.* The Intermountain Health Care Quality Assurance Tool described in this reading indicates the utilitarian value of making both intrainstitutional and interinstitutional comparative data available to administrators. Deficiencies in educational, structural, or management areas can be readily identified and feedback can be directed to the appropriate unit or hospital so that changes to alleviate the problems can be initiated.

- *That funding of research on multiorganizational approaches to cost containment and quality assurance be encouraged.* Throughout this reading, the advantages of the multiorganizational approach carry an implicit assumption that the capability of central administration to allocate resources among a set of hospitals results in a more efficient operation than is possible with a single institution. The increasing numbers of hospitals that are merging, or exploring the feasibility of merging, indicate that the perceived benefits of collaborative pooling of resources must outweigh those of the competitive and autonomous model that has been the norm for both public and private hospitals for a number of years.

These new suprasystems offer unlimited opportunities for intraorganizational and interorganizational comparative studies of the human and nonhuman factors that contribute to the quality and cost of health care. For example, longitudinal studies to answer questions concerning the relationships of differing structures and processes to the quality of care could be launched prior to amalgamation. Findings from such studies could be used as feedback for improvement.

REFERENCES

1. Barrett D: Multihospital systems: The process of development. *Health Care Manage Rev* 1979; 4(3):49-59.
2. Brown M, McCool B: *Multihospital Systems*. Rockville, Md, Aspen Systems Corp, 1980.
3. Cochran J, Fourkas T: *Hospital Consortia*. Scaramento, California Hospital Association, 1979.
4. Frist T, Campbell J: Outlook for hospitals: Systems are the solution. *Harvard Business Rev* 1981; (September-October):130-141.
5. Mason S (ed): *Multihospital Arrangements*. Chicago, American Hospital Association, 1979.
6. Zuckerman H: Multi-institutional systems: Promise and performance. *Inquiry* 1979; 16:291-314.
7. Mueller D: Organization for quality assurance in a hospital system, in *Multihospital Arrangements: Public Policy Implications*. Chicago, American Hospital Association, 1979.

Part IV

Future Directions

20. Some Future Directions in Quality Assurance

JANELLE C. KRUEGER and ROICE D. LUKE

A concluding reading can serve two functions: to summarize the major points made by the authors or to delineate future directions. We choose here merely to suggest future quality assurance needs in the areas of education, research, and policy. These are derived from or suggested by the writers of the preceding chapters. Our comments, although brief, capture the key points we believe need attention.

The Joint Commission on the Accreditation of Hospitals (JCAH) has been instrumental in shifting the emphasis of quality assurance programs from measurement and assessment techniques to organization behavior and the relationship between cost and quality. The new standard (1981) is a step forward. However, much work remains to be done in the operationalization of the new emphases. For example, the conceptual and operational sides of organization behavior need to be developed, giving emphasis to the design of quality assurance programs, the linkage of quality assurance activities to the authority structure of health care institutions, and the methods of bringing about change in the behavior of health care professionals. What is needed is an infusion of organizational theory, management science, change theory, decision making, and so on, to further our understanding of quality control and improvement. In addition, the linkage between quality and cost control needs to be more clearly established. This will require theoretical and practical input from such areas as economics, finance, marketing, program evaluation, quantitative analysis, and public policy.

It should be apparent that the problem of quality assurance is a single but important example of broader managerial and policy considerations in the health care field. In other words, the quality assurance function should not be considered simply as a narrow clinical or technical concern but rather as a complex organizational problem requiring the integration of multiple disciplines and organizational functions. To this end, we offer the following specific recommendations in the areas of education, research, and policy.

EDUCATION

Clearly, our approach to teaching quality assurance must be altered if the above-mentioned change in emphasis is to be accomplished. An important beginning point is the teaching of quality assurance at the graduate level. However, of equal importance is the retraining and reorienting of people who are involved in quality assurance at the institutional level.

- The teaching of quality assurance in graduate programs of health, nursing, or medical administration should emphasize the organization behavior and quality/cost considerations of quality control and improvement. This is not to suggest that the technical aspects of measurement and assessment should not also be taught but that much greater emphasis on the former topics is needed over what is commonly taught in graduate programs.
- Given that the design of quality assurance programs is still very experimental and developmental, the teaching of quality assurance at the graduate level should extend beyond the conceptual and applied aspects of program design to include the scientific or research foundations of quality assurance activities.
- Should specific courses in quality assurance be developed, the instruction should generally be interdisciplinary. Disciplinary areas that should be represented include the variety of specific areas within the social, clinical, quantitative, and applied sciences.

Because of the difficulty of altering deeply entrenched perspectives on quality assurance at the level of practice, continuing education programs should also be mounted that emphasize the organization behavior and quality/cost aspects of quality control. In the development of such programs, priority should be given to the training of people (clinical and nonclinical) who hold top-level management positions in health institutions. These are the individuals who will have the best opportunity to shape the development of programs for assuring the quality of care at the institutional level. The JCAH should be encouraged to take a lead role in this effort as it expands its educational programs.

RESEARCH

Many of the authors of chapters identified specific research questions that needed further work. We do not wish to restate those questions but instead suggest what to us seem to be general themes or areas in which particular priority should be given.

- Research needs to focus on the effects of organization structures and environment on the quality of care provided in health care institutions. Particular emphasis should be given to the effect of power relationships and incentive structures, especially if the design of policy relating to quality assurance is to be made more effective.
- As hospitals and other health care institutions develop programs to control both cost and quality, evaluative research efforts need to be supported for the purpose of assessing the effectiveness of such efforts.
- The problem of bringing about change in professional workers is at the root of quality assurance activities. Research is thus needed into the behavioral aspects of professional work, with emphasis on those techniques and structures that are likely to impact health professional performance.
- Research into the measurement of quality must certainly be continued. Added to that effort, however, must be the study of methods for *valuing* quality improvement or differentials. This is essential if we are to be successful in linking quality assurance to the areas of reimbursement, regulation, program evaluation, institutional marketing, and clinical management.

POLICY

Some changes described or proposed in this book also suggest a need for new or expanded policies. It is apparent that these should be developed both by the JCAH and by federal and state governments.

- An increasing number of hospitals in the United States are now, or are exploring the possibility of becoming, a part of some form of multi-institutional group. In fact, many free-standing hospitals that are not members of formally organized multihospital groups can reasonably be considered, for purposes of quality assurance, to be part of broader community hospital systems. Focus of quality assurance activities at the multi-institutional level shows promise of providing a more cost-effective and comprehensive program than would be possible with the resources of a single institution. JCAH policy has not yet fully taken multihospital relationships into account in the design of its standards. Thus, the JCAH should be encouraged to broaden its focus on single institution review to consider the multi-institutions or community linkages individual hospitals might have.
- The new JCAH standard leaves somewhat unclear the organizational dimensions of quality assurance programs. As the JCAH gains further experience with its new standard, it should be encouraged to view quality assurance programs in the broader context of the structure of institutional and clinical

authority. Care should be taken to prevent the focus of quality assurance review to emphasize mere information system linkages, committee structures, and quality assurance program staffing.

- As public policy emphasizes deregulation and encourages the use of competition and the incentives of reimbursement for purposes of cost control, careful consideration should be given to the use of the same mechanisms to accomplish the aims of quality assurance. It is obvious that the lead for this development rests with federal and state governments and the health insurance industry.

These recommendations are not meant to be all inclusive. However, we feel that if an advance is to be made in assessing the quality of care in this country, the points keyed in these recommendations should be given priority. Since the early 1950s significant progress has been made in some specific although important areas of development in quality assurance. The unimpressive performance of quality assurance efforts once implemented, however, clearly suggests that a refocus of effort is needed in the coming years.

Index

Sheldon, A., 263
Sherman, R. E., 226
Shifts (nurse), 248
Shoemaker, F. F., 163, 165
Shortell, S. M., 87, 128, 136, 138, 271
Shukla, R., 254
Shultz, R. L., 194
Simmons, H., 223
Slevin, D. P., 194
Smith, M., 159
Social services, 53
Somers, A. R., 45, 51
Somers, H. M., 51
Specialization, 111
   heteronomous organizations and, 54
   nursing and quality care and, 253
   quality care determinants and, 131, 132
   surgical, 95
Staffing
   multi-institution systems and, 288
   patient classification and nurse, 243-244, 246-247, 250
Standardization, nursing and quality assurance and, 254
Standardized mortality ratio (SMR), 110, 111, 112-115, 116, 119. *See also* Mortality
Standardized normal tissue removed (SNTR), ratio, 111, 116
Standards, 72
   autonomous organizations and, 42
   change and, 161
   evaluation, 265
   JCAH quality care, 3, 148, 217, 226, 236, 243, 282
      current quality assurance and, 29-30
      evaluation of, 21-26
      information and, 231
      intent of, 27-29
      problem solving and, 30
      revision of, 26-27
      statement of, 34-37

support service review and, 30-32
   multi-institution systems and, 282-283, 285, 288
   nursing and educational, 254
   review and, 222
Stanford Center for Health Care Research, 85 n., 88, 129
Starfield, B., 128
Stearns, G,. 217
Steers, R. M., 128 n.
Steiner, G. A., 205
Stolley, P., 223
Stross, J. K., 118
Study on the Efficacy of Nosocomial Infection Control (SENIC Project, CDC), 201-202. *See also* Nosocomial infections
Stull, R. J., 263
Sunk costs, 152. *See also* Costs
Support service review, 30-32
Support structures
   autonomous organizations and, 43
   cojoint organizations and, 58-59, 61
   heteronomous organizations and, 52-53
Surgeons
   decision making and, 134
   medical staff study and, 109
      acute myocardial infarction (AMI) and, 107, 108, 110-115, 118-119, 120, 121
      appendectomies and, 107, 108, 110-112, 116-118, 119-120
      performance profile and chief of, 229
   quality care and, 137
   surgical staff and, 87-88, 92-94, 95-100
      outcome measures and, 89, 90, 95-98, 99, 100
Surgery
   quality care study and, 131
   "unnecessary," 219, 222-223
Swain, M. A., 257
Systems, quality assurance and, 217